Britcoms
FAQ

Britcoms FAQ

All That's Left to Know About Our Favorite Sophisticated, Outrageous British Television Comedies

Dave Thompson

APPLAUSE
THEATRE & CINEMA BOOKS
An Imprint of Hal Leonard Corporation

Published in 2016 by Applause Theatre & Cinema Books

An Imprint of Hal Leonard Corporation

7777 West Bluemound Road

Milwaukee, WI 53213

Trade Book Division Editorial Offices

33 Plymouth St., Montclair, NJ 07042

All images are from the author's collection unless otherwise noted.

The FAQ series was conceived by Robert Rodriguez and developed with Stuart Shea.

Printed in the United States of America

Book design by Snow Creative

Library of Congress Cataloging-in-Publication Data

Names: Thompson, Dave, 1960 January 3– author.
Title: Britcoms FAQ : all that's left to know about our favorite sophisticated, outrageous British television comedies / Dave Thompson.
Description: Milwaukee, WI : Applause Theatre & Cinema Books, 2016. | Includes bibliographical references and index.
Identifiers: LCCN 2016013993 | ISBN 9781495018992 (pbk.)
Subjects: LCSH: Television comedies—Great Britain—History and criticism. | Situation comedies (Television programs)—Great Britain—History and criticism.
Classification: LCC PN1992.8.C66 T57 2016 | DDC 791.45/6170941—dc23
LC record available at https://lccn.loc.gov/2016013993

www.applausebooks.com

To the cast and creators of *Look, Ma, It's Our Bus*, the greatest of all bad eighties Britcoms; and to the minds behind *That's My Birdbath!*, ornithological hygiene hijinks at their featherbrained best

Contents

Acknowledgments

Firstly, and before the vicar inadvertently grabs that lady's chest while reaching for some juicy melons, thanks to all the family and friends who spent this book's gestation trying to remember whether "him out of thingy" then went on to a career in Hollywood, or is now making jam commercials.

But especial thanks to Amy Hanson, for whom *Last of the Summer Wine* is the first day of a week spent as far from the TV as possible; Jo-Ann Greene, who watched one episode of *'Allo 'Allo* and has never been the same since; Chrissie Bentley, who likes her Britcoms uncut; and Chloe Mortenson, who compiled the episode guides with such grace and glee, before doing a Reggie Perrin (read chapter sixteen, you'll understand) the first chance she got.

To all at FAQ Central Headquarters, but most especially John Cerullo, Marybeth Keating, Wes Seeley and Gary Morris; to Karen and Todd; Linda and Larry; Betsy, Steve and family; Jen; all at Captain Blue Hen in Newark; Chrissie Bentley; Dave and Sue; Tim Smith, Gaye Black, Oliver, Trevor, Toby; Barb East; Bateerz and family; the Gremlins who live in the heat pump; and to John the Superstar, the demon of the dry well.

Introduction
What Is a Britcom?

t's British and it's a comedy.

It's not necessarily a sitcom, although it usually is. It's not always comical, although the studio audience seems happy enough.

It usually lasts around half an hour, although specials might go on for longer; and it usually challenges, illustrates or comments upon something that needs to be said.

Again, not always. But that is the criteria for the majority of shows that are featured in this book. Shows that say something about the world around them, or shows that don't say anything at all, because there's nothing that can be said. It's the story of the currents that swirl beneath them, the trends that gallop around them, the motives that lay behind them and the characters who appear within them.

Not all of whom are British, and not all of whom are comics.

But they're a part of the Britcoms all the same.

It's a mixed bag, then, but an illustrative one, a history of the hoots and howls that have kept a large percentage of the Western world smiling for sixty-something years.

And which will probably keep them smiling for sixty-something more.

A Little Bit of Background

Although the first regularly scheduled television broadcasts in Britain commenced in 1936, it was the early-mid-1950s before things truly took off. Blacked out throughout World War II, services resumed in 1945, but as late as 1951, just 9 percent of homes in England (and none whatsoever in Scotland, Wales or Northern Ireland) had a TV, all of them clustered around the two transmitters that were in operation, one in north London and the other in Birmingham.

The rest of the country simply got on without it.

It was the coronation of Queen Elizabeth II in June 1953 that turned the tide. The BBC, at that time the country's sole broadcaster, was televising the event live, and nobody wanted to miss out. People of a certain age still remember the excitement that surrounded the event; the rush to either purchase a television in time for the big day or, if that wasn't feasible, to befriend somebody who already owned one.

An episode in the BBC's *Doctor Who* in 2006, "The Idiot's Lantern," depicts the frenzy very well, entire extended families crammed into a single living room, clustered around the tiny glowing box that glowered in the corner, to watch the flickering monochrome images that were history-in-the-making. True, the episode then went somewhat off the historical record by introducing into this cozy scenario a merciless face-eating alien being, but *aside from that* . . . .

The Coronation kick-started television ownership; now, people had to find other programs they wanted to watch just as much. And they did. It is one of TV history's most trusted canards that, through those earliest years, people would watch anything and everything, simply because it was on, and that included the footage of a potter's wheel spinning round and round, and a lady playing the zither, both of which aired between the scheduled programs. Some even watched on as the evening's broadcast finished, and the picture faded to a tiny dot in the center of the screen.

Today, they might even say it was better than most of what we are subjected to nowadays. That dot was great.

That said, a glance at the schedules even for 1953–54 throws up some remarkable, and still fondly remembered, offerings. We received the first-ever small-screen rendition of *Robin Hood*, with Patrick Troughton (a future *Doctor Who*, incidentally) taking the title role. There was *The Quatermass Experiment*, a science fiction adventure that remains among the most influential shows of its ilk ever screened. *The Good Old Days* made its debut, a nostalgic re-creation of old time music hall that was still going strong through the 1970s and into the early 1980s.

The news and current affairs program *Panorama* debuted back then; and so did the first in the veritable raft of children's shows that themselves have been repeated, revived and recalled for more than sixty years: *Andy Pandy*, *Muffin the Mule*, *Rag Tag and Bobtail* and *The Flowerpot Men*, a pair of horticulturally inclined puppets whose vocabulary made the later Teletubbies sound like university lecturers.

It's odd to think that any child who sat down to watch the maiden episodes of any of those shows is now of pensionable age, but it's even odder to realize that they still know precisely what "ob-bob-flobbalob" means.

With so many riches to consume; with transmitters opening and their range increasing, television ownership rocketed. Once, a family would gather at the end of the day, seated around the kitchen table, the radio quietly murmuring on the sideboard, and they would talk—discuss their day, their school and work, the doings of the neighborhood, the health of Great Aunt Lil.

And then, one day, a television appeared, crouched in the corner of the living room, looking a lot like a fat one-eyed toad, and off went the radio, out went the table, and who gives a hoot about Great Aunt Lil? Everybody leaped into armchairs and couches, dinners balanced precariously on a small plastic tray, gathered around the small-screened god, and paying nightly obeisance (and a weekly rental fee) to its every burp and babble.

Family life as we knew it had been wiped out of existence. Conversation had been crushed. The radios fell silent (or adopted a nonstop diet of music).

The television had arrived, and, almost seven decades on, it is still here, its one eye still glaring out at the room (only many, many times larger); its babble still devouring everyone's attention (only many times louder). It is the first thing to be installed when you move into a new house; the last thing to be switched off before you go to bed at night.

It is all that many people live for, and the toll it has taken on society and culture would be positively unforgivable if we hadn't enjoyed its depredations so much. Viewers of Ricky Gervais's *The Office* are often heard to describe it as the ultimate condemnation of the meaninglessness of modern corporate life, peppered with bland conversation, idiot misconstructions and mindless catchphrases trotted out by fools who think they're funnier than they are.

It's not only the average office, however, that has devolved so darkly. And it wasn't commerce and corporations that caused it to do so. One only needs to reflect on how readily a politician's sound bite can become irrefutable fact if it's broadcast on enough news channels; how easily a song can become a hit if it's aired on-screen often enough; how readily a show can be deemed a "classic" if enough sheep sit and baaa before it.

Britcoms, and comedies of all other descriptions, are not a universal panacea to this; there are many that are as awful as anything else on television. And besides, other genres, too, have highlights that rise above the level of brainless mediocrity. But *The Office* makes its point regardless, and we can laugh at ourselves as we cringe at one another, and maybe that was always the goal of good TV. To show us the things we don't normally see.

Wipeout

With the television having so effortlessly become the axis around which the average family's existence now revolved, it was only fitting that Britain's first-ever soap opera, *The Grove Family*, should concern the activities of a "typical" British household; and that the first-ever British sitcom, *Life with the Lyons*, should follow that same homely formula.

Adapted, in 1955, from an already successful (and ultimately longer-running) radio show, and a couple of movies too, *Life with the Lyons* was also, in many ways, the first reality show. Its stars, Ben Lyon and Bebe Daniels, were a real-life husband and wife, Americans who settled in London during World War II, and who were already familiar voices from the radio show *Hi, Gang!*

Joined now by their own children, Richard and Barbara, *Life with the Lyons* was effectively a domestic sitcom scripted (by Bebe) around actual events in the family's real life, with matters aided and abetted by nosy neighbor Florrie (Doris Rogers) and their housekeeper Aggie MacDonald (Molly Weir).

Sadly, and igniting a discussion that will recur many times as this book continues, it is possible today to garner just the teensiest taste of what the show was actually like. British broadcasting's policy of wiping, junking and otherwise disposing of programs that appeared to have reached the end of their useful life accounted for many more significant casualties than *Life with the Lyons*.

Just six of the forty episodes transmitted between 1955 and 1960 survive today, one apiece from the first and fifth seasons, two apiece from the third and fourth. Fondly remembered the show might be, but memory is all we do have. (The radio show has fared somewhat better. While only three of the broadcasts remained in the BBC's own archives, an old-time radio collector came forward in 2011 with over two hundred recordings, apparently captured from Ben Lyon's own reels.)

The issue of what a broadcaster keeps and what it disposes of is one of modern culture's thorniest. Certainly throughout the first decades of its existence, since its founding in 1922, the BBC had no interest in preserving its output (it was not yet rebranded as "heritage"), and matters did not change once television came into the picture.

Indeed, in many ways, the very medium played a major part in its own destruction. Television was ephemeral, instant gratification. The vast majority of it was transmitted live, with no practical means of preserving the broadcast. Once it had been aired, therefore, it was forgotten. If a repeat was called for, the crew and cast would simply gather again and physically replay the action.

No reference copies were kept; there would be no filmed souvenirs. Like a concert or a theatrical performance in the days before cellphones became an instant movie camera, you either watched a show "live" or you didn't see it at all.

Later, once it became common practice to prerecord programming, the occasional show might be deemed worthy of retention and a tape would be archived in the bowels of the broadcaster's HQ.

For the most part, however, programs were intended to be screened just once, and any copies that might be made were created for the specific purpose of selling them overseas. Then, once that particular demand was satisfied, they would be deleted—from the catalog and from the shelves.

Of course, the policy makes sense. Today, we like to look back on the past as a golden age in which people appreciated culture, valued art, cared for the past. And so they did. Some of them. But money still ultimately dictated those values. The cost of storage (those old reels weren't small) was high; the cost of film (there were no digital recorders) was prohibitive; and what were they going to do with all those miles and miles of used tape anyway?

There were no VHS players or DVD box sets in those days and no public appetite for watching reruns, anyway. Oft-quoted today, but making sound sense at the time, when the BBC first began discussing its entrance into the home video market in the early 1980s, one executive asked incredulously, "why would people want to spend good money for a bunch of old repeats?"

Just as nobody would expect a boutique to retain last year's fashions on its racks in the hope of appealing to any passing nostalgics, or a supermarket to maintain past-their-sell-by date cookies in the hope that someone might like their snacks soft and stale, so nobody in broadcasting could ever even imagine a time when some rotten old show from donkey's years back might ever be welcomed into the home. And even if they had, there were union and contractual rules that rendered even the airing of a simple repeat an all-but-Herculean undertaking.

So, as the contracts they had signed with the casts and writers began expiring, and with them the rights to sell or otherwise exploit the holdings, what reason was there to keep the shows? They were useless.

Tapes would be wiped, their contents diligently scrubbed out of existence, and nobody really cared. Besides, everybody did it, the independent stations in the UK, the national conglomerates in America, TV stations large and small, rich and poor, hither and thither. Only in France did the national broadcaster actually have a legal duty to preserve a copy of every minute of broadcast footage, and it was an onerous obligation that they would gladly have been released from. When a show's useful life was over, the tape should be wiped and reused, and another show would rise from the magnetic ashes.

It's called the cycle of life.

Or it would have been had the public's perception of those old shows not begun to subtly change. Through the fifties, sixties, seventies . . . the golden age, in fact, of junking old tapes . . . the sight of an old repeat in the listings was indeed the cause of major griping.

The fact that the UK had only three channels throughout that time played its part, of course. The state-and-public-funded BBC's outright monopoly was broken in 1955 with the launch of independent television (ITV), funded by commercials rather than public subscription and taxes, and prompting a furious outburst from Lord Reith, the founder of the BBC three decades previous and still a staunch upholder of its purported purpose.

"Somebody introduced dog-racing into England," he stormed. "And somebody introduced smallpox, bubonic plague and the black death. Somebody is minded now to introduce sponsored broadcasting into this country . . . . Need we be ashamed of moral values, or of intellectual and ethical objectives? It is these that are here and now at stake."

A third channel and the BBC's second, the very sensibly named BBC2, arrived in 1964. But it would be 1982 before a fourth channel, the equally sensibly named Channel Four, was born, and so every repeat that was aired on TV effectively cheated you out of a 33 percent opportunity to watch something new.

Channel Four changed that, *not* because its content was dictated by reruns (of course, it wasn't; it hadn't been around long enough to make enough shows that could be repeated), but because its early economics demanded a certain amount of cheap and cheerful programming, which it gathered up from the relics of 1960s children's programming.

Old American favorites like *Mr. Ed*, *The Beverly Hillbillies*, *Lost in Space*, *Champion the Wonder Horse* and so forth were reborn, and they punched a button marked "nostalgia" that even the programmers had not known for certain was there.

Add to that the aforementioned home VHS market, kicking off likewise in the early 1980s; and add to that the fact that audiences who had grown up on the shows of the sixties and seventies had finally arrived at a station in life where they had the disposable income to relive their childhoods . . . suddenly the sheer enormity of what the nation's broadcasters had done came crashing home on both sides of the cash register.

The broadcasters, as they realized how much money they could now be making from sticking a few old *Bill and Bens* on a videocassette, for sale to the baby boomers; the public, as they remembered just how much they had loved those old *Quatermass* adventures; and the broadcasters again when they looked at the sales enjoyed by the old shows that *had* survived the cull, and multiplied the figures by the numbers that hadn't.

In Search of the Lost Canister

Standard practice was rewritten as a national scandal; administrative decisions as cultural vandalism. Indeed, by 1993, the loss of the nation's televisual heritage was regarded as such a major issue that the British Film Institute, the UK's national home for all archived film and television, created its own "Missing Believed Wiped" division, dedicated not only to cataloging every nonextant piece of British-made programming ever shot, but also to attempting to recover them.

It's a quest that has turned up some astonishing dividends from some most unexpected sources—from private collectors who, whether through employment, opportunity, or a lucky spot of dumpster diving, had acquired a few reels of old television shows; from forgotten basements and long-forsaken attics; from any place, in fact, where a few anonymous-looking film boxes could be stashed by someone for whatever reason, and then left to collect dust.

In 1994, one private collector came forward with a veritable mountain of 16mm telerecordings, including lost episodes of *At Last the 1948 Show*, *Comedy Playhouse* and *No, That's Me Over Here!* Another appeared with a single episode of *Till Death Us Do Part*—most of which will be encountered later in this book.

An appeal on the BBC's *Treasure Hunt* series brought more film out of the woodwork; while a UK-based company, Television International Enterprises Archives (TIEA), exists at least in part to scour the vaults of foreign television stations in search of further elusive reels and assist in their preservation and digitization.

Of course, the media headlines focus on the so-called "big money" rediscoveries: in 2013, the fiftieth anniversary of the series *Doctor Who*, a search of archives in Nigeria revealed a cache of 1960s episodes, including two (near-) complete missing adventures from the tenure of Patrick Troughton.

But "lesser" discoveries are regularly being made: that same year, TIEA also restored two missing installments of the astronomy show *The Sky at Night*, while 2010 saw over one hundred hours of lost British drama unearthed by the Library of Congress in Washington, D.C. And in 2014, two further episodes of *At Last the 1948 Show* were found among the effects of the recently deceased David Frost, among them the original version of the famous "Four Yorkshiremen" sketch.

It was "a crucial find," BFI television consultant Dick Fiddy said. The show "represents a key moment in the history of British television comedy featuring the combined talents of some of its greatest exponents. These gifted comedians, all in their twenties and thirties, were let off the leash and allowed to experiment with style and content, resulting in shows which have had an enduring influence on comedy worldwide."

Just as the junking of shows was not immediate, neither was it all-inclusive. Sometimes, an entire series would be lost; other times, an episode or two might be retained for whatever reason.

In some cases, a mere handful went astray. In the 1980s, for instance, the BBC discovered that its archive of *Steptoe and Son* (the UK model for America's *Sanford and Son*) was short of fourteen episodes; one from 1965 and thirteen from 1970. By the end of the decade, however, all had been retrieved from the personal collection of the show's cowriter Ray Galton.

Some shows survived through the tenacity of its creators—*Dad's Army* producer David Croft ferociously guarded that show's vast archive—and sometimes, a sheer fluke saw their efforts undone. One day while Croft was on vacation, a request came through to wipe five of the tapes. Someone else gave their approval, and suddenly the collection was no longer complete. And so on.

Today, we read of these events with the utmost incredulity. But again it must be remembered that nostalgia for old television programs is a relatively recent phenomenon—brought on, of course, by the advent of home video and DVD. Prior to their arrival, television truly was as ephemeral as the BBC insisted, and while there would always be an audience for certain shows, it was new editions, or recent favorites, that were most welcomed.

Besides, in the case of the fifties and sixties shows, with color television now firmly entrenched in British households, there was no appetite whatsoever for black-and-white TV, and no tolerance for it either. So it was disposed of.

The year 1978 was the last in which programs were routinely wiped. The home video revolution may not have been imminent but it was certainly approaching, and the first farsighted minds were applying themselves to the possibilities that it engendered. There was, too, a growing awareness that television played as great a role in the country's culture as did film and music, perhaps even more so.

Many more people, for example, watch a single television program than purchase even the biggest hit record. Indeed, the combined sales of the five best-selling 45 rpm records in British musical history ("Candle in the Wind 1997" by Elton John, "Do They Know It's Christmas?" by Band Aid, "Bohemian Rhapsody" by Queen, "Mull of Kintyre" by Paul McCartney's Wings, and "Rivers of Babylon" by Boney M) are not even close to the audience that tuned in for *one single episode* of *Dad's Army* in 1972, when it was averaging sixteen million viewers a week.

So, while the accountants and legal teams got to work unraveling the red tape that inevitably surrounded the future retailing of old TV, the BBC got to work re-creating the library that it had so happily spent the last half century junking.

It was not an easy task. But the host of DVD box sets that now loiter on our shelves stand as testament to the perseverance and patience of those doughty campaigners. And, though they still have a long way to go before their job could be called complete, one would need to live for an awful lot of years simply to watch all the jewels that they have recovered.

Beginning, because one has to start somewhere, with all thirty-seven surviving episodes of *Hancock's Half Hour*.

We're still eighteen short of the full collection, but no matter. The world of Britcoms starts here.

Britcoms
FAQ

Meet the Lad

The Improbable Rise of Tony Hancock

ancock's Half Hour is the greatest British sitcom of all time. And Anthony John Hancock was the greatest British comedian. Born in Birmingham on May 12, 1924, he grew up in the seaside town of Bournemouth, where his father John not only ran the Railway Hotel, but also performed there as a comedian.

Dad's influence was strong on the boy; aged fifteen when the Second World War broke out, Hancock joined the Royal Air Force in 1942 and immediately found his way into one of the twenty-four Ralph Reader Gang Show units that toured the various theaters of war, entertaining the troops.

Number Nine, to which Hancock was assigned, concentrated in the main on North Africa and Italy, a raucous training ground for any comedian, but one in which Hancock readily flourished, despite his tender years (he was just twenty-one when the war ended).

Hancock's humor was never overt, neither as a military youth nor, a decade later, as a radio and soon-to-be TV star. Chubby of form, lugubrious of face, a veritable Eeyore among the Tiggers, Poohs and Kangas of the comedic mainstream, Hancock rarely told jokes. Rather, he spun out stories, detailing situations whose comedy lay as much in the listener's interpretation of what he was saying as in the way he said it.

Black comedy exists throughout our world and often springs from the most unintentional wells. The military, beholden as it is to so many blindingly petty rules and regulations, was an endless source of material for someone as observant as Hancock proved to be, and later, back in civilian life, the equally petty Jobsworths (as in "it's more than my job's worth"—the lament of low-ranking officials the world over) of society proved an equally tempting target.

Particularly as many of the men entrusted with the task of ensuring society kept ticking over—traffic wardens, hotel doormen, minor council officials and so forth—were themselves ex-military, accustomed to believing their word was law. Later, Captain Peacock of *Are You Being Served?* and Foggy of *Last of the Summer Wine* would perfect the absurdity of this stance. But it was the character Hancock was slowly assuming, and who would blossom across his broadcast career, who drew the blueprint for those future creations.

He may have portrayed the Everyman, but Hancock's fame still afforded him a new Aston Martin. Which must be why he's waiting at a parking meter.   *Alamy*

From Wings to the Windmill

Demobbed in late 1946, Hancock's early attempts to break into the world of peacetime community were doomed to failure, a dispiriting run of bad luck that perhaps culminated the day he burst into a theatrical agent's office, announced himself as "Anthony Hancock, comedian," and then proceeded to slip on a loose rug and tumble backwards to the floor. Related later in life by the downtrodden but so-defiant television star, it was an extremely funny anecdote. At the time it was simply humiliating.

Salvation came when Hancock was recruited to a Gang Show revival that toured the UK under the aegis of Ralph Reader and the Air Ministry. Reunited with many of the men with whom he had performed during the war, and earning introductions to others who had worked in other Gang Show units, Hancock remained with *Wings*, as the show was called, until late 1947.

He got through the festive season by appearing as one of the Ugly Sisters in a Christmas pantomime production of *Cinderella* in Oxford, and proved so popular that he was retained to appear in the same repertory company's next show, Noel Coward's *Peace in Our Time*. And it was there that his genius for extracting comedy from even the most unpromising situation truly came to light.

Hancock played three roles in the play, including a sadistic Nazi officer who, he was told, was to be played absolutely straight, without an iota of humor or comedy. He might have succeeded, too, had the audience not recognized him from *Cinderella* and fallen about laughing at his every gesture or word.

Still, when the season ended, he was back on the unemployment lines, honing his future act by literally living it—a pokey flat, a shabby wardrobe, a miserable face and an unfailing faith in his own abilities.

Occasionally a crumb would be thrown in his direction—odd club and cabaret engagements, a stint as an impressionist and so forth. But the majority of his time as a starving artist was spent genuinely starving.

He was not, of course, alone in this. Postwar Britain groaned beneath a surfeit of young comedians, many of whom—like Hancock—had learned their trade in the military, whether with the Gang Shows or ENSA (the Entertainments National Service Association), or independently as a regimental clown.

Names like Eric Morecambe, Ernie Wise, Harry Worth, Eric Sykes, Michael Bentine, Spike Milligan and Peter Sellers (whom Hancock had come to know during the last months of service) were all on the outside looking in, pushing for the breaks that would raise them out of the one-off pub gigs and into more rarefied atmospheres.

One might assume they were fierce rivals—gigs were sparse, money was tight, opportunity was limited. In fact, quite the opposite mentality prevailed. Perhaps drawing from the communal spirit of their shared military service . . . or perhaps because society was less riven by jealousy and backbiting back then . . . a powerful bond existed between them all, a sense that they were all in it together.

Meeting regularly at a pub across the road from the legendary Windmill Theatre on Archer Street, off Shaftsbury Avenue in London's theatrical West End, these wannabe comics would exchange tips, offer advice and encouragement and, should one of them find himself in work for a short time, share in the largesse with a few drinks and some coins, knowing that when the boot was on the other foot and it was someone else's turn to be in the money, they would be just as generous.

There was a reason, of course, why Archer Street was their chosen point of call—and that was the proximity of the Windmill. Although the theater is best remembered today for its policy of nude-or-thereabouts dancing girls (who did not, in fact, dance; censorious law at that time insisted that nudity could be shown only in the form of unmoving tableaux), it was also a proving ground for a vast number of comedians, many of whom would be called upon at the last minute to fill a gap in the evening's running order. A head poked around the pub door would effectively see the cream of out-of-work English comedy all looking hopefully back up at it.

At the same time, the Windmill was a ruthless employer. Everybody, the comedians included, knew that the audience was there for just one reason—to ogle the naked ladies on the stage. The Windmill's proudest boast was that it never missed a single night's performance throughout the duration of World War II, not even at the height of the London Blitz. "We never closed," boasted the theater's publicity. "We never clothed," lisped back the jokers, but the joke, too often, was on them.

Open for close to twelve hours a day, from quarter-after-noon to shortly before midnight, the Windmill required comedians only to keep audiences amused while the girls changed their costumes or took a rest—a necessity that the audience already resented. If a comic couldn't keep them entertained until the ladies came back to the stage, the crowd would entertain itself by making the poor soul's life a misery, and many is the forgotten comic (and famous one too) who came to such grief on the Windmill stage that they came close to abandoning their ambitions altogether.

Hancock had already auditioned for the Windmill, placing his name on the list of potential employees that owner Vivian Van Damme kept forever to hand; he had recently worked up a new act with pianist Derek Scott, revolving around the vagaries of a seaside concert party. And suddenly, he found himself with a hit.

Van Damme booked the duo for five weeks of performances, six shows a day, six days a week, and while audiences were initially uncertain, within a couple of days, word had got around. The Windmill had an act that was almost as entertaining as the dancing girls. *Almost. . . .*

Other gigs followed; other eyes saw the act. The BBC caught wind of Hancock and Scott and offered them an audition. Phyllis Rounce, one half of the International Artistes Representation agency, caught the show, and became Hancock's agent. The duo appeared on *Worker's Playtime*, a daily half-hour variety show that the BBC targeted directly at those factory and office workers whose employers permitted them to listen to the radio while working.

They played cabaret and nightclubs, upper-class ballrooms and working-class pubs, and all the while, Hancock was gathering material, lifting it straight out of the characters he saw in the audience or ran into backstage, then refining it at home with his writing partner and roommate, Larry Stephens (later a writer on *The Goon Show*).

He parted with Derek Scott, who wanted to concentrate more on his musical ambitions, and launched out as a solo act—tentatively at first, but with increasing confidence, not only in himself but also in his agent. When Hancock's debut on another BBC radio show, *Variety Bandbox*, proved an absolute fiasco, it was Phyllis Rounce who convinced the Beeb to give him another try.

He also landed a regular role as a scoutmaster in a weekly show called *Happy Go Lucky*, and it was there that he met the two men who were to shape his future, playwrights Alan Simpson and Ray Galton—themselves destined to become giants of British comedy over the next couple of decades, but for now, still struggling to get a foothold, just a few years after they first met in the TB ward where they were both patients.

Hancock was growing more and more popular. He appeared again on *Worker's Playtime*, this time performing a Galton and Simpson script; and later was a star of *Forces All Star Bill*.

Educating Anthony

Hancock's greatest early success, however, was as the long-suffering tutor in *Educating Archie*, a half-hour radio comedy starring ventriloquist Peter Brough and his mischievous sidekick Archie Andrews . . . a dummy. And before you raise your eyebrows in disbelief—*a ventriloquist on the radio? How absurd!*—remember this.

It was not the fact that Archie was a dummy that gave the show its popularity. It was the fact that it was genuinely funny, no matter who (or what) was doing the speaking. Archie was already a hit from live performances; so long as the audience heard "his" voice, it didn't matter that he was not living flesh and blood.

Like Hancock, the act had already been through the mincer of BBC variety shows; *Educating Archie* launched in June 1950 with a cast that included Max Bygraves, Hattie Jacques and a thirteen-year-old Julie Andrews. Hancock joined the cast for its second season, in August 1951, and within weeks his catchphrase—"flippin' kids"—had been adopted throughout the nation.

He even, for a time, became known to the newspaper-reading public as "Tony 'Flippin' Kids' Hancock," as critics fell over themselves to praise his performance, while he also ignited a lasting friendship with costar Hattie Jacques; once his own show got under way, Hancock lost no time in adding her to his team, while Ms Jacques would also strike up a longtime working relationship with *Educating Archie*'s cowriter, Eric Sykes.

It was the wildfire success of his catchphrase, and the fear of the typecasting that would inevitably follow, that prompted Hancock to leave the series after just one season (he was replaced as tutor by Harry Secombe). He returned to live work, appearing on a variety tour with singer Nat King Cole (not as a double act, of course), a stint on the West End stage in Jimmy Edwards's *London Laughs* and more.

Moving to television, he had a regular six-minute sketch in the hour-long magazine program *Kaleidoscope*, playing "a would-be rescuer of damsels in distress" named George Knight.

Until finally, the inevitable happened. The BBC called, offering him his own radio program. *Hancock's Half Hour* was born.

The importance of radio in the development of British, and indeed international, comedy can never be overstated, and not only because, until the mid-1950s, it was effectively people's only form of broadcast entertainment.

Television, as we have already seen, was making voracious inroads into the market by the early-mid-1950s, but still it took a large bite out of the average family budget, whether a "TV set" was rented by the week ("hire purchase") or bought outright—a 14-inch GEC television cost around £65 (around $160, but a staggering $1,300 today), at a time when the average worker's weekly wage was around £10 (around $350 in modern terms).

Add to that the annual cost of the license fee (payable by every household that owned a television)— a nonnegotiable £3 per year, as compared to just £1 for the radio-only equivalent; add to *that* the knowledge that your new purchase was capable of receiving only one television channel and would,

This memorial to Tony Hancock glowers out over Birmingham's Old Square. The odd appearance of the statue is, in fact, what it looks like.
Copyright © Oosoom/Wikimedia Commons

therefore, need to be either adapted or replaced if and when a second channel was authorized; and then remember that even the best-cared-for set was prone to any number of glitches and gremlins, and it was small wonder that many people viewed the whole thing as a passing gimmick and stuck to the faithful old "wireless" instead.

In terms of sheer entertainment, after all, the radio offered far more variety than a haunted fish tank ever could. The generation of comics who, just a few years earlier, had been huddled in a pub, hoping the Windmill would call them in, had finally broken through. The wealth of talent that passed through the *Educating Archie* cast list was exploding everywhere— Frankie Howerd's *Fine Goings On—And More*, Derek Roy's *Happy Go Lucky*, Peter Ustinov's *In All Directions*, David Tomlinson's *A Life of Bliss*, Morecambe and Wise's *You're Only Young Once* and many more to follow.

Including, as we will discover in a later chapter, *The Goon Show*, thirty minutes of surrealism and silliness that effectively rewrote great swathes of the British comic landscape.

Those that Hancock had not already redesigned.

Many, but by no means all, of these shows and performers would move on to television—*Life with the Lyons* was the first to make the transition, and Tony Hancock would follow; *Hancock's Half Hour* was radio-only for two years, 1954–1956, before a TV show of the same name came along to run concurrently.

Heaven's Half Hour

The Greatest Thirty Minutes of All

Both versions of *Hancock's Half Hour*, on radio and television, concerned the adventures—or, more appropriately, the *mis*adventures—of one Anthony Aloysius St. John Hancock, resident of 23 Railway Cuttings in the London suburb of East Cheam.

Like Hancock himself had once been, this version of Hancock was often (but not always) portrayed as a struggling comedian, although in truth, his station in life was of markedly less significance than his personal vision of that station.

Every two-bit military officer who had ever crossed Hancock's path was wrapped up in there; every sneering upper-crust society maven; every bumptious official and officious bumpkin.

What an appalling creature he was, this self-centered egomaniac, this absurd social climber, this pathetic, gullible, pretentious, bloviating little man. Years later, John Cleese would effectively re-create the Hancock of the *Half Hour* as Basil Fawlty, an equally ridiculous little man with pretensions to a higher station in life, ingratiatingly crawling to those he perceived as his betters (witness the *Fawlty Towers* episode "A Touch of Class," when he falls for a confidence trickster's aristocratic bearing; or "Gourmet Night," when he becomes obsessed with the notion of attracting "the right kind of person" to his somewhat sordid seaside hotel).

Unlike Fawlty, however, for whom it is difficult to truly feel even a modicum of sympathy, Hancock demanded it. His drive to better himself was absurd, of course, but he did not pursue it solely because he felt he *deserved* better, but because the life he was actually living was so impenetrably pathetic.

The friends he had, and the characters with whom he interacted, were precisely the ones he deserved; Bill (Bill Kerr), the Australian best friend who unkindly insists on referring to Hancock as "Tub" (short for "tubby"); Moira (Moira Lister), his ever-suffering housekeeper; and an overexcitable,

John Cleese prepares to say something unpleasant.   *Photofest*

nightmarish nemesis played by Kenneth Williams, already perfecting the über-camp, prissily prim, snide and slimy, and, most of all frightfully annoying "everyman" who would himself become a star before the decade was out, but for now seemed content merely driving Hancock to exasperated distraction.

And then there is Sid, played by Sid James, a happy-go-lucky petty crook, a con man and a permanent thorn in Hancock's side, whether as the inadvertent architect of the next disaster to befall him or as a willing instrument in that disaster. As, for example, the time when Hancock decided that if he was ever to be recognized for the comic genius he was, he needed to emigrate to a country less blinkered. No less than eighty-three different nations have rejected his application before Sid suggests Hancock get a new passport.

"But I've already got a passport," replies Hancock.

"That's no good. You've tried emigrating under your own name . . . use this passport. This'll get you out."

He hands Hancock a new document. It's the prime minister's.

Sid would become a constant in Hancock's life, both on radio and on television, where their misadventures effectively became a two-man show with added extras.

And what a show it was. With a cast of such effective comedians, it would have been easy for *Hancock's Half Hour* to look to its already established acts and persona to carry the comedy, effectively creating a variety show regardless of any linking material.

Through his early years of struggle, Hancock was writing with Larry Stephens (later to find fame behind the scenes for the Goons). Now, however, he had a new team, Galton and Simpson, and they had a whole new theory of comedy.

No more laugh-a-minute individual showcases, the default setting for so much broadcast humor. Instead, they set about deftly weaving the cast's disparate personae into a single whole, each episode carried by a solitary plotline; despite, and not because of, the ensemble's own abilities.

Williams, in particular, had long since established himself as a character whose brilliantly realized mannerisms were capable of stealing the show away from almost anyone—later in the decade, and on through the sixties too, he was among the stars of the *Carry On* series of movies, and in almost every one he appears, his facial expressions, vocal outbursts and exquisitely delivered lines outplay almost everyone else on the set.

He also remains one of the few people on earth who could make even a casual greeting like "good morning" sound simultaneously threatening, lascivious, derogatory and facetious.

Hancock's Half Hour didn't rein him in, not in the slightest, and often it encouraged him to even greater heights. His performance as the "Yodeller of Dulwich" in the television episode "Alpine Holiday" is a masterpiece of madness, effectively driving the audience to the same depths of despair as Hancock himself is very visibly feeling.

It is difficult today to convey just how wildly popular *Hancock's Half Hour* was. In an age before viewing figures were tabulated on anything approaching the industrial scale that they would later be, we have only anecdote to

speak of a show's drawing power. But it is said, and has never been contradicted, that you knew exactly when *Hancock's Half Hour* was on, because
you'd be sitting somewhere watching it.

Complaints that the television show somehow diluted the madcap purity
of the radio were swiftly deleted. On the radio, for example, "The Pet Dog"
saw Hancock purchase his girlfriend Andrée (Andrée Melly) a puppy from

Sid James and Barbara Windsor prepare to carry on Christmas.

Sid's newly opened pet shop, only to discover that it won't stop growing. Soon it is as big as he is; soon, it is even bigger.

There was no way that such a catastrophe (or should that be a dog-astrophe?) could be realized on television at that time. But Galton and Simpson were not deterred. They scaled back the surrealism and replaced it with realism, and proved that that, too, could be as rich a vein. (The ever-growing domestic pet would not be forgotten, however. A decade and a half later, *The Goodies* revisited it for "Kitten Kong"; while Sid's sales patter would likewise be revised for *Monty Python*'s parrot sketch).

Streets emptied, pubs cleared, the most popular restaurants bemoaned empty tables, movie houses might as well not have opened. Hancock dominated the medium like few other performers ever would.

Both the BBC and the newly launched ITV independent network benefitted from his popularity.

Even before *Hancock's Half Hour* moved to moving pictures, Hancock starred in a six-part sketch program for ITV, titled *Jack Hylton Presents The Tony Hancock Show* and written by Eric Sykes and Larry Stephens. Debuting in April 1956, the show predated *Hancock's Half Hour* by a full month, but is frequently overlooked as not a moment of the show has survived. (A second season later in 1956 has also been lost.)

Once established at the BBC, however, Hancock's paymasters bent over backwards to keep "the lad," as he was known, happy. Hancock's perfectionist streak had long railed against the practice of broadcasting the show live; in 1959, the BBC finally acceded to his demands that it be prerecorded, the first comedy show ever to be afforded that luxury. Likewise, Hancock became the first entertainer ever to receive a four-figure salary for a "mere" thirty-minute show.

When he tired of working with Sid James, convinced that their long-running partnership was in danger of becoming a true double act, the BBC offloaded James to another show, *Citizen James*. Other cast regulars, too, were disposed of, while Hancock even eventually dropped Galton and Simpson, adamant that their vision of comedy was too dependent on catchphrases and cheap laughs.

The BBC barely raised an objection.

When a motor accident left him with insufficient time to learn his lines, the BBC provided him with a teleprompter and simply bowed to the inevitable demand that followed—that the machine be available for every show, to save him from learning any lines whatsoever.

Face to Face

Yet the more popular Hancock became, the less secure he grew, a paranoia that reached its public apex when he was invited to appear on the interview program *Face to Face.*

Hosted by a former politician, John Freeman, *Face to Face* is often described today as a remorseless, relentless and, most of all, inquisitorial ordeal, in which Freeman—usually seen only from behind—quick-fires searching and sometimes painful questions at his guest, who contrarily is usually shown in unforgiving close-up.

In fact, although nobody would accuse Freeman of giving his guests an easy ride, the majority of his subjects came through unscathed. Bertrand Russell, Dame Edith Sitwell, Adlai Stevenson, Carl Gustav Jung and King Hussein of Jordan were among those who faced Freeman's face, and they answered his questions calmly and thoughtfully.

The show's reputation, then, is based on just two episodes. One, on September 16, 1960, saw TV presenter Gilbert Harding reduced to tears as he discussed his relationship with his mother. The other, on February 7, 1960, saw Hancock essentially transform a television chat show into a painful, pitiful display of self-excoriation.

Even today, it is disquieting. Hancock, having first agreed to "come clean" about the man behind the show, seems comfortable at the beginning, lightly self-effacing, smiling. When Freeman asks why he became a comedian in the first place, Hancock's answer includes the line "looking like this, it was perhaps the only thing I could do."

"Yes, but let's go a bit deeper than that," Freeman drills, playing on the insecurities with which Hancock's workmates were already familiar, demanding a definition of comedy in general, and in Hancock's hands in particular; teasing out "meaning" in the humor; analyzing the ingredients that constitute his own brand of comedy and then pouncing when Hancock admits that his targets not only include the things he dislikes about the world around him, but also those that he dislikes in himself.

"What are they?"

Hancock's health was discussed; the fact that he and his wife had no intention of having children ("flippin' kids"); the fact that he was one of the best-paid celebrities in the country. And all the while, Hancock is visibly growing less and less sure of himself; more and more awkward. His smile fades, his manner becomes solemn. "The lad" appears visibly to age before the camera's merciless glare.

Afterwards, it is said the BBC itself hesitated about screening the interview, worried about the effect it might have on Hancock's popularity. As it turned out, they did not need to worry. It was Freeman who felt the sharp end of the critical stick, berated for so brutally treating the nation's favorite son.

In the days when a letter to a newspaper was still regarded as the most effective means of stating one's case in the face of widespread public opprobrium, Freeman finally wrote to the *Daily Telegraph* to effectively plead his innocence. "I judged, I believe correctly, that more of Hancock's complex and fascinating personality would appear on the screen if he was kept at pretty full stretch. I hope viewers generally did not equate that with hostility because I am sure Hancock didn't."

Besides, it is not as though Hancock's definition of what truly constitutes humor was that far from the mark, either in execution or popularity. He viewed it, he said, as a beast that is not so far from real life as many people—lesser-talented comics and scriptwriters, perhaps—seemed to think.

It certainly was not merely a matter of making people laugh with slapstick capers and clever catchphrases; of conjuring absurd situations and peopling them with people whose every line was effectively meaningless beyond its own comic absurdity—a school of comedy that later writers Douglas Adams and Steven Moffat (whose mother-in-law, Beryl Vertue, succeeded Phyllis Rounce as Hancock's agent), to name but two, would fall prey to at different points in their careers.

Genuine comedy revolves around following real-life situations to their inevitable conclusions, with every one of the emotions that entails. A genuine comedian, therefore, was one who could bring humor, or at least levity, to those situations, no matter how unpromising they might seem.

True, Hancock's first feature film, *The Rebel*, was generally overlooked, often regarded as an overlong *Half Hour*, without the benefit of the attendant *Hancock*. But the final season of the television show itself would feature several shows that are still regarded among the best he ever made, and that despite him having done away with almost every recognizable feature of the earlier show, cast, title and even location included.

That's Nearly an Armful

No longer based at number 23, or even in Cheam; and titled now an unequivocal *Hancock*, the lad's fare well not only included "The Bowmans," a spot-on parody of the top-rated, and astonishingly long-running, BBC radio soap *The Archers* (the everyday tale of simple farming folk); but also introduced us to "The Radio Ham" and "The Blood Donor."

In the first, Hancock has succumbed to the joys of amateur radio, chatting with fellow enthusiasts around the world when his leisure is suddenly interrupted by a mayday call from a yachtsman. It should be the simplest thing in the world for Hancock to take down the distressed mariner's position and alert the rescue services. But of course, it isn't.

Even more popular is "The Blood Donor," in which Hancock does indeed go to a clinic to donate blood, without quite comprehending exactly what the procedure involves. He is astonishingly put out when, having undergone a prick on the finger to ascertain his blood group, he discovers that the orange juice and cookies are not immediately forthcoming; that first, he has to be drained of a pint.

"A pint? Why, that's very nearly an armful!"

A classic Hancock grimace inviting you to relive a classic *Hancock* episode.

Both episodes are classics, a point that was made, and perpetuated, by their release (in rerecorded form) as a long-playing record later in the year; indeed, across the years before VHS finally commenced the slow liberation of classic TV from the vaults, the gramophone was the only way that fans could relive favorite episodes of a great many shows.

Hancock would see four LPs released during his lifetime, the first (*Pieces of Hancock*) offering up excerpts of four past shows; the remainder, *The Blood Donor* included, serving up the soundtracks to two shows apiece—"The Wild Man of the Woods" and "A Sunday Afternoon at Home" on *This Is Hancock*; "The Missing Page" and "The Reunion Party" on *It's Hancock*. It is no surprise, even today, to see these same stories routinely proclaimed among Hancock's finest half hours, although to adhere to that wisdom is to seriously overlook some genuinely remarkable, and inspiring, shows.

Of course, the scourge of missing episodes haunts the series. Not one episode from the first season survives today, and just one from season two—the aforementioned "The Alpine Holiday." Five stories apiece from seasons three and four escaped the wiper; only seasons six and seven survive in their entirety, for a total of thirty-seven episodes. Which is better than many shows can manage, but does leave us primarily reliant on imagination, memory and scripts to realize what we are missing.

Those that do survive, however, offer more than adequate testament to the reverence with which their maker (and his coconspirators throughout the bulk of the show's lifetime) is held, ensemble pieces in which there are no weak links, no wasted dialogue, no wasteful space.

Hancock and the BBC parted company in 1961, the same year as he broke with Galton and Simpson, after disagreeing with them on the form of his second feature film. They went on to create what became *Steptoe and Son*, one of the most beloved sitcoms of the 1960s; Hancock began work on the movie *The Punch and Judy Man*, playing a struggling seaside entertainer desperate for a better life but, like the *Half Hour* hero before him, destined for failure.

So was the feature film. Spread over thirty minutes at a time, the sometimes relentlessly downbeat struggles of a pathetic little man caught the public imagination because at least part of you hoped that he might turn it around in the end. The movie allowed for no such happy ending; less a piece of light entertainment than it was a commentary on the sheer futility of life, *The Punch and Judy Man* is a fabulous movie, not only for its performances, but also for its evocation of British seaside life in the early 1960s.

But boy, is it depressing.

The Curtain Falls

In 1963, Hancock with new writers Godfrey Harrison, Dennis Spooner and Richard Harris, and Terry Nation launched a new season, again titled *Hancock,* for independent television.

Following the course of the BBC series, each episode was a stand-alone sitcom, featuring Hancock in a variety of situations from which all manner of chaos could be unleashed—working in a department store, witnessing a bank robbery, building a DIY wardrobe and so forth.

But whereas once, Hancock's presence alone was worth an extra decibel on the laugh track, and the sheer teamwork surrounding it could iron over any cracks, one cannot help but feel there was a disconnect between artist and writers; that Hancock flourished best in a situation where he knew his writers and they knew him.

It is impossible to disregard the talents of the men he now worked with—by the end of the year, Terry Nation would have created the Daleks for *Doctor Who*; and Dennis Spooner would be writing excellent episodes of nigh on every decent British show of the sixties. But though they wrote great shows, they did not write great Hancock shows. He deserved better and he needed better, too.

More salt was rubbed into his wounds when *Steptoe and Son* was launched and effortlessly overtook Hancock in the popularity stakes—even leading some critics to declare that it was Galton and Simpson, and not "the lad," who was the true star of the *Half Hour.*

Hancock was in decline, now. Although he continued a regular on British television, it was as the host of a couple of variety shows, neither of which are at all memorable. Alcohol was his constant companion, and his constant downfall; his performances were faltering, his timing was shot. His private life was dissolving, his friends were deserting him. When Hancock traveled to Sydney in March 1968, there to make a new television series for Australia's ABC network, *Hancock Down Under,* many in the industry regarded it as his last chance.

It was one that he would not take. With just three episodes completed, on June 25, 1968, Hancock died from the effects of a lethal combination of vodka and amylo-barbitone tablets. Notes found in his Bellevue apartment made it clear that it was a suicide.

"Things just seemed to go too wrong too many times," he wrote in one of them.

Hancock has never been forgotten. In 2002, among the myriad "best of" polls conducted to mark the millennium, BBC radio fans voted him the greatest British comedian of all time. Movies and dramas have been written around different elements of his time on this earth, with his tangled private life (two marriages, two divorces and a now well-publicized affair with the wife of actor John Le Mesurier) likewise prompting books and articles aplenty.

Comedians Paul Merton, David Pibworth and Kevin McNally are among the latter-day talents who have taken on Hancock's role in fresh visits to the Galton and Simpson canon, while several generations of subsequent funnymen could lay claim to, or have been credited as the beneficiaries of, different aspects of Hancock's cultural legacy.

Not one of them, however, can grasp it all, no matter how sincere their efforts, or their love of the original.

For not one of them has what Hancock had.

An astrakhan coat, a homburg hat and a comic genius that matched up to every ideal he believed the genre should embrace. If only he had realized that fact.

Aaah, He's Fallen in the Water

The Madness of Saint Milligoon

More than any other show in this book, perhaps, people either love *The Goons* with an undignified passion or they loathe it with a preternatural intensity. There is no (or, at least, very little) middle ground.

Certainly, listening to the shows some sixty years after they were created, it is impossible to deny that they have dated, and in some cases very badly. But is that because people don't find the same things funny anymore? Or because *The Goons* have been so thoroughly assimilated into the body politic of comedy that there is not an utterance, not a squawk, not a single, simple, sound in the show that has not been repeated, restyled, redressed and reinvented by somebody else?

It's a little like searching for the moment when the phrase "it was a dark and stormy night" was first declared a cliché, because when it was first penned as the opening sentence to a novel (by Victorian author Edward Bulwer-Lytton), it was one of the most dazzlingly original and atmospheric first lines ever penned. That's why so many other people borrowed it, copied it, ran with it; and *that* is why it became a cliché. The phrase itself was superb; it was its popularity that turned it into a joke.

And so it is with the Goons. The modern connoisseur of cutting-edge comedy has probably had its fill of hearing three or four people saying stupid things in a variety of silly voices. Particularly when they realize that they're actually watching the local news. (We will encounter this same dilemma again, later, when we revisit *Monty Python*.)

Where *The Goons* (and *Python*) triumphs is in the sheer freshness of the material. This was its first airing; the first time Britain at large had been privy to the innermost workings of a group of minds schooled not in the creative ferment of one of the military's entertainment units, but in the barrack rooms and mess tents of the fighting men, and based not on a reflection of life in all its petty absurdities, but on flights of fancy that only circuitously . . . *very* circuitously . . . returned to reality.

Or, as founding Goon Spike Milligan put it, "it is critical comedy. It is against bureaucracy and on the side of human beings. Its starting point is one man shouting gibberish in the face of authority and proving by fabricated insanity that nothing could be as mad as what passes for ordinary living."

Walking Backwards for Christmas

The Goons has been described as the most famous radio show in history, at least in the UK. Even abroad, however, cabals of enthusiasts still meet to rejoice in recordings of the episodes that have survived—and there's a lot, although (as always) not them all. Close to 150 episodes are available, derived in their entirety from the show's fifth through tenth seasons, plus a selection of rerecorded shows from the fourth. The remainder, the history of *The Goons* between its launch of May 28, 1951, and September 1954, were wiped.

Scripts survive, though, and those same enthusiasts are known to reenact them, silly voices and all.

And were those voices silly!

There were four Goons to begin with. Spike Milligan and Harry Secombe first met while serving in the Royal Artillery during the Second World War. According to a much-repeated anecdote, they were introduced when Milligan's unit, on top of a cliff, somehow allowed a howitzer to fall off the edge and come crashing to earth close by the spot where Secombe was seated in a wireless truck.

The dust was still settling when a truck pulled up and a voice called out "has anyone seen a gun?"

"What color was it?" Secombe replied.

Friendship blossomed immediately.

Following the war, Milligan and Secombe both moved onto the London comedy circuit, snatching work where they could and hanging out with everybody else at the pub in Archer Street; Tony Hancock was among their closest friends, and his cowriter Larry Stephens, too. Peter Sellers, another of Hancock's friends, entered this same ferment after being introduced to Milligan and Secombe at the Hackney Empire; Michael Bentine encountered Secombe at the Windmill Theatre.

Harry Secombe, Peter Sellers and Spike Milligan line up as *The Goons*.

Any permutation of available comics could, theoretically have become "the Goons"; by the late 1940s, however, the quartet of Milligan, Secombe, Sellers and Bentine were a team, based at the Grafton pub in Victoria and entertaining themselves and anyone else in range with lengthy, impromptu and uproariously bizarre sketches.

Painfully aware that a lot of great material was simply being thrown into the air, never to be heard again, the Grafton's eponymous landlord, Jimmy Grafton (himself a renowned scriptwriter), prevailed upon them to begin recording these outbursts and circulating the tapes as well. One came to the attention of BBC producer Pat Dixon, who, knowing that all four performers already had a foot in the door of BBC light entertainment, began championing the full team in the corridors of power.

The BBC agreed to commission a single season from the quartet, but, by all accounts, was less than enthusiastic about the show. On paper, all was conventional enough, a typical thirty-minute variety show that combined humorous sketches with musical numbers, with Secombe already a proven musical talent. Possessed of a rich baritone, he would later enjoy a sizable career both on record and in musicals.

But he would not really be exercising his baritone in *The Goons*—or *The Crazy People*, as the BBC insisted on retitling it. None of the four would appear as themselves. Rather, a stable of characters had developed across their years of struggle, each with its roots in a certain kind of person whom one of the four had met; sometimes even a specific individual.

All, however, were then taken to the point of caricature, and beyond. And that was the beauty of the show. To an alien, or a twenty-first-century novice, Sellers's Major Dennis Bloodnok and Henry Crun, Milligan's Eccles and Minnie Bannister, and the inventor Osric Pureheart, who might be voiced by any of the team, are just funny names with silly voices. To the listening public, they were instantly recognizable.

Early reviews of the show echoed the BBC's trepidation. The show was recorded live onstage, and was as reliant on visual humor as it was verbal. The studio audience, for the most part, was in stitches of laughter. But critics complained that the action was too fast, the voices too difficult, the caricatures too obscure.

The public disagreed. The first show was heard, it was estimated, by around 354,000 people. The seventeenth, the last in the season, attracted an audience of 1.8 million.

The success was instantly rewarded with a Christmas special, playing on the story of Cinderella, and weeks later, on January 22, 1952, the show's second season got under way. The team was also permitted to revert to its original name. The show was now, and forever more would be, titled *The Goons*.

Milligoon in Excelsis

Because no earlier episodes exist, it is often said that *The Goons* did not really find their feet until the fourth season. That was the first in which single story lines appeared, each bearing its own unique episode title (beginning with "The Dreaded Piano Clubber"); and the last to feature Tony Hancock's ex-partner Larry Stephens as Milligan's regular cowriter; henceforth, Milligan would do much of the writing alone and handle his own script editing too. (Jimmy Grafton filled that role previously.)

By this time, too, the team had been reduced to a trio, as Bentine departed (perfectly amicably) following the second season, to concentrate on his own career; and Peter Eton replaced Derek Main Smith as the producer. Musical interludes, hitherto performed by such conventional talents as Max Geldray, the Ray Ellington Quartet and the Stargazers, had been eased out, to be succeeded by the team's own efforts (the Goons' "Ying Tong Song" would be a UK hit in 1956 and again, as a reissue, in 1973).

Season four was also the first season to be recorded after Milligan suffered the nervous breakdown (brought on by overwork) that removed him from much of season three, but which allowed him valuable time and space in which to reconsider what *The Goons* was all about.

However, if the convergence of so many different events conspired to turn *The Goon Show* into the program that we now know so well, that is not to say that the earlier series were in any way deficient.

With an audience now numbered in the millions, it would be absolutely disingenuous to claim that they all listened in in the hope of the show at some point getting better. They listened because they already loved it, and it is impossible to say whether or not they loved it any more as a result of the changes. To argue otherwise is akin to claiming that *The Taming of the Shrew* was Shakespeare's first decent play, simply because you've not read any of the earlier ones.

As aforementioned, season four no longer exists in its original form. Such was the popularity of *The Goons*, however, that the BBC later requested a series of *Vintage Goons*, re-creating fourteen of the season's thirty episodes and thus allowing subsequent generations to thrill again to such capers as "The First Albert Memorial to the Moon," "The Kippered Herring Gang" and "The Great Ink Drought of 1902."

(Still lost, however, is a June 1954 special in which Harry Secombe was reunited with the dummy Archie Andrews, and Milligan wrote for the first time with Eric Sykes. *Archie in Goonland* sees Peter Brough and his loquacious costar tumble down a mousehole and find themselves in the midst of a rodent-led plan to destroy London.)

In adopting what we now call its "classic" format, a single thirty-minute story line, *The Goon Show* was free to expand beyond all previous boundaries. In an age when royalty was still regarded as untouchable in the realm of comedy, Peter Sellers excited any amount of ill-tempered comment when he introduced the Duchess Boil de Spudswell to another one-off special, "The Starlings," and revealed her to sound exactly like the Queen.

At a time, too, when the public image of law enforcement remained locked in a cozy world of respect and politeness, Milligan's Ned Seagoon and Sellers's Hercules Grytpype-Thynne enjoyed this particular exchange:

Grytpype-Thynne: "This batter pudding hurler . . . [has] made a fool of the police."

Seagoon [a policeman]: "I disagree. We were fools long before he came along."

Grytpype-Thynne: "You silly, twisted boy."

Although the Goons seemed to operate wholly in a world all of their own insane invention, the show was, in fact, extraordinarily topical. "The Starlings" was based on a real-life newspaper report in which a local council was soliciting suggestions on how to rid itself of an infestation of that very bird; Milligan's response was to apply exploding bird-lime to all public buildings and rely on the sound of detonation to scare them away. Sadly, this succeeds only in damaging the buildings; the only guaranteed way of chasing off the birds, it seems, was by catapulting rice pudding at them.

When actor A. E. Matthews, one of *the* grand old men of English film, was noted in the press for opposing attempts to erect a lamppost outside his country cottage home, Milligan invited him to appear in an episode in which a pair of servants, looking after a home a lot like Matthews's own, discover a giant hole growing in the garden.

Close to ninety years old, Matthews gamely agreed—without appearing to have any idea of what the show actually was. In fact, it isn't even certain that he was given a script. Rather, he seems to have been told to simply be himself and react to what goes on around him in any way he pleased. The result, "The Evils of Bushey Spon," is one of the most delightfully chaotic of all surviving *Goon Shows*, if only for the sheer calm and common sense that Matthews displays in the face of such madness.

"The night before last, I was on the television," he announces, for no particular reason, at one point.

Minnie Bannister—the rest of the cast remained resolutely in character—promptly rebukes him. "Oh sir, we told you not to go. It was very cold that night, you shouldn't have gone out." Henry repeats her admonition, only for Matthews to snap "you're over-acting. Leave it be."

Brilliant!

On another occasion, reports that the BBC was undergoing an economy drive prompted the introduction of a bagpipe record being slowed down and then sped up again, as Seagoon boards a taxi. This, the show's announcer Wallace Greenslade explains, is because "the BBC . . . have discovered that it is cheaper to travel by bagpipes. Not only are they more musical, but they come in a wide variety of colors."

And when BBC television scored a massive hit with a magnificent adaptation of George Orwell's *1984*, in December 1954, *The Goons* promptly unleashed *1985*, in which the Big Brother Corporation crush opposition by introducing its foes to the dreaded Room 101—a listening room into which the theme music from other radio shows is piped incessantly. This fearful organization's initials, of course, were probably not arrived at coincidentally.

Another popular TV show, adapting the adventures of Robin Hood, would also be spoofed during season four, while the sitcom *Life with the Lyons* was also a favorite target—its title music is among those that drive dissenters insane in Room 101, while its catchphrases were frequently deployed as purposeful non sequiturs during other adventures.

But Ben and Bebe Lyon would take their revenge. When a solid four minutes of laughter needed to be edited from the recording of *The Goons*' "The Terrible Revenge of Fu Manchu," Ben Lyon promptly requisitioned it to splice into the soundtrack of his own show!

A Goonish Legacy

The Goons ultimately ran for ten seasons before closing shop in January 1960—a run that is all the more remarkable when one considers that for at least half of its run, it was in serious competition with television. (Other radio shows could boast far longer lives, but scarcely touched *The Goons* in terms of popularity.) Yet the Goons themselves never made the switch to the small screen during the show's own lifetime.

Later, in 1963, *The Tele-Goons*, would run for one season, carving original broadcasts down to fifteen minutes and peopling them with puppets, while Harry Secombe revisited "The Whistling Spy Enigma" for his 1966 solo series. The Goons themselves would reconvene in 1968 to make a TV version of "Tales of Men's Shirts," and again in 1972 for "The Last Goon Show of All."

By that time, however, all four Goons had long-established careers of their own, with one of their number, Peter Sellers, now verging on movie superstar status; with another, Harry Secombe, rejoicing in his musical doings; with Michael Bentine a madcap television regular; and Spike Milligan basically off being Spike Milligan in a variety of hit-and-miss ventures. *The Goons* was a long way away for them all, but it had never *gone* away.

To the end of their lives (Sellers died in 1980, Bentine in 1996, Secombe in 2001, Milligan in 2002), all four members of the team could scarcely give an interview without the Goons raising their collective head; could not make a public appearance without hearing one of the characters' voices raised in greeting; could not even read the memoirs of their contemporaries without being reminded of their own inestimable impact on the world of British comedy.

In Maxime Ventner's biography of Milligan, *Spike Milligan: His Part in Our Lives,* John Cleese is quoted as saying "in comedy, there are a very small number of defining moments when somebody comes along and genuinely creates a breakthrough, takes us into territory where nobody has been before. The only experiences to which I can compare my own discovery of *The Goons* are going to see NF Simpson's play *One Way Pendulum* . . . or, later on, hearing Peter Cook for the first time. They were just light years ahead of everyone else."

In Cook's collected works, *Sadly I Was an Only Twin,* we discover that he would feign sickness at school simply so he could listen to *The Goon Show.* And there may or may not have been just a soupçon of Goonsy reminiscence when, at the Secret Policeman's Ball in 1979, Cook found himself running out of comical euphemisms for a homosexual.

"Well," Billy Connolly is said to have responded. "You could always try 'a player of the pink oboe'." Twenty years earlier, with Britain still reeling beneath the repercussions of the so-called Cambridge Spy Ring's defection to the Soviet Union, and the apparently significant revelation that at least one of its number had been gay (a popular theme of Soviet blackmail plots), *The Goon Show* immortalized a secret agent whose codename was Pink Oboe.

Beatle John Lennon told the *New York Times,* "I was twelve when *The Goon Show* first hit me, sixteen when they finished with me. Their humor was the only proof that the world was insane."

In every generation, in every aspect of entertainment, the Goons lurk on. Prince Charles, the Prince of Wales and heir to the British throne, is a confirmed Goons fanatic. There is a character named Minnie Bannister in *Superman III* and a star system named for Bloodnok in *Shrek.* An early nineties pop band called itself Ned's Atomic Dustbin.

And every time a child refers to an illness as "the dreaded lurgi" (a Goonsian construct that may or may not have been short for "allergy"), which in Britain, they have done for fifty years, they are referencing the greatest sickness of them all.

We should all catch a dose of Goons fever.

Your Majesty Is Like a Cream Donut

It's Not Funny, It's Satirical

The story of the "satire boom" that swept the world of British entertainment in the early 1960s is a well-worn one. Responsible for bringing the world a veritable shopping list of talents, tyrants and institutions, the following is a mere snapshot of all that this unprecedented outbreak of comedic observation unleashed:

The twice-monthly news magazine *Private Eye*, still going strong after fifty-plus years.

Beyond the Fringe, the post-Oxbridge revue that developed in the halls of England's greatest universities, and eventually wound up on Broadway, and which shocked all comers when Peter Cook became the first person in living memory to impersonate a sitting prime minister, Harold MacMillan, onstage.

David Frost, regarded as among the most trenchant television journalists of his generation.

Dudley Moore.

Alan Bennett.

Monty Python's roots lie in the boom, and so do the Goodies'. (For more *Fringe* frolics, see chapter four.)

And, at the forefront of all this hangs *That Was the Week That Was*, a weekly BBC show that can in many ways be regarded as a precursor for everything from the anarchic puppet show *Spitting Image*, with its incisive and even brutal treatment of the great and the good of the day; and the Jon Stewart-era *Daily Show*, for its no-nonsense analysis of what the network news wasn't telling people.

That Was the Week That Will Be

TW3, as it conveniently became known, was the brainchild of Ned Sherrin, a BBC current affairs producer, acting on the success of his earlier show, *Tonight*—an hour-long magazine program that itself caused something of an uproar with its less than deferential treatment of the day's leading politicians.

This was new territory for the BBC or, indeed, any other aspect of the media. The assumption that "our leaders know best," while not necessarily the opinion of the journalists and newsmen, was nevertheless ingrained in society. (Half a century on, two seasons of the superlative BBC drama *The Hour* offered up an exquisitely realized examination of the broadcasting mores of the day.)

Sherrin and other members of the current affairs team were working as hard behind the scenes to shatter this attitude as the cast of the theatrical revue *Beyond the Fringe*—Cook, Moore, Bennett and Jonathan Miller—were working onstage; harder, in fact, because they not only had to convince the public of their stance, they also needed to convince their own bosses.

Fortunately, current events themselves were also at work, undermining the government's hitherto formidable carapace. The humiliation of the Suez Crisis in 1956; the unfolding revelations of the aforementioned Cambridge Spy Scandal; scandal after scandal was suddenly being unearthed; controversy after controversy, misstep after misspeak.

When the publishers of D. H. Lawrence's novel *Lady Chatterley's Lover* went on trial for obscenity in 1960, how could one not laugh when the government's chief prosecutor asked the jury, in all seriousness, whether it were the kind of book "you would wish your wife *or servants* to read."

Servants? Who had servants in 1960?

Oh, right. People like the chief prosecutor.

The watershed, however, arrived two years later in the form of the Profumo Affair, a bitter betrayal of both the country's security *and* its morality that ultimately reeled in, in no particular order, the Secretary of State for War (Profumo himself); a Soviet Naval attaché; a model; a hooker; a socialite; one of the wealthiest families in the land; and one of the most bumbling attempted cover-ups ever attempted.

The British press was effectively gagged, even as foreign newspapers ran with the unfolding details. Only *Private Eye*, hitherto a more or less underground organ of disaffected carping (as the satire movement in general was perceived to be), chose to break the embargo, dropping a stream of

Host David Frost and singer Lance Percival on the set of *TW3*.   *Alamy*

increasingly inflammatory hints as to what and, more importantly, who was involved in the scandal.

Finally, in 1963, it all came out, and heads would roll, cell doors would slam and governments would teeter. Before that, though the media—which was in no mood whatsoever to maintain the pretenses that had hitherto shored up the country's self-styled lords and masters—had a field day. Comedians, not least of all.

Launched in November 1962, *TW3* was the BBC's contribution to the ensuing merriment. Mining the comedic underground for cast members—*Beyond the Fringe* had already spawned a "satirical" nightclub, the Establishment; other venues were regularly staging "satirical" revues of their own—Sherrin pieced together a cast headed by a young but still improbably smarmy David Frost, together with cartoonist Timothy Birdsall, political commentator Bernard Levin, and comedians Kenneth Cope, Roy Kinnear, Frankie Howerd, Willie Rushton, Al Mancini, Robert Lang, and Lance Percival. Music was supplied by Percival (a weekly calypso reflecting on current affairs), David Kernan and Millicent Martin.

Behind the scenes, scriptwriters included John Albery, John Antrobus, poet John Betjeman, John Bird, future Pythonites Graham Chapman and

John Cleese, Peter Cook, author Roald Dahl, Richard Ingrams (the editor of *Private Eye*), Lyndon Irving, Gerald Kaufman (a Labour Party politician), Frank Muir, David Nobbs (creator, in years to come, of the mighty Reginald Perrin), Denis Norden, Bill Oddie (*The Goodies*), Dennis Potter, latter-day *Goons* alumnus Eric Sykes, Kenneth Tynan, and Keith Waterhouse (a ferociously socialist newspaper columnist and author of the novel *Billy Liar*).

And, before the cameras, nothing was sacred.

Modern audiences would likely be unimpressed. Nothing ages so fast as current affairs humor, as an evening spent watching mid-eighties *Spitting Image* reruns, or even one of last year's *Daily Shows*, will prove. Can you even remember half of what they're talking about? At the time, though, they were at least effective, and oftentimes infinitely more devastating.

Reel back close to sixty years, to a time when *nothing* like this had ever been screened. Forget making jokes about the Queen; you wouldn't even make fun of her pet corgis. Politicians were sacrosanct, the aristocracy was respectable, scandals were scarcely whispered about.

Then along came *TW3*, a riot of parodies and lampoons so effective that, ultimately, the ruling class was reduced to such figures of fun that many of them would never shake off the caricatures that were created around them.

Writer Bill Oddie later admitted that many of the show's jokes were simply revisions of older, existing material—only instead of telling a "mother-in-law" joke, the writer would substitute the name of a top politician. Still, the result was often just as funny and sometimes even better.

Topicality was the show's goal. Scripts were not finalized until just hours before the show's Saturday night broadcast (a trick that both *Spitting Image* and *Drop the Dead Donkey* would echo in later decades), allowing events to slip almost instantaneously from the evening news to the *TW3* mincer.

Nor did the show shy away from the most controversial issues of the day.

When the Home Secretary, Henry Brooke, announced he intended deporting a young Jamaican girl for the crime of shoplifting (only to relent when the papers got hold of the story), *TW3* ran a spoof interview with him (Willie Rushton played Brooke, interviewer David Frost played himself) in which all of Brooke's past absurdities were dragged out—including his decision to ban the American Nazi George Lincoln Rockwell from ever entering the country, *two days* after the man gave his first speech on British soil.

"[That] August was a busy time for you," Frost consoled him. On another occasion, Brooke informed the House of Commons that he had approved the extradition back to the United States of the spy Henry Soblen. "He is fit to travel," Brooke announced, "and I must act as I have said I will."

"Which is rare," Frost mused, spitefully enough, before delivering the killer blow. "Alas, Henry, Dr. Soblen took an overdose of drugs and let you down."

A decade-plus later, such comedy remained entrenched. Touring the UK in 1974, Monty Python's Flying Circus, Cleese and Chapman included, performed a lengthy skit parodying typical television coverage of a General Election, its impact granted additional *gravitas* by the fact that the country had just been through one—and would face another before the year was out. Even more scathingly, few people listening to it could disagree that Python's projection for victory . . . "another four years of Silly government" . . . was now horribly close to the truth.

Introducing such immortals to the hustings as Kevin Phillips Bong and Jethro Q Walrustitty, "Election Special" is a succession of quick-fire puns, well-mannered digs and quite ferocious insults, many of which were, on this occasion, targeted ruthlessly at real-life political candidates.

A renowned racial scaremonger, Enoch Powell, saw his constituency won by the unequivocally named Rastas O'Dingah O'Dingah. Tarquin Fintinlinbinwimbimlinbin-Bus Stop-F'tang_F'tang-Ole-Biscuit_Barrel was patently modeled on any one of several double-(or more) barreled Conservative bastions; and the little pink pussycat who beat the Liberal Party in Barrow was, in fact, a veiled acknowledgment of the rumors of homosexuality that now swirled around that party's leader, Jeremy Thorpe.

All of which, when laid bare, is utterly meaningless today, but remains cloaked in a veneer of glorious satirical commentary when regarded in its own right.

TW3 could never have gone that far (even Python's election special was never performed on television), but it was undeniably scathing and astonishingly popular nevertheless. Audiences that averaged around twelve million represented one-fifth of the entire population of the country. But the BBC remained unhappy with it. Most of the show's scripts were frowned upon in one circle or another, all the more so since the nature of the show ensured that some would not even be submitted for approval before the program aired.

There was also the show's constant habit of either under-running or over-running its allotted late-night space. Finally, the powers that be acted, adding one more show to the schedule, reruns of the thriller *The Third Man* Now TW3 would have to fit its time slot. Or so the schedulers thought. Frost and Sherrin responded by giving the new show their own unique form of prepublicity—by reading out the entire plot of the forthcoming episode. Three weeks later, *The Third Man* slipped quietly from the schedule.

So parochial a program could not, for obvious reasons, hope to resonate with an American audience. However, as if to prove that not everything is a laughing matter, a twenty-minute *TW3* tribute to John F. Kennedy, broadcast the very day after his assassination, Saturday, November 23, 1963, would be picked up by NBC for US consumption, and even led to a hit single. Millicent Martin's musical tribute, "In the Summer of His Years," was covered by Connie Francis and became an American hit in the new year.

However, *TW3*'s days were numbered. Despite its popularity with the viewing public, it remained the most frequently and vociferously complained-about show on the network. The BBC had already demanded that the show tone down its constant references to what Director General Hugh Greene termed "sex" and "smut," but disrespect and rudeness continued unabated.

When David Frost compared the newly appointed leader of the Conservative Party, Alec Douglas-Hume, with his Labour Party opposite Harold Wilson as a battle between "Dull Alec" and "Smart Alec" (an English term for "smartass"), the BBC received almost a thousand complaints by phone and mail.

Powerful names, too, were allied against the show, from the vice-chairman of the Conservative Party (who accused Frost of nurturing an uncontrollable hatred of the prime minister), to the government of Cyprus, who thought jokes about the country's ruler Archbishop Makarios violated "internationally accepted ethics." Even the Boy Scout Association stuck the knife in, after a sketch seemed to suggest its founder Lord Baden-Powell was not among the most heterosexual of men.

The final straw, however, came when the vice president of the BBC's own Board of Governors, Sir James Duff, insinuated that he was considering resigning his position, so deeply did he loathe *TW3*. After thirty-seven episodes spread across two seasons, *TW3* breathed its last on December 28, 1963. The official reason was, 1964 was an election year, and the BBC was expected to be politically balanced in its output. Few impartial viewers could deny that *TW3* was an equal opportunity taunter, as the Dull versus Smart Alec debate amply proved. But the very nature of government insisted that the ruling Conservatives would bear the brunt of the show's scorn, and that was enough.

Not So Much a Revival, More Another Program

Besides, although the cancellation of *TW3* readily mollified the show's critics, the BBC turned out not to have tired, after all, of either satire or the satirists. On October 15, 1964, the election was fought and won by Harold Wilson and Labour. A month later, on November 13, Ned Sherrin, David Frost, Willie Rushton and Bill Oddie were back with *Not So Much a Programme, More a Way of Life*.

Again, current affairs were the primary target; again, the program mined the richest seams of British comedic talent—the poet P. J. Kavanagh, Eleanor Bron, John Bird, Patrick Campbell, John Fortune, Rod Hull (later to find fame as one half of a double act with a psychotic emu puppet) and Michael Crawford (still years away from his superstardom as Frank Spencer) were all involved.

Accusations that the show was simply the son of *TW3*, meanwhile, were dismissed by staging the action on a vivid, all-white set, a stylish contrast to the darkened nightclub setting of its predecessor; and by scheduling no less than three episodes a week, on Friday, Saturday and Sunday nights.

That was the first mistake. With the best will in the world, it was difficult for any writing team to maintain a high-quality output across such a demanding schedule, and the show quickly gained a reputation for being somewhat hit-and-miss. However, when it worked, it was every bit as successful as *TW3*, with Eleanor Bron's recurrent Lady Pamela Stitty not only emerging as the "star" of the show, but also providing the blueprint for more or less every vapid female aristocrat to appear on-screen since then. (And, one might add, for a lot of their real life counterparts, too.)

Neither was there any lessening of complaints. In cultural terms, the "satire boom" could now be said to be over; it perished, it seems, with the removal of the spectacularly bumbling Conservatives from office, and their replacement by the commoner touch of the socialists.

But politics and world affairs remained a source of considerable glee, if one only cared to look past their direr connotations, as John Bird discovered when he appeared as Kenyan President Jomo Kenyatta. He was commenting on the somewhat bitter election campaign that the British had just endured and suggesting that Kenyan troops should be stationed in the UK to oversee its peaceful transition to a more stable government. Precisely the kind of thing, in fact, that Western leaders suggest whenever a so-called "underdeveloped" nation elects a leader that London and Washington don't approve of.

Immediately, the Kenyan High Commission was up in arms, protesting everything from Bird's mock-African accent (and his waving of a flyswatter) to a perceived slight on their leader and his policies.

The BBC refused to apologize. In spirit, if not in these actual words, the Kenyans were informed that they had clearly not understood the sketch, which was far more a comment on British than African politics; that they had probably not even listened to what was being said—and, if they had, they had taken it so far out of context that they might as well be complaining about a different program altogether.

How different from today, when context is often the very last topic addressed when the witch-hunt wagon sets off in search of artificial offense. How different from the modern media, which will happily throw the most innocent soul to the wolves of "popular opinion," rather than actually stand up for itself. In those days, the BBC stood firm, and the complainants stood down.

But the show was not out of the woods. Viewing figures were in no way comparable to *TW3* at its peak, and the press in general was unimpressed, constantly referring back to the old show as the model it should be replicating (and overlooking the howls of protest that those same critics would have uttered if it had).

Even Peter Cook, who might have been expected to show some solidarity with *NSMAP*'s aims, delivered a brutal parody of it for a flexidisc given away by *Private Eye*, an inflection-perfect impersonation of Frost, accompanied by a barrage of rude noises to represent one of the program's beloved live discussions.

Ultimately, however, the show would be undone by its own commitment to comedy. The Catholic church's stance on contraception was a hot topic of controversy at the time, as the birth control pill continued its relentless drive into everyday life; Donald Webster's sketch revolved around a Catholic priest collecting donations from his parishioners and pausing to inquire after the number of children one of them has now had.

"Twenty-five," she tells him proudly, but the priest is aghast. Clearly she is not pregnant now—has she, perhaps, sinned? Is she using contraception?

"Why, no, father," she replies. It's just that the family is now so poor that her husband can no longer afford to get drunk, which in turn means he can no longer "do his duty."

Horrified, the priest hands her back her donation and tells her to buy her husband some beer instead.

In the eyes of the Catholic church, that was bad enough, but worse was to follow: a studio discussion in which the bluntness of the sketch was compared with the church's own policy of insisting that even the poorest nations should be denied contraception, and thus contributing directly not only to poverty, but to wider issues of starvation and overpopulation.

It was a debate that had already played out in the corridors of the United Nations—whose idea it had been to distribute free contraception to the so-called Third World—and in those newspapers and magazines that followed the controversy. But clearly that was no defense. A late-night light entertainment program, it seemed, had no business discussing such affairs.

The Catholic church was outraged; the British Parliament sided with it. Public apologies were demanded, from the BBC (whose director general would write a letter of regret) and from Frost (who refused outright), and the furor was still percolating a month later when *NSMAP* delivered its next zinger. And this one would be fatal.

On the face of it, a musical comedy about the abdication of King Edward VIII should not have been too much of a problem. The events in question occurred back in 1936, almost thirty years before, and in many ways represent one of the great love stories of the twentieth century; the heir to the throne relinquishing the kingship so that he might marry the woman he loved. Who, unfortunately, was an American divorcée, at a time when such creatures (divorcées—and, come to that, Americans) were barred from the throne of the United Kingdom.

And that was it, a simple song and dance that was absolutely nothing to make a song and dance about. Apart from the fact that Buckingham Palace had announced the death of Edward's sister, the Princess Royal, just four hours before the show was broadcast.

This time, maybe there was cause for complaint. The sketch could have been held back a week as a mark of respect to the family; and of course today, there would be no question about doing so. But it was aired as scheduled, and with another firestorm of opprobrium raging around it, the BBC pulled the plug on *NSMAP*. It would complete its scheduled run (on April 11, 1965), but the expected second season was cancelled outright.

The Third Channel

And still Ned Sherrin and the BBC persisted, replacing *NSMAP* in October 1965 with *BBC-3*, hosted by the avuncular Robert Robertson, and again featuring the likes of John Bird, Eleanor Bron, Bill Oddie, Millicent Martin and Alan Bennett, alongside roly-poly Roy Dotrice and the desert-dry comic genius that was Leonard Rossiter.

It was, perhaps, hoped that the show would prove calmer, and less prone to outrage than its predecessors. Robertson, in particular, was one of the country's most respected broadcasters, his warmth and on-screen friendliness far removed from the self-aggrandizing braggadocio of Frost, while the political humor was gentler. Even the prime minister, Harold Wilson, was said to be an avid viewer, a fan in particular of John Bird's weekly homilies—delivered, though they were, in the character of . . . Harold Wilson.

But still outrage awaited, and it ensnared the most unexpected member of the cast, Robert Robertson, as he hosted a live discussion onstage of censorship—at that time a very real, and voracious, beast that dictated every action, every gesture and every word delivered on a theatrical stage.

Playwright Kenneth Tynan was among the guests, a vociferous opponent of the Lord Chancellor's office that oversaw the censorship and a skilled self-publicist too. So he very likely knew exactly what he was doing, and what the reaction would be when, before an audience of live television cameras, he made the trenchant observation that he doubted whether there were "any rational people to whom the word 'fuck' would be particularly diabolical, revolting or totally forbidden." And then followed up by declaring that "anything which can be printed or said can also be seen."

It was the first time the word "fuck" had ever been spoken on British television. You can *imagine* the outcry.

As a forum for live debate, *BBC-3* was a lively beast, then. As a comedy, however, it continued in the same when-it's-good-it's-very-good-*but* fashion as its predecessor, with even the normally reliable Alan Bennett guilty of filling space with some overlong material, and Bill Oddie, oddly, largely confined to providing the musical numbers—no hardship for him, as he later went on to score a number of hit singles with *The Goodies*, but still a peculiar use of his manifold talents.

There again, it's hard to fault Sherrin's judgment in deploying Oddie thus; we are talking, after all, of a man who later took the traditional northern English folk song "On Ilkla Moor Baht 'at" (which we will meet again later in this book) and transformed it into a yearning rock epic to stand alongside Joe Cocker's "With a Little Help from My Friends" in the annals of howling, yowling anthemic majesty.

So, Oddie sang, Robertson discussed, the others played out their sketches and *BBC-3* ran for one season and then sank. A replacement, *The Late Show*, debuted a year later, with Bird and Bron joined by the future

Dame Edna Everage, Australian comic Barry Humphries, among others, but it too lasted just one not-so-memorable season. Its final episode included a sketch about the Irish writer James Joyce, in which the recurring line "satire is dead" could not help but feel like a statement of fact. In terms of television comedy, it was.

But nobody really minded. Not when there was so much else to laugh at.

This Bloke Came Up to Me

Pete, Dud and the Pursuit of Perfection

According to Peter Cook, the miracle of life is achieved in a very particular manner.

First, the father-to-be sits in a chair. Then, moments after he has vacated it, and it is still warm from his body, his wife (they have to be married for this to work) also sits it. Something "very mysterious, rather wonderful and beautiful" then occurs; and, "sure enough, four years later . . . ."

Dirty Uncle Bertie has nothing to do with any of it.

The world of Peter Cook (and, for that matter, his longtime comedic partner Dudley Moore) was a very strange place. A place where war wounds left hereditary blemishes. Where an order of nuns spends its days on trampolines, and where aristocratic women can break a swan's wing with one blow of their nose. Where breasts are referred to as busty substances (but those belonging to deceased historical personages are more accurately termed "musty" ones); and where it is perfectly feasible for a grown man to find employment removing lobsters from Jayne Mansfield's bottom.

Cook also once claimed to have once met Princess Anne, and introduced himself as Hollywood great Stewart Granger. "You're not," replied the princess, and she was correct.

Peter Cook has been described, by no less a quipster than Stephen Fry, as "the funniest man who ever drew breath," a fact that an evening spent in the company of his writings, broadcasts, recordings and movies may or may not validate.

Certainly not everything he did was deathless. Like Spike Milligan, another challenger for that title, much of Peter Cook's career was spent laboring beneath the burden of *being* Peter Cook; of knowing, wherever he went, that there would be an audience hanging on his every word, waiting for him to utter *the funniest thing they had ever heard*. And he hated to disappoint them, which invariably meant that he would. It's hard to be hilarious every minute of the day, although Cook came closer than most.

The Trouble with Herring

Throughout the mid-1980s, listeners to a late-night phone-in show on a London local radio show had long since grown accustomed to callers having one topic, and one topic only, that they wished to sound off about—often in the most minute and tedious detail. So when a Norwegian insomniac named Sven began phoning in to bemoan his countryfolk's obsession with fish, interspersed with laments for his runaway wife Jutta, nobody really thought anything of it. Just another sleepless weirdo.

One night, he would discuss how refreshing it was to hear a phone-in whose topic was not exclusively fish-related. On another occasion, he called in during a "guess that sound" competition, to suggest that it was the sound of fish. Another night, he was explaining how Norway deals with the problem of football hooliganism—by showing pictures of fish on a giant screen.

And all the while, nobody knew that Sven was Peter Cook. Not the listeners, not the station switchboard and certainly not the show's host, Clive Bull. He did, after a while, suspect that Sven might not actually be all he said he was—the fishy references were growing too bizarre for that. But he played along regardless, and while a mutual friend did eventually spill the beans, Bull kept his knowledge to himself. And so Cook, or rather, Sven, continued on, liberated from the demands of being *Peter Cook*, free simply to be himself.

So if anyone ever tells you that he wasn't so funny in his later years as he was when he was younger . . . they're wrong. Sven was one of his greatest creations of all.

That much of Cook's comedy was improvised, or at least gave the impression of being so, is undeniable. He fed off people's reactions, whether it was an audience's laughter, when he appeared alone, or his onstage partner's own reactions, when he worked with others (even Clive Bull could effectively be termed his straight man), changing thoughts in midstream according to whatever else was happening around him.

Rarely do you see Cook simply adhering to a prearranged script; never do his eyes glaze over as he slips into autopilot. Always he was studying his surroundings, searching for that one word or gesture that might catapult him away in a whole new direction, while his costars struggle to catch up.

Few could, but one usually did—Dudley Moore.

Through the years during which Cook and Moore seemed inseparable—
that is, most of the sixties and pockets of the seventies—the double act of
"Pete and Dud" was best characterized by two somewhat shabby men seated
on a bench, on a bus, at the zoo, or even in a rather tatty annex of Heaven,
talking about "stuff." Geckos one week, art the next, St. Paul's Letters to
the "Ephiscans" the next, "Dear Ephiscans. Stop enjoying yourselves, God's
about the place. Signed Paul."

And every week, there would be that telling moment when Moore would
crack up, as if the stream of invention ushering from his partner's lips had
caught even him by surprise. And if Moore could not control his laughter,
what chance did the rest of us have?

Peter Cook and Dudley Moore—the one a towering, handsome and
almost aristocratic-looking wit, the other a short, dark, clubfooted pianist—
met as members of *Beyond the Fringe*, in which Cook was the only professional
comic; he already had a revue running in the West End, *Pieces of Eight* with
Kenneth Williams.

Beyond the Fringe was essentially a sequence of sketches, each written
by one or more members of the team, each playing to an individual's
strengths—so Moore's were musical; Bennett's were character-driven . . .
and Cook's were surreal, pointedly addressing those questions that most
of us have probably asked ourselves at one time or another, but never really
expected to be answered.

Such as—what, precisely, does a doomsday prophet say when he realizes
he got his dates wrong yet again? ("Never mind, lad, same time tomorrow.
We must get a winner one day.")

What does a talent agent say to a one-legged man, applying for the role
of Tarzan? ("I've got nothing against your [one] leg. The trouble is—neither
have you.")

What should Britain do about national security during the eight-year
wait for a practical nuclear deterrent, the American Polaris system, to be
delivered? ("Keep our fingers crossed, sit very quietly, and try not to alienate
anyone.")

And effectively birthing the British satire movement with that aforementioned word-perfect impersonation of the prime minister.

Cook's rise beyond *Beyond the Fringe* was mercurial. He established
a comedy club in the heart of London, and the Establishment became
to satire what Greenwich Village was to the folk boom. He was a major
contributor to, and investor in, the newly launched *Private Eye*; and history
rightfully records him as both parent and midwife to such television shows

as *That Was the Week That Was* (see previous chapter), *At Last the 1948 Show* and *Monty Python's Flying Circus*—not to mention a signal influence on the career of David Frost, whom Cook delightedly rechristened "the Bubonic Plagiarist."

Returning from *Beyond the Fringe*'s American sojourn, Cook moved into television as one of the stars of the magazine program *On the Braden Beat*. But then the BBC offered Dudley Moore his own one-off musical television show, a pilot for a possible series. Moore jumped at it, of course, and promptly recast it as a double act, inviting Cook to both write sketches and star alongside him in what became *Not Only . . . But Also*—the home for some of Cook's most memorable characters.

Not Always . . . But Often . . .

The Braden Beat had already seen the introduction of EL Wisty, a ruminative semiparanoid whose monologues ranged from his plans for world domination to the need to train bees in espionage work. Now we met Sir Arthur Streeb-Greebling, a scientist of sorts, whose projects include teaching ravens to fly underwater, teaching flowers to work and the study of worms. What, exactly, about worms he is studying, he does not seem too sure. But he studies them regardless.

"Pete and Dud," too, were born, their flat caps and raincoats soon becoming as iconic a comic standard as Charlie Chaplin's little tramp outfit, or Laurel and Hardy's trademark hats—and that despite also being the favored uniform of an entire generation of working-class grandfathers gathered in the pub, behaving in much the same way as this pair.

But whereas the conversation of these elderly souls was meandering, pedantic, meaningless, that of Pete and Dud . . . well, it was also meandering, pedantic and meaningless.

That's why it was so funny.

Dudley is reminiscing on a lost love.

"She used to get the 5.45 25B [bus]. 'Course, she used to come out at 5:45, and I used to leave work about 5:00 nowhere near where she was. So what I used to do, I used to get on a 62A up Chadwell Heath, then I used to get the 514 trolley down to the Merry Fiddlers, then I used to have to run across that hill down by the railway bridge, over that field where the turnips were, over by the dye works, then I used to leap over the privet hedge and hurl myself onto the 25B as it came round Hog Hill. There wasn't a bus stop there, but it used to have to slow down because it was a very dangerous curve. I used to leap onto the platform and spend about twenty minutes trying to get my breath back. 'Course, I never spoke to her."

But their ramblings transfixed the nation regardless—late-night phone calls from an amorous Betty Grable; the convenient falls of gauze that obscured the "appropriate places" of Rubens's paintings of naked ladies ("it must be a million one to chance . . . that the gauze lands in the right place at the right time"); the ease with which burglars can be mistaken for visiting angels ("she went down on her knees praying to it, and he was in the kitchen whipping away her silver"); and the poetic abilities of a housefly that may or may not be a reincarnated poet.

THE COMPLETE
BEYOND THE FRINGE
JONATHAN MILLER ■ DUDLEY MOORE ■ PETER COOK ■ ALAN BENNETT

THE FULL 1961 FORTUNE THEATRE SHOW PLUS HIGHLIGHTS FROM THEIR BROADWAY PERFORMANCES - ON 3 CDs

Beyond the Fringe gets the box set treatment—(*left to right*) Jonathan Miller, Dudley Moore, Peter Cook, Alan Bennett.

"Mr. Thomas [has] got this bluebottle in the bathroom. He thinks it's Keats . . . so he keeps going into the bathroom, takes it in marshmallows and marmalade. The bluebottle's getting very fat."

Royalty was another favorite topic.

"Do you know," asks Pete, "at this very moment, Her Majesty is probably exercising the royal prerogative."

"What's that then, Pete?"

"Don't you know the royal prerogative? It's a wonderful animal, Dud. It's a legendary beast, half bird, half fish, half unicorn, and it's being exercised at this very moment."

Other elements in the show included prefilmed segments, such as a spot-on parody of the puppet action show *Thunderbirds*, with Cooke and Moore playing a variety of the show's best-known (and very obviously string-driven) characters; and musical interludes that featured acts as varied as Cilla Black and Julie Driscoll, Brian Auger and the Trinity.

Not Only . . . But Also ran to a total of three seasons, with a series of four hour-long specials titled *Goodbye Again*, airing on the independent network in between seasons two and three, while Cook and Moore also took time away from television to pursue their movie ambitions—*The Wrong Box* in 1966, Moore's *30 Is a Dangerous Age, Cynthia* in 1968 and, in between times, their masterpiece.

Bedazzled was an indeed dazzling reinvention of the legend of Faust, with Cook playing the devil and granting Moore a series of wishes (most of which revolve around his love for Eleanor Bron)—which are then gleefully sabotaged. It was not a commercial hit, but it remains a beloved facet of the late sixties "Swinging London" subculture, with Cook's musical number "Bedazzled" more or less prefiguring the entire early 1980s synthesizer movement as well. (In 2000, the movie was remade, surprisingly well, with Brendan Fraser and Elizabeth Hurley respectively in the Moore and Cook roles. The devil's pet hellhounds, by the way, are named Peter and Dudley.)

Goodbye Again, too, underperformed when compared to the earlier show, with a variety of external influences also playing on its fate—the UK at this time (and for several decades after) had two weekly television listings magazines, the BBC's *Radio Times* and the independent network's *TV Times*. Although the same information was published on a daily basis by the newspapers, many people relied on the magazines to plan out their viewing priorities. It was *Goodbye Again*'s bad luck to be aired at a time when the *TV Times* was on strike.

But the quality of the show, too, suffered—Cook had never been a temperate drinker, and was now approaching (if not already in the grip of) alcoholism. His timing, still perfect by other people's standards, had nevertheless slipped, and for the first time, he was reliant on the auto-cue. No less than his idol Tony Hancock, he got his words "right," but his instinctive impetuousness was gone.

Goodbye Again remains crucial viewing, however, again loaded down with excellent material, while also utilizing the fast-developing talents of John Cleese, but there was an inescapable sense that the duo was nearing its sell-by date.

Both the final BBC season of *Not Only . . . But Also . . .* and an attempt to repeat the success of *Beyond the Fringe* with the two-man stage show *Good Evening* were little more than exercises on treading (and reheating) water, and had Pete and Dud's career ended there, or even with their 1978 movie reunion in a remake of *The Hound of the Baskervilles*, their legend might have remained locked firmly in the 1960s.

What's the Worst Job You've Ever Had?

Between 1976 and 1978, however, the pair also convened in the recording studio to exercise their latest joint creation, Derek and Clive—a latter-day Pete and Dud, to be sure, but a pair whose outlook, aspirations and, most of all, capacity for extraordinarily foul language knew no boundaries whatsoever.

In 1972, American comedian George Carlin introduced the world to what he called "the seven dirty words"—those oaths and ejaculations that could not, under any circumstances, be repeated on any broadcast medium (unless you were Kenneth Tynan): the F-word, the C-word, the other C-word, the MF-word, the P-word, the S-word and the ornithological word. And that was Derek and Clive's vocabulary, an LP-length avalanche of effing c's and essing p's, first recorded in 1973, at a late night ad-lib following what Cook described as "what seemed like the millionth performance of *Good Evening* in New York."

Tapes of the performance circulated the music industry, becoming an underground secret (and obsession) among the rich and famous. Cook and Moore themselves were astonished, and a little shocked, too—the entire thing had simply been a means of letting off steam inside the cauldron of monotony that was a "greatest hits" stage show. Asked, once the secret became public knowledge, how two renowned and respectable satirists could resort to such base and crude humor, the pair very patiently explained that they had not *resorted* to anything. They were simply saying what was inside them . . . what is inside a lot of people.

Derek and Clive, Cook told the *Sheffield and North Derbyshire Spectator* newspaper in 1976, "are probably both mechanics, strongly [right wing], like a drink, are embarrassed by women, like football and the whole world's gone mad. Life ended for them with the Big Bopper. They don't like [homosexuals] or having to pay taxes when the country goes down the toilet. There are a lot of Derek and Clives about."

They were also shockingly successful. Unleashed upon the public in 1976, *Derek and Clive Live* became one of the best-selling comedy albums ever released in the UK, and that despite there being barely a minute of playing time that could be broadcast without any form of censorship.

From "The Worst Job I Ever Had" (the aforementioned retrieval of crustaceans from Jayne Mansfield's posterior) to "This Bloke Came Up to Me and Said," in which Carlin's C-word is repeated thirty times in the first eighty-five seconds, *Derek and Clive Live* caused outrage, shock and, of course, uncontrolled mirth in every quarter. It was also later revealed that no less than three regional British police forces considered bringing obscenity prosecutions against Cook and Moore, although with punk rock also newly unleashed upon the British Isles, doubtless their attention strayed elsewhere before they could act.

Three Derek and Clive albums were released (the second and third were fairly dull and way too predictable), and they marked the end of Cook and Moore's partnership (occasional reunions for onstage charity events notwithstanding). Dudley moved to Hollywood and became a superstar; Peter stayed in London and continued drinking.

He continued brilliant when the occasion demanded; became a sometimes regular on the chat show circuit, and made a handful of half-hearted television comebacks.

Half-hearted, perhaps, because he realized that he had already made his mark on comedy, and on television, too, and it didn't matter what he did in the future, people already knew "who" Peter Cook was. So he was content (happy is not, perhaps, the word) to allow them to remain blissful in that ignorance. He even helped perpetuate it.

Outraged when he learned that the BBC had wiped most episodes of *Not Only . . . But Also . . .* (even though he and Moore offered to fund their retention themselves), Cook was nevertheless later able to convince the corporation to produce half a dozen thirty-minute compilations of surviving elements (primarily from the first two, black-and-white seasons) as *The Best of What's Left of Not Only . . . But Also.*

Further archive footage emerged in the form of the DVD *The Very Best of Goodbye Again* (comprising around 50 percent of the original broadcasts), and scant though they are, even these pickings are sufficient to ensure Cook and Moore's legend, not only as comics in their own right, but also as a formative influence on every subsequent generation of British comedians.

Their respective deaths—Cook's in 1995 at the age of fifty-seven; Moore's in 2002, aged sixty-six—naturally saw the panegyrics rain down upon their memory and legacy, but for once, one searched in vain for a trace of pseudish disingenuousness, or even a droplet of crocodilian tearfulness, in the words that flooded out.

Both were, to paraphrase their own greatest Britcom achievement, not only genuinely loved, but also genuinely genius.

6

Busmen and Totters

Blakey, Stan and a Dirty Old Man

n the days before public transport in the United Kingdom became a privatized fiasco, slashing routes, raising fares and generally making the simple act of traveling from A to B as uncomfortable, inconvenient and expensive as possible, buses were the only way many people got around. This was especially true in those country communities far from the smoke of the cities, where only the wealthiest had their own transport, because the buses worked perfectly for everyone else. But it was also the case in the major cities, too, where the planners who laid out roads in decades, and even centuries, past had never dreamed that one day, armies of motorcars, taxi cabs, goods lorries and the like would be choking even the slimmest thoroughfares.

For many people, it was a lot easier to ride the buses, which frequently had their own dedicated lanes, than it was to add your hunk of immobile metal to the traffic snarl-ups that gridlocked the streets.

But what of the people whose job it was to actually drive, and maintain, those buses. What were *their* lives like?

That was the, to be honest, faintly unpromising question that lay at the heart of what contrarily became one of the most popular sitcoms of the late sixties and early seventies—one that ignited three movies, a stage show, a comic strip, a couple of Christmas specials, an American repurposing and a spin-off series, too. None of which is at all bad for a show that no less an authority than *The Guinness Book of Classic British TV* honors as the independent network's "longest running and most self-consciously unfunny series."

Unspoken is the fact that the BBC had already firmly rejected the show prior to ITV picking it up.

But that's *On the Buses* for you. Either you loved it, as great swathes of the British public seemed to do, or you loathed it, as successive generations of snotty critics have chosen to do. And it's true; watching all seven of the seasons that ran between 1969 and 1973 can become a little oppressive; more than that, it can remind contemporary viewers why they never really cared too much if they should miss watching it every so often. The show's plots were themselves a little like buses. You miss one, but there'll be a similar one along soon enough.

The Bus Now Racing Past Your Stop . . .

On The Buses succeeds, and is worthy of one's attention, for the sheer magnificence of the characters that sustained it.

Reg Varney, as bus driver Stan Butler, effectively played the same kind of character he always had, witty and wiry, a diminutive east Londoner who specialized in cheerful working-class roles (he was the foreman in *The Rag Trade*, an early sixties sitcom about the garment industry), a "never say die" everyman who took all the abuse that life threw at him and came up smiling every time. In *On the Buses*, he is clearly in his early fifties, but he still lives with his mother, still chases the dolly birds and still mouths off at his boss . . . who is one of the most ferocious monsters ever conceived for a show as innocuous as this.

Blakey—Inspector Blake to you (Stephen Lewis)—was the man whose job it was to ensure the straightforward and, more importantly, punctual operation of the bus garage when Butler works.

In less enlightened times, we might say he had a bit of the Hitler about him, and not only because the hairstyle and mustache came very close to matching. A Little Hitler, perhaps, obsessed with his own worth, drunk on his own power, a crazed fury who seethed with barely repressed anger every time he imagined that he had been crossed—and who *was* crossed more often than he realized, by Butler and his best friend Jack Harper (Bob Grant).

Jack is employed as a bus conductor—a dying (if not wholly deceased) art in these days of Pay as You Enter one-man vehicles. Working an old double-decker bus, Jack and Stan's passengers would board and then either seat themselves in the downstairs compartment or mount the stairs to the top deck—hence the vehicle's designation.

The conductor's job would be to walk the two decks, collecting fares and dispensing tickets, and making certain that nobody got away without paying. And, to make certain that he did not slack, another of the inspector's tasks was to undertake occasional spot checks on moving vehicles, demanding to see every passenger's ticket and then meting out instant justice to both the attempted fare dodger and the tardy conductor.

At home, Reg's mother Mabel (played in the first season by music hall veteran Cicely Courtneidge, but thereafter by Doris Hare) is kindhearted, bustling and prone to mother Stan a little too vigorously; but the home is also shared by Olive, Reg's sister and her husband Arthur—a couple so mismatched that even the writers, Ronald Wolfe and Ronald Chesney, were eventually driven to divorce them.

Blakey (Stephen Lewis) looms over the hapless minions who are *On the Buses*.

Arthur (Michael Robbins) is brash, loud and intolerant, forever criticizing both his wife and his brother-in-law; always ready with an opinion on anything and everything that goes on around him. The season-one episode "Bus Driver's Stomach," in which he lectures Stan on his admittedly poor diet (French fries with everything), quoting from a book that is as light on actual fact as Arthur himself, is typical of the man.

Olive (Anna Karen), on the other hand, is bland, tearful, obstinate and usually suffering and sniffling from one ailment or another. "You only married her for my [cigarettes]," Stan accuses, after Arthur helps himself to another one, and all Arthur can do is glance at Olive, as she snuffles into her omnipresent handkerchief, and grimace in apparent agreement.

She is also portrayed with such lank-haired, lumpy-bodied and disfiguringly bespectacled plainness that successive generations of reviewers would forever perform a double take when they discovered that actress Karen had previously taken the contrarily über-glamorous lead role in *Nudist Memories*, a cinematic featurette extolling the pleasures of naturism, 1961-style. Herself a former stripper, Karen also played a very convincing schoolgirl in the 1969 movie *Carry On Camping*—and that despite being thirty-two years of age when she was cast.

This quintet, stable throughout the show's lifetime, more than retained the viewer's interest even after the occasionally flimsy plotlines lost their allure. They became blueprints for any number of subsequent comedic characters, and touchstones for the actors themselves. Barely had *On the Buses* dropped off its last passenger than Blakey was retiring to Spain with his sister Dorothy, to tyrannize the locals in *Don't Drink the Water*, and there were still glimpses of the old manic madman years later, when Stephen Lewis joined the cast of *Last of the Summer Wine* as the dreadfully misnamed "Smiler" Hemingway.

Karen, too, bears the mark of Olive in her occasional roles as dowdy Aunt Sal, in the soap *EastEnders*—amusingly, in the show, she is the sister of the matriarchal Peggy Mitchell, played by Karen's costar in the *Carry On* movie, Barbara Windsor. She is also, sadly, the last living survivor of the *On the Buses* cast, with Lewis passing away in 2015, Varney in 2008, Grant in 2003, Hare in 2000, Robbins in 1992. (Rarely remembered for her early role in the show, Courtneidge died in 1980.)

Before this tragic sweep commenced, in 1990, the so-called "classic" lineup regrouped for a proposed sequel series, *Back on the Buses*; it did not, ultimately, appear, but the show did see several earlier sidelines. Three movies were released between 1971 and 1973, of which the first, *On the Buses*, became the top box-office success in the UK in 1971.

Two years later, a stage show ran for the summer season in Torquay, *Busman's Holiday*, starring Karen, Lewis and Grant; one wonders if they stayed at Fawlty Towers while they were in town? (Of course they didn't. It's make-believe. But it *was* set in Torquay.)

And the same year that *On the Buses* returned to the depot in the UK, it rolled out as a whole new show in the United States, with Dom DeLuise in a vague approximation of the Stan Butler role (Stan Beaumont, working in the lost luggage office), Beverly Sanders and Wynn Irwin as Olive and Arthur, Jack Knight as Reg's best friend, the oddly renamed Bummy Pfitzer . . . and no Blakey. *How* can you have *On the Buses* without Blakey?

You can't, and that's probably why they retitled it *Lotsa Luck*. They needed it. (And they didn't receive it. The show folded after one season.)

The Dirtiest Old Man

If one British import could not adapt to its (admittedly bizarre) reinvention as an American sitcom, others of the era were made of sterner stuff, even if the actual linkage between the two shows is sometimes difficult to determine.

Nobody comparing the US revisions of *Coupling* and *The Office* with their UK parents could mistake their genesis, regardless of how they perceived the new version. Roll back a few decades, however, and fans of *Sanford and Son*, *All in the Family* and *Three's Company* might as well be viewing a completely different show, from a completely different planet, were they to be sat down to contemplate *Steptoe and Son*, *Till Death Us Do Part* and *Man About the House*.

It is, however, a very pleasant planet.

Galton and Simpson's *Steptoe and Son* was not always particularly funny. Forensic examinations of dysfunctional relationships rarely are. One episode revolves around an elderly homosexual's advances; another opens, and then wallows in, the death of a horse, with the first minutes consumed by its owner's palpable, silent grief.

Let's see what the laugh track makes of that.

In half the episodes, Albert Edward Ladysmith Steptoe, the father, is either complaining that his son is heartlessly waiting for him to die or accusing the boy of having a woman stashed away somewhere, with whom he is planning to run away). In the other half, Harold Albert Kitchener Steptoe, the son, is bemoaning his father's thoughtless mistreatment of him.

As befits its authorship, it is the ultimate manifestation of Tony Hancock's vision of comedy as a reflection of reality at its rawest; of seeking and smiling at the tiniest spark of humanity, the merest fragment of triumph, before sinking back into a morass of unrelenting misery.

And it held British television transfixed across nine seasons, the first four running between 1962 and 1965; the remainder between 1970 and 1974. At its peak, fully half the country was watching, twenty-eight million people.

No, it was not always particularly funny. But it was unmissable, all the same.

Steptoe and Son was originally commissioned as a single episode in the BBC's *Comedy Playhouse* series—one of ten installments that Galton and Simpson wrote for the show during 1961–1962.

Very much a testing ground for new ideas, as well as a vehicle for proven writers' one-off notions, *Comedy Playhouse* launched as Galton and Simpson's own playground; its entire first season was their work and included the following plays: *Clicquot Et Fils*, starring Eric Sykes and Warren Mitchell; *Lunch in the Park*, with Stanley Baxter and Daphne Anderson; *The Private Lives of Edward Whiteley*, with Tony Britton and Raymond Huntley; *The Offer*, with Harry H. Corbett and Wilfrid Brambell; *The Reunion*, with Dick Emery and Patrick Cargill; *The Status Symbol*, with Alfred Marks and Graham Stark; *Visiting Day*, with Bernard Cribbens and a returning Wilfrid Brambell; *Sealed with a Loving Kiss*, with Ronald Fraser and Avril Elgar; and *The Channel Swimmer*, with Bob Todd, Frank Thornton and, again, Warren Mitchell.

All featured proven televisual talent; any could, in theory, have caught both the public and the corporation's imagination sufficiently to be viewed as the pilot for a new series. Just one, however, made that leap, and it was the one that Galton and Simpson themselves viewed as something of a makeweight, forced upon them by circumstances.

With the first three episodes of the series having overspent their budget, the pressure was on for the fourth to come in as cheaply as possible. The pair settled down, then, to write a half-hour comedy that required minimal set design, minimal cast; a "two-hander" featuring one established character actor, Wilfrid Brambell, and one best known for smoldering dramatic roles, Harry H. Corbett (Ronald Fraser was also considered for the part.)

Son and Steptoe: Harry H. Corbett (*left*) and Wilfrid Bramble (*right*) at the wheel of Hercules the horse.   *Alamy*

Neither were considered comedians, which was itself a novel approach but one that would pay dividends as the pair steadfastly avoided playing for laughs. It was up to the audience to decide when the performance deserved one.

"The Offer" was set in what the British call a rag-and-bone business on Oil Drum Lane in Shepherd's Bush, in west London, and depicted a trade that flourished into the 1970s, at least.

From their junkyard headquarters, so-called "totters" would set out daily on their horse and cart and tour the surrounding neighborhoods, calling out for householders to bring out their junk. A quick appraisal, a speedy sale, and then back to the yard to sort the treasures from the trash. (Tom and Barbara in *The Good Life*/*Neighbors* purchase their old iron range from a passing rag-and-bone man.)

The plot was less about the business, however, than it was about relationships—shattered, fractious relationships, a vivid and often vicious portrait of resentment, regret and sometimes, plain spite.

Old man Steptoe, as he would soon become known, has raised the thirty-something Harold single-handedly since the death of the boy's mother, many years before. Now entering his twilight years, he's looking for some reciprocation, the knowledge that the boy will care for him when he's too old to look after himself; his greatest fear, therefore, is that Harold will find himself a woman, marry and leave home. Leave him.

Harold, meanwhile, follows exactly in the footsteps of Tony Hancock; a working-class man of no particular charm or ability, who nevertheless aspires to better himself and shed the trappings of his humble origins.

We learn that Harold collects classical music and antiques, and prides himself (mistakenly) on his ability to speak knowledgeably on those subjects with even the most aristocratic connoisseurs. (A decade later, *Only Fools and Horses'* Del Boy would share the same trait.) That he dreams of mixing with the jet set and skiing in the Alps with the rich and famous. That he truly believes, without his grasping, whining parasite of a parent to hold him back, he could be flying as high as his ambitions.

Albert, of course, knows better, and never loses an opportunity to puncture his son's aspirations.

In "The Offer," we see what happens when Harold is offered what he perceives as a better job, and the lengths Albert will go to stymie it. A mere six months later, with *Steptoe and Son* on the screens in its own right, we watch Albert sabotage Harold's dinner date with a lady by setting all the clocks forward an hour, to make him think he's been stood up.

Later, when Harold plans a foreign vacation, Albert fakes a heart attack; while the long-ago death of his wife provides him with the most lethal ammunition of all. "I won't be on my own," Albert will quietly say, as Harold outlines another of his dreams of escaping his dreary life. "I'll go to the cemetery to visit your mother."

But Harold gives as good as he gets. Albert, he insists in one episode, is "morally, spiritually and physically a festering fly-blown heap of accumulated filth"; and, in another, "a dyed-in-the-wool, fascist, reactionary, squalid little, 'know your place,' 'don't rise above yourself,' 'don't get out of your hole'—complacent little turd."

Which really is no way to speak to your father, but we soon grow accustomed to that.

Of course, much of Harold's bitterness (for he is very bitter; far more so than dad) arises from the fact that this "complacent little turd" is actually a lot smarter than he lets on. Harold's learning comes from books; Albert's from life.

When Harold thinks he has found a rare oil painting, it is the old man who, with a single glance, brings him back to Earth. When Harold decides to learn television repair, he discovers Albert is already an expert. When Harold wants to learn to dance, Albert is the one who teaches him. The realization that experience will always, ultimately, trump "learning" might well be the source of Harold's most deeply rooted resentments.

So he pretends to forget the old man's birthday; he makes regular threats to murder him (and once, in his sleep, comes close to doing so) and he sabotages Albert's dream of remarrying—although when it is Harold's turn to fall in love with a pretty French girl and he brings her home to meet his dad, it transpires that Albert met her grandmother during World War I, and that relations *may* have become a little steamy. The implications of that encounter send all dreams of marriage out of both youngsters' heads.

True to another of Tony Hancock's theories, catchphrases did not necessarily abound, although it is hard to think of *Steptoe and Son* without hearing Harold groan "you diiiirrrtttyyyyy old man" in a voice soaked in contempt; or Albert responding to suspicions of his son's amorous adventures with an equally well-turned phrase. (A couple of years later, when Brambell appeared as Paul McCartney's grandfather in the Beatles' movie *A Hard Day's Night*, his reputation had clearly followed him—everybody comments on what a *clean* old man he is.)

For the most part, however, *Steptoe and Son* avoided any of the genre's most commonplace tricks and traps, if only by turning them upside down. Maybe Albert is a dirty old man—when Harold brings home an old "What the Butler Saw" peepshow machine, he is mortified when he discovers that his father was one of the actors. But Harold is no better. It is his idea to take his dad to the movies to see *I Am Curious, Yellow*—the then (1970) controversial Swedish film in which a couple are seen actually "doing it. Up a tree"; it is he who lives life in a semipermanent state of lust, forever on the lookout for "crumpet"; and when he finds some, his passions know no bounds. Again, the viewing public might well have learned a less than pleasant lesson—that every generation is destined to reenact its predecessor's foibles

Another intriguing element of the show, as it aged, was the gradual development of a surprisingly detailed backstory to the characters that, unlike so many other television shows, was only ever added to, as opposed to being constantly revised and contradicted according to the needs of an individual plot. Of course, this was largely because the same two writers, Galton and Simpson, handled the show throughout its lifetime. But still it was an achievement.

Wilfrid Bramble is such a clean old man in the Beatles' *A Hard Day's Night*.   *Photofest*

Albert was born in 1898 (but habitually trimmed three years off his age), the son of the local muffin man, who also founded the family business. It was he who painted the name "Steptoe and Son" on the gates of the junkyard, more than fifty years before—at a time when *Albert* was the son; or one of them, anyway. He had thirteen siblings.

Albert fought in World War 1 and the struggles that followed it; in France, he fought at the Battle of Mons; and, following the Armistice, he was with the British Expeditionary Force in White Russia. He had at least one child out of wedlock (the boy was raised in Australia), then married Harold's mother in the 1920s. Their son was born somewhere between 1925 and 1932 (the only historic date in the show that does seem to be delivered inconsistently); but became a widower in 1936.

The boy, Harold, followed in his father's military footsteps, rising to the rank of corporal in the army, where he served in both Korea and Malaya, before returning home to help with the business. He has been trying to get out of it ever since, but of course, he never will. Whether by callous manipulation, cynical brinksmanship or sheer animal cunning. Albert (almost) always wins out in the end, and Harold knows he will. Their relationship might appear to be built on mutual loathing, abuse and belittlement, but it is actually one of deep and binding love and dependency, as both prove time and time again, when danger threatens.

How easy it would have been for Harold to shop the old man when the taxman questioned Albert's weekly withdrawal of his (very) late wife's pension. But he doesn't. How desperately Albert tries to protect his son when Harold is befriended by an older, and somewhat effete, antiques dealer, without even suspecting that the gentleman's motives might not be as pure as he believes. And when the business's debts become too much to bear, Albert fakes his own death to collect on his life insurance, and bail them out again.

It was somewhat chilling, then, to learn that the two actors who so brilliantly played these parts were themselves less than friends, at least according to the 2008 documentary *The Curse of Steptoe*. There, Corbett was portrayed as a fractious, pretentious womanizer, forever at odds with the supposedly self-hating homosexual Brambell; who loathed his greatest role for the stereotype that it landed him with; and so on and so forth. It was gripping television, but it was gruelingly depressing, too.

Immediately, the pair's supporters rose in opposition. The documentary's depiction of constant infighting was dismissed, before the program even aired, by Alan Simpson. He informed *The Times* that throughout their twelve-year relationship, "we were unaware of any conflict between the actors save from the occasional gritting of Wilfrid's false teeth when Harry had the perceived audacity to give him a little direction. At all other times they were the acme of professionalism."

Shocking insinuations and headline-sized accusations delivered by the manipulation of the show's chronology were laid bare to the public; while Corbett's brother-in-law was so vociferous in his complaints that the BBC Trust Editorial Standards Committee not only ordered the documentary to be revised and edited before it could be broadcast again, it then made the same demand after the revised edition was screened, and further condemned the show by demanding that the recently released DVD be withdrawn from sale.

Of course, no amount of sensationalist revelations could dent the high esteem in which *Steptoe and Son* is held, even today; had the two actors truly hated one another, they disguised it well. Even in a single show where rage and loathing are the script's default setting, a degree of affection and respect *had* to be present, else the actors (not to mention the writers and crew) would have self-combusted.

Spread out across eight seasons, six years' worth of radio adaptations, two feature films, two Christmas specials and a stage show, the studio, network and even the viewers would have followed suit—then and now. With all eight seasons of the show surviving more or less intact (the fifth and much of the sixth seasons, shot in color in 1970–1971, exist only in black and white today), *Steptoe and Son* remains avidly watched and avidly dissected too—few, if any, subsequent shows have so boldly strayed from the parameters of their genre as *Steptoe and Son* at its best (which was most of the time); few have succeeded in making such cultural icons from such un-iconic characters.

Nobody regarded either Steptoe or son as a role model (or at least, one hopes they didn't); few felt anything approaching conventional sympathy or affection for the two men. Yet we loved them all the same—just as they, ultimately, loved one another.

America, too, loved *Steptoe and Son*, albeit in the heavily revised format that was duly translated as *Sanford and Son*. Sixteen original *Steptoe* scripts were adapted for the show, the earliest dating back to the English series's second-ever episode, "The Piano" (retitled "The Piano Mover"), although the irascibility and intolerance that fueled the American characters' relationship during the show's early episodes softened considerably as time passed. And with that softening, so *Sanford and Son* distanced itself from the confrontational fury of its forebear. Clearly, the British and American sense of humor is separated by more than the inability to pronounce "tomato" the same way.

7

The Moo and All Who Are as Silly as She

Alf Garnett and the Bleedin' Moral Fiber of the Nation

Albert Steptoe was not Britain's only "man you loved to hate" during the 1960s. Racist, homophobic, prejudiced and foul-tongued he may have been, but in a room with Alf Garnett, Steptoe would simply have been stepped on.

Even today, Garnett's outbursts can cause sensitive viewers to flinch back in horror, and not only because they were written in an age before political correctness relegated certain terms and attitudes to the garbage can. They flinch because he really *was* a horror. And because most of us knew someone just like him. Indeed, writer Johnny Speight later admitted that he based the character on his own father!

Till Death Us Do Part was another show to emerge from *Comedy Playhouse*, first appearing during its fourth season in 1965.

Again, the pilot was swiftly transformed into a series; it was first broadcast on July 22, 1965; the series proper kicked off the following June 6, and would ultimately run until 1975, before reappearing as *In Sickness and in Health* a decade later. And Alf barely shut his mouth once throughout that entire span.

Played with mercurial timing by the great Warren Mitchell, Garnett is the archetypal Cockney, proud of his roots, patriotic to a fault, an east Londoner through and through. He loves the Queen, West Ham United soccer team and the sound of his own voice. He hates blacks, browns, yellows, and any other colored skin that should cross his field of vision.

But he is not necessarily racist. He is *everything*-ist. Women, Unions, young people, old people, gays, straights, babies, progress . . . one of the most affecting depictions of Garnett ever shot was reserved for the 1969 movie *Till Death Us Do Part,* in which Garnett first relives his youth and war years, but which ends with him returning to the same landscapes as an old man, and contemplating the changes that have befallen them. The houses that have been demolished, the pubs that have been closed, the stores that stand derelict, awaiting the wrecking ball.

And suddenly we realize *why* Garnett is the way he is. Because, however misguidedly, and however stubbornly, he is desperately trying to hold on to the values that he was raised with; where policemen were figures of respect and not "pigs" to be sworn at by passing yobs; where the yobs themselves were lifted from the street and taught discipline and loyalty in the armed forces; where short hair and suits were the order of the day, because a man had pride in the way he dressed; where people looked out for one another, and the kindness of strangers was as reliable as that of friends.

You can maybe see his point, as well. People were, perhaps, happier in an age when local businesses were locally owned, as opposed to the

Chairman Alf and his Silly Moo.   *Alamy*

outposts of some faceless multinational corporation; where local landmarks were cherished and utilized, instead of being earmarked for exciting new developments; where government governed, rather than did whatever its wealthiest supporters told it too; and where everybody, as Garnett would have put it, not only "knew their place," but were happy to remain there. And if their place happened to be in some far-flung corner of the British Empire, then so be it.

He probably regretted the invention of penicillin, too, and mourned the days when the swimming pool closed because someone had just contracted polio from it, but that is beside the point. Alf Garnett had experienced his own vision of Utopia, and he raged against its loss.

Understand that, and whether you agree with him or not, you understand who he is.

Harder to fathom is why his family remain with him.

Else, his wife (Dandy Nicholls), is as likely to answer to the name "silly old moo" as she is to her own, so long has she suffered Alf's tantrums and rages. His daughter Rita (Una Stubbs; decades later, Mrs. Hudson in the BBC's *Sherlock* series) does her best to oppose him, although less in word than in deed—why else would she have married Mike (Anthony Booth), a card-carrying socialist, proudly unemployed, long-haired and scruffy? And why else would she then have continued living at home, knowing that Mike's very existence was an affront to all that Alf believed holy?

Ironies abound elsewhere. A staunch soccer fan, even his fellow supporters proved unwilling to tolerate his abuse during one game—and that at a time when English soccer in general was just beginning to suffer the depredations of real-life hooligans, racists and thugs.

He railed against Jews, but actor Warren Mitchell himself was Jewish.

And he was an avid supporter of the "Clean Up TV" campaign, housewife Mary Whitehouse's evangelical quest to drive smut, bad language and questionable content from the nation's television screens, at the same time as *Till Death Us Do Part* effectively waged a one-show campaign to infuriate her.

Indeed, Whitehouse regularly highlighted *Till Death Us Do Part* as a clarion example of the BBC's failure to uphold simple moral values. Apparently she used to count up how many times Garnett deployed the minor expletive "bloody" in each episode, and then write a letter to the BBC to reveal her findings.

"She's concerned for the bleedin' moral fibre of the nation!" Garnett enthuses admiringly, although one wonders how she felt, not only when she discovered that Garnett was such a loyal supporter, but also when he ever-so-slightly pronounced her name wrong. Dropping the 'aitch as was his linguistic prerogative, it came out "White-*arse*." As in *ass*.

T*** d**** u* d* p***

Not that arses and bloodies were Garnett's sole contribution to the vernacular of the age. He had a healthy repertoire of racist epithets, but again demonstrated his even-handedness by describing his Liverpool-born son-in-law as "a randy Scouse git"—"randy" meaning oversexed; "git" meaning despicable jerk; and Scouse being a standard insult for Liverpudlians, derived from "lobscouse," a cheap meat stew that was once popular among the city's poor.

Such explanations were apparently necessary, too. Visiting England and watching the show, the Monkees' Mickey Dolenz was so delighted by the phrase that he promptly used it as the title for a song he was writing. (Presumably, English-born bandmate Davy Jones declined to translate it for him.) Equally hilariously, the ensuing record was released as "Alternate Title" in the UK, and became a massive hit.

Till Death Us Do Part initially ran for three seasons, totaling twenty-five black-and-white episodes, between 1966 and 1968, just ten of which survive intact (a handful of others exist either as audio recordings or extracts). It then left the screens while the cast pursued other activities and Johnny Speight launched the ill-fated *Curry and Chips*.

This new show was ostensibly an assault on racism, with Spike Milligan cast as a half-Irish Indian seeking work in London and running into any number of barriers on account of his skin color. Even a Jamaican coworker looks down on him and taunts him, and the show's spoken objective of illustrating just how hypocritical and ignorant such attitudes are, was indeed achieved.

Unfortunately, it simply wasn't funny; and more than that, it often seemed to go out of its way to alienate its viewers—Milligan fans among them. It's not easy watching your idol play a character barely more animate, or likable, than a showroom mannequin.

Other viewers objected to the unrestrained racism, or the constant bad language (fifty-nine "bloody's" in one thirty-minute episode), and though a full season was shot, and has since been released on DVD, *Curry and Chips* ran for just six episodes before independent television's own watchdog, the IBA (Independent Broadcasting Authority), demanded it be pulled from the schedules. Overturning the traditional lament of "missing, believed wiped," here was a rare example of "unwiped, but we wish it was missing."

The show did not survive, but the hybrid did; following *Till Death Us Do Part*'s return, Alf was confronted with a "Paki-Paddy"—and in truth, the joke wasn't any funnier this time than it was first time round.

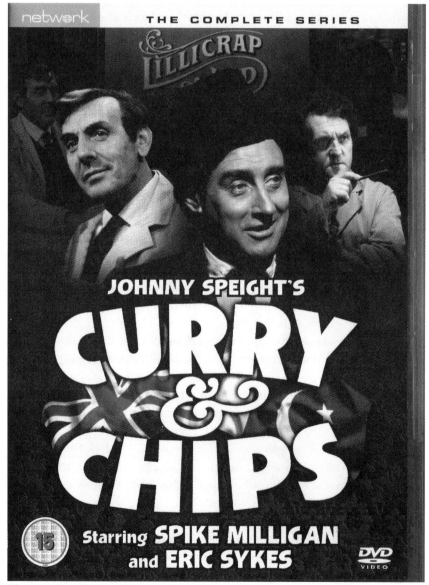

It's pretty dreadful, but if you really need to watch *Curry and Chipsi*, it's here.

Till Death Us Do Part commenced its comeback when it reappeared (for the first time in color) for a one-off in 1970, to coincide with that year's General Election. It reemerged again in 1972, then wound down with three seasons aired during 1974–1975.

The breaks in transmission, while predicated upon any number of factors (not least of all the cast and writer's own availability) in many waves paved the way for Garnett's still-resonant reputation. Even within the space of a decade, different eras heralded different concerns; fresh iniquities for Garnett to rail against and, to the dismay of his opponents, new linguistic horizons in which to cavort.

While his language today would scarcely shock a country priest, let alone induce a lorry driver to put his foot through his television screen (as allegedly occurred just a year after Alf's final show, when the Sex Pistols appeared on the *Today* news program and reiterated Kenneth Tynan's breakthrough oath), still the very tone of Garnett's voice was sufficient to put many people's backs up, as if they knew that only the law of the land prevented him from speaking the words he really wished to say.

Neither would the show end on any kind of upbeat note. When actress Dandy Nichols was taken ill and could no longer appear in the show, she was written out in the most dramatic fashion—not with death, but by walking out on her husband and moving to Australia.

Garnett soldiered on alone for a while, with neighbors Min and Bert (Patricia Hayes and Alfie Bass) bearing the brunt of his bad behavior, but with ratings flagging, and Mitchell himself tiring of the role, Johnny Speight fashioned the most apocalyptic finale he could. A man who proudly had never dodged a day's work in his life was made redundant; and one who truly believed that marriage was "till death us do part" was shaken by the arrival of a telegram from Else. She wanted a divorce.

The old world, the old values, that Garnett had fought so brutally to uphold had finally been destroyed.

Or had it?

Although the BBC had no interest in reviving Alf Garnett, a 1980 Christmas special was broadcast on independent television, under the title *The Thoughts of Chairman Alf at Christmas*—a one-man show in which Warren Mitchell proved he had lost none of his old acidity.

The following year, with Alf and Else apparently reconciled, and Rita now the proud (or, perhaps, merely mischievous) mother of a punk rocker son, a new series ran beneath the title *Till Death . . .* and, while it was scarcely a success, being dropped after just half a dozen episodes, 1985 saw the Garnett clan reappear on the BBC in a new series, *In Sickness and in Health*.

Age had caught up with them. Alf had mellowed, or perhaps simply abandoned himself to the inevitable, and Else was now confined to a wheelchair. It wasn't bad, just not as good as it ought to have been, and there were thoughts that it might just fade away following Nicholls's death on February 6, 1986, aged seventy-eight.

It didn't.

A second season, which opened with Else's death, was itself largely built around Garnett's attempts to adjust to life without her—oft-cited, but remarkably touching all the same, is the scene where Alf returns to the empty house following the funeral, and softly caresses his wife's wheelchair. "Silly old moo," he says sadly.

Other characters would come and go, and occasionally sparks of the old Alf Garnett would appear. A lot of the fight had gone out of him, though. He maintained his old distaste for race, but his epithets sounded forced, even false. He lived now in a truly multicultural society, and no matter how he disliked it, he had learned to accept it too. Four further seasons of *In Sickness and in Health*, broadcast between 1987 and 1992, saw him come close to marrying again, but his heart was clearly not in it.

Falling out with his bride-to-be over the inclusion of the word "obey" (as in "love, honor and . . .") in the wedding vows, he is left standing at the altar with just one regret. He had wasted a Saturday afternoon, which would have been better spent watching soccer.

The final season, in early 1992, in some ways compensates for the downbeat ending to the original series—Alf strikes it rich. But in many ways, it is hard to regard *In Sickness and in Health* (or, indeed, the short-lived *Till Death . . .*) as anything more than minor adjuncts to the brilliance that was the original (pre-1975) *Till Death Us Do Part*.

Other shows and other shockers had come along to supplant it; if anything, it now had more in common with the similarly geriatric *Last of the Summer Wine*, or the later *One Foot in the Grave*, just one more sitcom revealing the vagaries of the older generation, largely targeted *at* an older generation.

Cutting-edge comedy, as it was beginning to be termed, was the province of the young, now, and one day it would also be the remit, both individually and collectively, of *The Young Ones*. Before that could occur, however, there needed first to be some other young ones: Eric and John, Terry and Terry, Graham and Michael. And, lest we forget, Monty.

And Now for Something Prototypically Pythonic

The Expurgated Version, Of Course

The Spanish Inquisition, the Battle of Britain and spurious Hungarian phrase books are seldom ranked among the first things you think of when considering classic themes for television comedy.

Nor are self-defense classes, the correct identification of trees and the collected work of Marcel Proust. But to the generation that came of age during the early 1970s, and for those who grew up in their wake, there will forever be a wet patch in the underpants of memory whenever they consider a goldfish with whooping cough.

Half a century is now close to elapsing since *Monty Python's Flying Circus* made its bow on British screens (a little less in America), and its legend remains writ so large that when the surviving cast members regrouped to tour in 2014, their routines were in as rude a state of health as ever they had been.

So much comedy does not age well; time dulls the sharpest cutting edge, and it is not only topicality that falls prey to the years. Delivery, too, changes, which is why an entire generation of seventies-era comics, telling jokes whose very subject matter (immigration, homosexuality, mothers-in-law) has long since fallen into disrepute, are now regarded as dinosaurs.

It's . . .

Monty Python is a part of that tradition. A forensic trawl through their repertoire will unearth any number of jokes, references and asides that could never be repeated by, for instance, an up-and-coming modern comedian; and many more that rely upon a precise awareness of then-current affairs, too—the "Spot the Braincell" game show spoof to name but one.

But . . .

Cultural historians counter this inbuilt redundancy by explaining that *Monty Python* was as much in the business of deconstructing the humor of the age as it was in building that of the future, and perhaps there is truth in that.

But a decade's worth of Twitterstorms remind us that the general public rarely responds well (or, at least, intelligently) to irony, however it is presented, while the media enjoys few things so much as unearthing a public figure's past indiscretions as clickbait for a fresh witch hunt. So why has *Monty Python* never been taken to task for unleashing the "N-word"? Why is *their* homophobia funny when, for instance, Bernard Manning's is reprehensible? How come Python can get away with blowing up penguins, when Facebook catches fire whenever a celebrity appears in an old fur coat?

Ummm . . . Because it's funny?

Again, we say, these jokes are fifty years old; as old in the mid-2010s as a vaudevillian prankster of the 1920s was when *Python* first appeared. Did Monty-maniacs unwind after an evening in the cheese shop by reciting classic Chester Conklin routines to one another? And if you don't know who Chester Conklin even is; well, that's the point, isn't it.

What of *Monty Python*'s original audience? Late teenage or early twenties at the time, it is now embracing retirement, which means it has probably already experienced the other side of the gang's greatest comic inventions and been employed indeed in cheese shops and pet stores, felled trees in British Columbia and learned how to react if attacked with a pointed stick.

Life lessons dressed up as jokes, disguised as surrealism, and reinvented as cultural artifacts around the same time as the pupils realized that what *Monty Python* presented as the height of humor was actually a sharply honed commentary on what life really had in store. It is Spike Milligan's "one man shouting gibberish in the face of authority," as enacted by a crowd of people. But ordinary living remains madder.

Television comedy grew up alongside the Pythons.

Who, watching prime-time reruns in the mid-1960s, for example, could ever have foreseen a day when the mannered sophistication of *South Park*,

At Last the 1948 Show delivers (*left to right*) Tim Brooke Taylor, John Cleese, Graham Chapman and Marty Feldman into the grasp of Ami MacDonald. *Alamy*

the dry intellect of *Beavis and Butthead* or the suave satire of *Married with Children* could even find a place in American television listings, let alone a respectable Nielsen rating?

About as many people as could think warmly of an age in which lumberjacks in lingerie, moistened bints lobbing scimitars and Hungarian tourists whose nipples are exploding were staples of evening viewing.

Yet, like those hunters who think it'll be fun to shoot an armadillo and end up getting killed by the ricochetting bullet, you mock *Monty Python* at your peril. It remains mesmeric, four seasons, or forty-five episodes, of cult comedy that have spun off an industry of CDs, DVDs, computer games movies, stage shows, books, toys and just recently, a vinyl box set that was so expensive that its price alone seemed like a Pythonesque joke.

"I'd like to buy this collection of old English comedy albums, please."

"Very good, sir. That will be $300. $330 if you have to pay sales tax. $370 if you would like it delivered tomorrow. $750 if you would like to buy two, in case one should get eaten by lemurs . . . "

"But . . . I can buy exactly the same discs at the thrift store for a buck apiece."

"Yes, sir. But you don't get the box to put them in, do you."

The Frost Report

The roots of *Python*, as has already been remarked, lay within a tangled but very specific skein of British broadcast comedy that dated back to the satire boom of the early 1960s, with the roots of Python's humor tracing back even further, to *The Goon Show*'s policy of allowing trenchant comment disguised as unbridled silliness to masquerade as humor to the delight of a nation.

Whether they listened religiously or not (and the chances are that they did), the *Python* team were all of an age to have grown up alongside *The Goons*—on radio, on record and in the day-to-day interaction of friends who knew every catchphrase, voice and intonation off by heart.

Hailing from Britain's halls of higher learning, the Universities of Oxford and Cambridge, with their own tradition of comic revues blossoming through such stage and TV shows as *Beyond the Fringe*, *TW3*, *BBC-3* and so forth, most of the individual Pythons were already familiar names, if not faces, from the last few years of television.

The late sixties testing ground for so many of the following decade's comic superstars, the surviving episodes of *At Last the 1948 Show* make it onto DVD.

In Cambridge, John Cleese first emerged as one of the writers behind the 1961 revue *I Thought I Saw It Move*; Graham Chapman debuted (alongside Cleese) in the following year's *Double Take*; over at Oxford, Terry Jones appeared in 1963's intriguingly titled "****," and was then joined by Michael Palin for 1964's *Hang Down Your Head and Die*; and, by 1965, all four were writing for *TW3* host David Frost's *The Frost Report*, where they were joined by a younger Cambridge alumnus, Eric Idle.

The last, and perhaps most fondly remembered, of the post-*TW3* satirical shows; successful because it did not necessarily portray itself *as* satirical, and just allowed its commentary to speak for itself, *The Frost Report* ran for twenty-eight episodes during 1967–1968, with a cast that included (alongside Frost), Cleese, the Ronnies Corbett and Barker (soon to become a popular TV double act in their own right), the delightful Sheila Steafel and Nicky Henson.

Other writers, meanwhile, included the ubiquitous Bill Oddie, fellow future-*Goodie* Tim Brooke Taylor, Frank Muir, Denis Norden, Barry Cryer, Marty Feldman, Dick Vosburgh and Antony Jay (later creator of *Yes Minister* and *Yes Prime Minister*).

With so many writers on board, there was no single comedic direction for the show. Rather, it was a tangle of ideas, notions and funny-bone-jarring genius that is most frequently regarded today for bringing the future *Pythons* together, but which also honed so many other talents, too—reawakening memories of Kenneth Williams's devotion to bedeviling Tony Hancock, the big-eyed Marty Feldman emerged as Mr. Raymond Pest, frustrating and infuriating all he encountered.

In the Bookstore sketch (written by Chapman and Cleese), Pest's search for a copy of that most elusive book *Ethel the Aardvark Goes Quantity Surveying* would certainly influence a stream of subsequent Pythonic retail experiences . . . this after having already requested *Thirty Days in the Samarkand Desert with a Spoon* by A. E. J. Elliott, *The Amazing Adventures of Captain Gladys Stoat-Pamphlet and Her Intrepid Spaniel Stig Among the Giant Pygmies of Corsica Volume Two*, several misspelt Dickens titles by one Edmund Wells and a copy of *Olsen's Standard Book of British Birds*.

Pest: "The expurgated version, of course."

Assistant: "I'm sorry, I didn't quite catch that."

Pest: "The expurgated version."

Assistant: "The expurgated version of *Olsen's Standard Book of British Birds?*"

Pest: "Yes. The one without the gannet."

Assistant: "The one without the gannet?! They've all got the gannet it's a standard bird, the gannet, it's in all the books."

Pest: "Well, I don't like them. They've got long nasty beaks. And they wet their nests."

Other classic sketches included the six-foot-five-inch Cleese in suit and bowler hat, the five-foot-eight Barker in a trilby and the five-foot-one Ronnie

The assembled width of the News team spreads onto this surprisingly innocuous-looking LP.

Corbett in overalls, commenting on their relative status in the British class system; Cleese reminding his secretary, Sheila Steafel, of her beauty, letting down her hair and removing her glasses, moments before she shortsightedly mistakes an open window for the door; and Frost warning us all of the dangers of overrelying on computers (a problem even then!) by telling of the man who planned his holiday with one, and is now going skiing in the Congo.

Perhaps best of all, though (at least among the single season of episodes that exist—all thirteen of season one remain intact; season two is altogether lost), was another comment on the British class system, as Ronnie Barker meets . . . for the first time, it seems . . . the son he packed off to boarding school the moment the tyke was weaned. He is now a young man in his early twenties.

> Barker: "I didn't quite catch your name."
>
> Palin: "Sebastian, sir."
>
> Barker: "Sebastian?"
>
> Palin: "Yes, sir."
>
> Barker: "Sebastian?" (breaks down laughing). "We christened you Sebastian? My God, we must have been drunk. No, sorry, sorry, bloody rude that, bloody rude. You see I'm not very good at names and I might have to introduce you to your mother."

The final episode of *The Frost Report* was broadcast in June 1967; the cast reconvened for a Christmas special that December. All, however, had already moved on, with Cleese, Feldman and Brooke Taylor now starring in *At Last, the 1948 Show*, a sketch-heavy show made by David Frost's own production company. It was titled, incidentally, to illustrate how long it took the average television company to make up its mind whether or not a show was worth commissioning, although in this instance, of course, it had not taken long at all.

The show launched on February 15, 1967; would undergo two seasons before closing on November 7, 1968; and, while memory and commentators are still prone to credit *The Frost Report* with sketches first sighted on *1948* and vice versa, that is to the advantage of both shows.

There was a consistency to the humor, or more accurately to the humorists behind it, that confirmed what a lot of people already suspected—that a great new wave of comedians was about to explode onto the mainstream scene, and it was now a matter only of when, not if, they chose to do so.

We Apologize for the Break in Transmission . . .

At the same time as *At Last the 1948 Show* was enjoying its heyday, Idle, Jones and Palin were working in what the schedulers, at least, believed was children's television—a half-hour slice of anarchy called, with skillful deliberation, *Do Not Adjust Your Set*. That was the standard message delivered when technical difficulties interfered with broadcast. Now it was a warning that the next thirty minutes would offer something completely different.

Do Not Adjust Your Set should never, however, be regarded as simply another few cobbles on the road to *Python*. In fact, until the show's rebirth on DVD, many people's fondest memories revolved not around the future Pythons, but around the continuing adventures of Mrs. Black and Captain Fantastic, a weekly superhero serial parody starring Denise Coffey and David Jason; and the musical interludes delivered by the Bonzo Dog Doo Dah Band—in comedic terms, still the most creative and brilliant musical

The Bonzos have been anthologized so often that it hurts. But this CD box set contained (almost) everything you could desire.

act ever to play tubas in the moonlight, while introducing the Incredible Shrinking Man on euphonium.

Again, two seasons plus a Christmas special were aired between December 1967 and May 1969; again, the survival rate was spotty, as the demon wiper took out all but ten episodes (nine of which are available on DVD), while the most commonly circulating copy of the 1968 *Do Not Adjust Your Stocking* Christmas special suffered an almost 50 percent trimming after David Jason demanded his performances be cut before it could be repeated in 1986.

And Now for Something Else

I dle, Palin and Jones were not the only future Pythons involved in *Do Not Adjust Your Set*. A couple of episodes also featured input from a new arrival on the scene, American cartoonist Terry Gilliam, and by the time *Do Not Adjust Your Set* adjusted sets for the final time, the quartet was already deep in discussions with Cleese and Chapman over a new show—one that would not only ferment the weird chemistry that had already bound them together in so many past projects, but that would also offer challenges they had never faced before.

The vision was of a comedy show within which short sketches, bizarre cartoons, one-off jokes, silly songs and more would flow as a near seamless whole, one merging into another (or not) according not to some artificial link, but by the mood of the players at the time.

There would be no punch lines. Visual puns and what amounted to stream-of-consciousness word or image association would lead one sketch into the next. A character from one, as yet unseen, sketch might invade another while it was still in full flow, demanding a cessation to the silliness. Faceless announcers would interrupt the action, or maybe it would be Cleese himself, clad in finest BBC suit and desk. The studio audience would be replaced by stock footage of an audience full of old ladies.

That's Not Funny, It's Milligan

They were not stepping wholly into the unknown. Spike Milligan's *Q5* also launched in 1969, and John Cleese readily admitted that it was a signal inspiration. Speaking for Python's 2004 autobiography, he explained how he and Chapman "both happened to watch Spike Milligan's *Q5*, and one or the other of us phoned up and said kind of jokingly but also rather anxiously, 'I thought that's what we were supposed to be doing?' And the other one said, 'That's what I thought too.'

"We felt that Spike had got to where we were trying to get to, but if you'd asked us the previous day, we couldn't have described very well what that was. However, when we saw it on the screen we recognised it, and in a way the fact that Spike had gone there probably enabled us to go a little bit further than we would otherwise have gone."

That said, Milligan's efforts, while applauded for their imagination and adventure, were never a huge comedy hit; like so much of the ex-Goon's television work, the notion that he was trying too hard to be Milligan, playing not to his strengths but to the audience's understanding of those strengths, was difficult to shake—all the more so since *Q5* followed hot on the heels of the rankly lamentable *Curry and Chips*.

Back with Cleese and co, and the proposed new show's debt to Milligan notwithstanding, BBC producer Barry Took (whom the team knew from *The Frost Report)* was sufficiently enthusiastic to win them a thirteen-show commission.

As is so often the case, however, others within the BBC were less over-whelmed by the anarchic promise of Took's protégés. One high-up doubter even dubbed the whole affair "a flying circus," a derogatory name that the sextet—who had hitherto been conjuring with such titles as *Owl Stretching Time* and *Bunn, Wackett, Buzzard, Stubble and Boot*—immediately claimed for their own.

Whose *Flying Circus?* For a time, the team was seriously considering the name *Gwen Dibley*, after Palin spotted it in a Women's Institute magazine and found it curiously entertaining.

But then Idle came up with "Monty"; Cleese contributed "Python," and following a short period of reasoned consideration, during which everyone tried to conjure something better, that was the name that was delivered to the BBC: *Monty Python's Flying Circus*. And it was perfect. Nobody involved was named Monty Python. There was no flying. It was not a circus.

The Curtains?

The first season of this new show was broadcast on October 5, 1970, at 11:00 p.m. "Whither Canada?", as the episode was titled, comprised seven basic sketches, including two parodies of contemporary television ("It's Wolfgang Amadeus Mozart" and "It's the Arts"), blueprinting one of the show's most popular ongoing targets.

In the years to come, viewers would be introduced to such shows as *Boxing Tonight*, in which a heavyweight champion takes on Sir Kenneth Clark, presenter of the monumental TV series *Civilisation*; *Communist Quiz*, in which leading (and late) members of the Communist Party take part in a general knowledge quiz, in the hope of winning sundry attractive housewares; *Anagram Quiz*, in which the winner receives a blow on the head; a live documentary about molluscs; *Blackmail*, in which unsuspecting contestants are invited to pledge increasing amounts of money to prevent their greatest indiscretions being revealed; *Ken Russell's Gardening Club*; Sam Peckinpah's Tennis Match . . . . But that first night, already, precedents were set.

The *Daily Telegraph* newspaper responded to what the BBC described as a "nutty, zany, comedy show" the following morning. "The comedy was sophisticated and had much of the delightful absurdity which has not been seen on television since the *Marty* [Feldman] show," enthused reviewer Norman Hare.

"It took toll of interviewers and other features of television that need the sending up process."

Neither was Hare the sole supporter of that aspect of the show; nor were the most obvious targets its sole victim. Cleese later spoke of someone telling him that, after half an hour spent in *Monty Python*'s company, the regional magazine program that followed could not help but seem equally hilarious.

Neither was Hare's reference to Feldman entirely gratuitous. Palin and Jones had both written for the two broadcast seasons of *Marty*, and at least one Python sketch, the current affairs type exposé of young men who get their kicks from dressing up as mice, had originally been written (but rejected) for the Feldman show a year or so previous.

Monty Python's delight in mocking the viewing habits of its public reached an early peak with the introduction of the Colonel, a stiff-backed voice of reason whose admonitions to "stop this, it's silly" parroted the vocal minority whose outraged complaints swamped the BBC switchboard every time the corporation broadcast anything out of the normal. *Monty Python's Flying Circus*, of course, was simply begging for their opprobrium.

The Colonel, played by Chapman, first appeared in episode one's Joke Warfare sketch, in which the British develop a joke so funny it is impossible to hear it without keeling over dead. He came into his own, however, deeper into the maiden season, interrupting army recruit Eric Idle's discourse on why he doesn't fancy the idea of getting killed.

"That's a very silly line. Awfully bad."

Graham Chapman and Michael Palin discuss the Mouse Problem for Monty Python.   *Photofest*

The BBC were very slow in appreciating the success of *Python*, particularly once the more open-minded Director General Hugh Greene quit, to be replaced by a considerably less tolerant regime. Viewing figures were low, a consequence not only of the late hour but also of different regions of the country being free to choose what they aired that late at night; many parts of Britain knew of the show only from its coverage in the London-based press.

Indeed, without the support of the media, it is doubtful that the BBC would have even considered commissioning a second season. Instead, with its cult status, at least, assured, they invited the team to press on.

Already a number of what would prove seminal sketches had been delivered: Eric Idle's "nudge nudge wink wink" assault on an unsuspecting businessman; a succession of sexually explicit children's stories; a self-defense class featuring murderous, fruit-bearing assassins; and the appearance of sundry Nazi leaders at a small bed and breakfast, arguing over the best route across the country.

There was also an airing for a sketch that has since become synonymous with *Monty Python*, featuring Michael Palin, John Cleese and a disputedly deceased parrot.

Peculiarly, in view of its subsequent ubiquity, "The Pet Shop" was not an especially successful sketch. In its original format, in fact, the actual debate over the parrot's animation was swiftly subverted by the action's rapid progress through a brief argument over whether or not the town name "Ipswich" is a palindrome of "Bolton," before the Colonel turns up to condemn the whole thing as "silly." But the deceased parrot had a lot more life in it.

Season two would be no less perplexing for those who found themselves agreeing with the Colonel. Originally broadcast between September 15 and December 22, 1970, the outing again has its share of classics; in April 1971, a Python compilation even won the prestigious Silver Rose at the Montreaux Festival, a mighty accolade indeed for a show that completely baffled its own bosses. But still the censors' scissors were never far away, and with very good reason.

A sketch revolving around a cannibalistic funeral home was permitted onto the screens only if it was arranged for the audience to show its vocal distaste at the concept.

A piece that combines wine tasting with urine, "The Wee-Wee Sketch," was banned outright, while one of Gilliam's cartoons (of a prince who foolishly ignores a malevolent black spot that is growing on his body) was redubbed for future broadcasts in case it upset cancer sufferers. Instead, in some misguided attempt at alleviating the inherent tastelessness of the original concept, it targeted victims of gangrene.

Other moments, however, remain pristine. The Spanish Inquisition (which nobody expects) effortlessly made the transition from televisual entertainment to cultural mainstay, as comfortable chairs became a ready synonym for hideous torture.

John Cleese's silly walks took on such a life of their own that they torment their creator to this day; and Doug and Dinsdale Piranha, as every British viewer instantly realized, parodied the recently jailed Kray Twins, London gangsters whose criminal empire held London society enthralled, even as their activities grew increasingly more brazen.

Finally imprisoned, the Krays' influence remained pervasive; the arrival of one of Doug Piranha's "associates" at the end of the sketch, to suggest politely that it should be brought to an end, was an echo of the Krays' own continued ability to squash unwanted publicity with a few well-chosen words in the appropriate ear—or "shell-like," as Londoners are alleged to prefer.

Immanuel Kant and Other Fables

By 1971, *Monty Python* was established. A record deal would see a string of LPs bring audio highlights of the show into every willing living room; a publishing deal allowed the world to enjoy such colorful sprawls full of stupidity, smut and inspired genius as *Monty Python's Big Red Book* (naturally, it was blue) and the *Brand New Monty Python Bok*.

A movie, *And Now for Something Completely Different*, sliced and diced the best of the first two seasons in an ultimately misbegotten attempt to introduce the show to the United States (it would be two years more before the show reached these shores); and work was under way on the third season, for broadcast beginning in fall 1972.

It was not the happiest of teams by now. Cleese, in particular, was losing interest in the TV series, in the belief that *Monty Python* had gone as far as it could in that particular medium, and announced his intention of quitting at the end of the new season (he would, however, remain on board for stage shows, movies and vinyl).

There was no shortage of inspiration, however; indeed, there so much material being written that Python were now including unaired material on their LPs. Cleese and wife Connie Booth's "A Fairy Tale"; the highwayman Dennis Moore; the Peckinpah sketch and Idle's "Eric the Half a Bee"

Monty Python's Upper Class Twits of the Year—the winners' rostrum.   *Photofest*

all rated among the comedy highlights of 1972, together with a sketch in which innocent soccer players are turned into Scotsmen by blancmanges.

Throughout, the *Pythons'* pataphysical ability to grasp slivers of contemporary society and twist them out of their customary orbit remained incisive. Characters like the bellowing Gumbies, the squawking Pepperpots, a nestful of shrill-voiced working-class housewives with names like Mrs. Scum and, somewhat unfortunately, Mrs. Niggerbaiter; a party of bellowing architects and, of course, the Colonel were by their very nature absurd.

But they also adopted a life of their own because, ultimately, they were drawn from life, exaggerated stereotypes of everyday Britain. Only occasionally would the show touch upon mentions of actual living people (a handful of now largely forgotten politicians and thespians), but few viewers failed to make the required connections.

Cleese's departure from the series ensured that there would be a long wait for a new television series; in the meantime, a new LP that revolutionarily contrived to place three sides of content onto two sides of vinyl (two sets of grooves ran side by side), a pair of German-language specials and a British tour kept the *Python* pan bubbling, with the latter claiming—most disingenuously, as it transpired—that many of the featured jokes were making their farewell tour effectively serving as a best of *Python*, both in their own right and hitherto.

Included in the repertoire, which surely rates as the ultimate "best of" that Python ever compiled, "The Four Yorkshiremen" sketch reprised a routine first debuted on *At Last the 1948 Show;* "Albatross," "Nudge Nudge," "Pet Shop" and the "Lumberjack Song," rose from past popular favorites, and all of it led up to the Python's farewell.

The fourth, and final, season of *Monty Python's Flying Circus* aired in Britain between October 31 and December 5, 1974, and, true to the absent Cleese's fears, ran into immediate press criticism, only some of which was predicated on the absence of the cast member who, to many viewers, *was* Mr. Python.

Rumors that the BBC itself felt that way, and had seriously considered canceling the show, only added to the sense of doom that surrounded the series. *Monty Python* would never return to the small screen again.

Yet of course there were highlights—and there would be more to come. Shrugging off the low-key reaction to the series, the full team reconvened on the big screen, in the epic *Monty Python and the Holy Grail* (itself subsequently reborn as the musical *Spamalot*)—twisted parodies of the Arthurian legend that rank among the team members' most successful ventures ever. Further tours, more LPs, more movies (the Bible-baiting *Life of Brian* and *Monty Python's Meaning of Life*), and more television, in the form of the various team members' own projects.

Both individually and collectively, then, *Monty Python's Flying Circus* occupies a unique place in the annals of British comedy. While a great deal of what was once considered daring has now become so integral a part of the comic landscape that it is all but meaningless today, still great swathes of the show's dialogue and humor have become one with the language.

The Spanish Inquisition, the Dead Parrot, "Nudge Nudge" and the cheese shop with no cheese are instantly recognizable even to people who have never seen the original sketches, while the sold-out audiences that greeted the team's (less the sadly deceased Chapman) most recent reunion knew the words to the sketches as well as the players themselves.

Other comics have developed universally loved and repeated catch-phrases. *Monty Python*, which deployed such things only to illustrate how unnecessary they were, have catch-paragraphs. Catch-pages, even.

Can there be any higher tribute than that?

Who Do You Think You Are Kidding . . .

War Can Be a Laughing Matter

The irascible Albert Steptoe and the belligerent Alf Garnett were not the nation's only grumpy granddads, nor were they its most popular. Old folk were also the focus of another long-running Britcom, perhaps the best-loved of them all. *Dad's Army* not only ran for nine seasons and eighty episodes broadcast between 1968 and 1977 (even longer than the war that it depicted); it was then followed by what appears to have been an eternity of reruns, radio adaptations, DVD box sets, and even (unseen at the time of writing, but it's always hard to hold out much hope for such things) a 2016 movie starring Toby Jones, Bill Nighy, Tom Courtenay, Michael Gambon and Catherine Zeta-Jones.

Set in what was then the not-so-distant past of 1940, and the opening rounds of World War II, *Dad's Army* was writers Jimmy Perry and David Croft's reimagining of the Home Guard, a volunteer service comprising men who were otherwise exempt from military service, but still wished to do their bit. This included those who were employed in professions deemed crucial to the war effort, men considered too old for the regular fighting services (forty and over) or those whose health had deemed them unsuitable.

Originally called Local Defence Volunteers, the Home Guard was established primarily to combat the very real fears of a German invasion of Britain—within eight months of the war breaking out, after all, the Nazis occupied the entire European coast facing the island, and that summer of 1940 saw the Battle of Britain raging in the skies, as the enemy tried to soften up the British defenses in preparation for *Aldertag*, or Eagle Day.

The invasion never came. The Royal Air Force defeated the Germans in the air through the summer and autumn, and while the winter saw the country subjected to a merciless bombing campaign, the Blitz, Britain neither surrendered nor crumbled. By spring 1941, Hitler had shifted his attention to the invasion of Russia. He thought that might be a softer target than the British Isles.

The Home Guard remain on alert, however, not standing down until December 1944, and being formally disbanded twelve months later. Its legend, however, grew—*not* a heroic legend of pitched battles and ultimate sacrifice, but a more homely one, the story of butchers, bakers and candlestick makers who donned a uniform and were prepared to fight for the love of their country, and the safety of their friends.

As the service's original name implies, Home Guard units were fiercely local, drawn from the immediate community—of course they were; with the country on permanent lookout for enemy spies, what could have been more suspicious than a total stranger asking to join the local defense force?

Or likely to create so many hilarious misunderstandings?

Dad's Army was a sitcom, then; an often breathtakingly deft balance of slapstick comedy and scripted humor, frequently understated, and never (or at least rarely) seeking out the easiest, cheapest laugh in any given situation.

But it was a tribute, too, a celebration of a perhaps unsung, and often underrated line of defense. Poorly equipped by their military overlords,

Dad's Army on parade—(*left to right*) Arthur Lowe, John le Mesurier, Clive Dunn, John Laurie, Arnold Ridley, Ian Lavender and James Beck.   *Alamy*

the Home Guard improvised its arsenal—everything from farming imple-
ments to vintage firearms, souvenirs of past conflicts. There were, as *Dad's
Army* illustrated, volunteers old enough to have served in the colonial wars
of the nineteenth century, battling Zulus, Boers and, as Corporal Jones
constantly reminded us, sundry other "fuzzy wuzzies." Who, he continues,
as he brandishes his bayonet, "don't like it up them."

The cast of the show reflected the makeup of the average Home Guard
unit. Respected veterans of stage and screen one and all, the officious
Captain Mainwaring, a bank manager by day, was played by Arthur Lowe
(aged fifty-three); Sergeant Wilson by John Le Mesurier (fifty-six), Lance-
Corporal Jones by Clive Dunn (just forty-eight, but expertly made up to look
almost twice that age). Arnold Ridley (Private Godfrey) and John Laurie
(the doomy Private Frazer), the oldest of the privates, were seventy-two and
seventy-one respectively.

Younger troop members included the medically unsuitable Pike, played
by twenty-two-year-old Ian Lavender, and whose overprotective mother is
having an affair with the sergeant—Pike's "Uncle Arthur"; and a greasy
black marketeer, a "spiv" in local parlance, named Walker (John Beck,
thirty-nine when the show started). An overenthusiastic air raid warden (Bill
Pertwee) completed the regular cast.

Their Finest Hour

Largely filmed on England's east coast, in a small town called Thetford,
Dad's Army was likewise set far from the hubbub of the cities, in the fictional
town of Walmington-on-Sea—well chosen because, of course, that particular coastline was regarded as the most vulnerable to invasion.

Beaches that once had thronged with families were now strictly off-
limits, a tangle of barbed wire, tank traps, mines and sundry other fearsome
obstacles. Further barricades awaited on the streets of the town itself, while
the fear of vast enemy artillery capable of launching shells across the English
Channel added fresh menace to the already prevalent airborne terrors.

All of these factors played into *Dad's Army*; though the show strived for
affection as much as accuracy, still it is difficult to watch it without gaining
some understanding of the sheer stressfulness of day-to-day life during the
years it depicts. Even the opening credits were accompanied by a glorious
pastiche of the typical morale-boosting wartime song, "Who Do You Think
You Are Kidding, Mr. Hitler," although modern sensibilities regarding the
use of swastikas in popular entertainment (even the markings on planes

in war movies are now routinely erased) would quail at the accompanying imagery. There's hordes of the things!

Further accuracy was drawn from writer Perry's own experiences in the Home Guard, with both situations and characters drawn from his service—Lance Corporal Jones, Perry revealed, was wholly based on one of the men with whom he served, while the character of Pike was modeled on Perry himself! His mother, too, insisted on him wearing a scarf on chilly nights, to ward off the possibility of illness.

Dad's Amy began in the days of black-and-white television, with the early episodes relating to the formation of the Home Guard itself, and the early trials that the force faced—in the first episode, Mainwaring is reduced to giving the men armbands in lieu of uniforms; in the second, he is forced to requisition weapons from the local museum; in the third, arms are finally provided, in the form of antique muskets.

Captain Mainwaring offers up a succinct summary of the spirit that fired the Home Guard in the opening moments of the pilot episode.

"The massive Nazi war machine is pushing its way across Europe, laying waste neutral countries with a savagery unmatched in history.

"When Hitler comes up against British troops, it's a different story. They fight him every inch of the way, giving as good as they get. Is Tommy Atkins [a popular nickname for the British soldier] downhearted? We'll say he's not! Why should he be with a leader like this?

"We all have our part to play, and every effort is being made to confuse the enemy. So, look out, Adolf. Every day, our defenses are strengthened, and if they do come, let's give them a sharp welcome!"

Surprisingly, in the light of the show's eventual success, and the affection in which it is still held (at one point, more than a quarter of Britain's population was regularly watching), these first episodes came in for considerable criticism.

There were fears, for example, that the show intended belittling the Home Guard, assumptions based on its portrayal of the very real difficulties that local units faced. The shortage of weaponry, for example, really *was* remedied by providing the men with wooden "rifles"; the shortage of troops to man the barricades *was* disguised by the deployment of dummies; and, even within their own communities, the needs of the local platoons often *were* at odds with the locals' attempts to maintain some semblance of regular, prewar life.

The characters, too, were exquisitely drawn, but caricatured just enough to arouse the ire of those who believe television should reflect life exactly.

The unwaveringly patriotic Captain Mainwaring had been a lieutenant in the regular army during World War 1 (albeit without seeing active service), and retained his eye for discipline; Sergeant Wilson, too, was a veteran, only he had not only seen battle, he had also risen to the rank of captain, a fact that Mainwaring never forgot, but was constantly trying to negate.

Dad's Army's Clive Dunn on the cover of the UK television listings magazine *TV Times*.
© *www.timeincukcontent.com*

This, in itself, reflected a certain inequality that was prevalent in the Home Guard, where the highest ranks were often awarded to the men whose civilian standing commanded respect (bank managers were once regarded among the most important people in a community), regardless of their actual experience and suitability for command.

Mainwaring: "You . . . went to public school . . . didn't you?"

Wilson: "You know, I can't help feeling, Sir, you've got a little bit of a chip on your shoulder about that."

Mainwaring: "There's no chip on my shoulder, Wilson. I'll tell you what there is on my shoulder, though: three pips, and don't you forget it."

Jones, now owner of the local butcher's store, had fought in the Sudan under Lord Kitchener; Godfrey, contrarily, had been a conscientious objector throughout World War 1, but served as a medic—a role he reassumed in the Home Guard. And Frazer was a former navy man, present at the Battle of Jutland, and forever looking on the blackest side of things, dire forebodings that he would utter in an almost impenetrable Scots burr.

Always good for a chilling anecdote was Frazer. Hark, for example, to the tale of the old empty barn, relayed, of course, in a voice that oozes mystery and suspense.

Frazer: "Captain Mainwaring. Did I ever tell you the story about the old, empty barn?"

Mainwaring: "Um. No."

Frazer: "Would you like to hear the story about the old, empty barn?"

Mainwaring: "Um. Yes. Listen everybody. Frazer's going to tell us the story about the old empty barn."

Frazer: "Right. The story of the old empty barn. Well. There was nothing in it."

He regularly bordered on the realms of mutiny, too; indeed, it is later revealed that Frazer had earned at least one promotion during his naval career, only to be reduced back to the ranks after decking an officer with a boat hook.

He remains a law unto himself in the Home Guard, too. Thankfully, Mainwaring usually knows how to deal with him.

Frazer: "I am refusing to obey."

Mainwaring: "You'll be in charge of the liquor permits, Frazer."

Frazer: "I'm right behind you, Captain."

Or not.

Mainwaring: "You should consider it an honor and a privilege to use this Lewis gun."

Frazer: "If it was a privilege, none of us would ever be getting a look in; you and the Sergeant would be doing it all the time."

There is no hint, however, that these men do not realize the seriousness of their current situation, nor the ends to which they are expected to go. Facing down what they believe to be an invading army, Mainwaring turns to his troops and tells them, "It'll probably be the end of us, but we're ready for that, aren't we men?"

"Of course," Frazer replies.

Against this doughty fighting force was ranged . . . not the enemy Germans, but the petty concerns of local life. The warden, Hodges, lives only to ensure that every light in town is extinguished at dusk, a role that he believes is far more vital to the war effort than Mainwaring's mob playing soldiers. The local priest, the Reverend Timothy Farthing, spends the entire conflict quietly regretting the day when St. Aldhelm's church hall was ever requisitioned for the Home Guard's use; and his verger, Maurice, is openly hostile toward the soldiers.

Farthing: "Mr. Mainwaring, if you can do your blood-curdling bayonet practice in the middle of my responses, I can do my Jubilate in the middle of your inquiry!"

Equally trying is the platoon's relationship with the nearby Eastgate platoon, a considerably more polished outfit than the Walmington setup, under the command of the ferocious Captain Square (Geoffrey Lumsden), a man mercilessly prone to unleash a withering bark of "you blithering idiot" at anything that crosses him.

It is these battles that *Dad's Amy* focused on, although the war itself is never far from view. Invasion scares were common during the early months of the war, with rumors spreading even faster than any genuine hostile force could hope to travel.

But it was not only weaponry that the Home Guard had a shortage of. If, as popular slang put it, "the balloon" should "go up," they had few viable fortifications, either. So-called pillboxes, reinforced concrete blocks with slitted windows, dotted the coast, but they were small, built for just a hand-ful of defenders. Larger forces, if they wished to keep together, had to fight from wherever they could —in one case, Private Godfrey's cottage.

On another occasion, a pair of Luftwaffe airmen are captured after their plane was shot down, a happenstance that allowed the show to portray another aspect of wartime reality. A number of Polish citizens had arrived in Britain following their own country's conquest in 1939, and many of them joined the military; these include an officer from GHQ (General Headquarters) who happens to be visiting Walmington during this latest crisis, and who is now mistaken for a German as well! (A similar scene was replayed in the movie *The Battle of Britain*, about a year later, with an English farmer proudly "capturing" a downed Polish airman.)

Don't Tell Him, Pike

One of the best remembered of all *Dad's Army*'s encounters with "real" Germans, however, occurred in the sixth-season episode "The Deadly Attachment," when the platoon are ordered to guard a captured U-Boat crew—which has little difficulty in turning the tables and, in turn, captur-ing the platoon.

Even before that, however their captain (Philip Madoc) has put the wind up Mainwaring and Co.

"I am making notes, Captain. Your name . . ." as he lowers his voice to a sinister pitch, "will go on the list. And when we win the war, you will be bought to account."

"You can write what you like," responds Mainwaring. "You're not going to win this war."

"Oh yes we are."

"Oh no you're not."

And so on until Pike pipes up with a chorus of "whistle while you work, Hitler is a twerp."

"Your name will also go on the list," announces the captain. "What is it?"

Mainwaring adopts his most commanding tone. "Don't tell him, Pike."

"Pike," says the German smugly.

"Don't tell him Pike" has since ascended into the uppermost annals of comedy catchphrases, despite not actually being a catchphrase—a 1999 BBC poll went even further, viewers voting it the third-funniest television moment in the corporation's history.

Even funnier than the story of the old empty barn!

But this single episode's popularity is misleading. Certainly throughout the early 1970s, *Dad's Army* was truly all conquering, cast and writers firing on all cylinders. Any episode from seasons four through six can be spotlighted as an example of the show at its best, from "Sgt.—Save My Boy," in which Pike contrives to entangle himself in barbed wire in the middle of a minefield, to "Getting the Bird," in which we not only see Wilson reunited with his lost daughter, but also cringe as the wily Walker tries to offload 250 suspiciously deceased pigeons to Jones's butcher's shop as "off ration meat."

Another classic played on the men's resentment of Mainwaring's love of his own voice, a conflict that reaches its apex when the exasperated Captain tells Frazer that he should try doing the job for a day. Of course, the Scotsman jumps at the chance and promptly initiates a new discipline. Mainwaring is appointed the platoon's bagpiper.

And then there's the one where they convert Jones's butcher's van into an armored car.

The first chip to appear in *Dad's Army*'s armor, however, had nothing to do with the quality of the show; it was the sudden death, on August 6, 1973, of James Beck—a heavy drinker, he was taken ill while opening a village fete, and discovered to be suffering from pancreatitis. The last episode in which he appeared was "Things That Go Bump in the Night," another magnificent story, in which the platoon run out of petrol and are forced to shelter for the night in what they think is a deserted house, but which actually turns out to be a military dog training center.

"Private Walker"'s absence was explained away in the next episode, in which Mainwaring receives a note apologizing for his nonappearance at parade; he is in London, concluding "a deal." We never hear of him again, and while *Dad's Army* was never consciously an ensemble production, the loss of that one character did upset its balance a little—not so much that it damaged the show's popularity (it continued on for another four years, after all), nor its overall quality.

But an intregal spoke of a beautifully rendered wheel was missing, the sassy disregard for orders and discipline that Walker so exquisitely injected into the group dynamic.

Telling, too, may have been the commissioning of a second war-based series by writers Perry and Croft, *It Ain't Half Hot, Mum*, in 1974. Set in the very different surroundings of the Indian and Burmese jungles during the last months of the war, and with a similarly unique cast of leading characters fronting the surely unpromising premise of a Royal Artillery Concert Party, the show nevertheless gnawed at many similar scenarios as *Dad's Army*, albeit with very different resolutions.

The suspicion that the rise (and swift popularity) of the new show drew the writers' attention away from the old may be baseless, but it is also understandable.

That said, *Dad's Army* was clearly coming to an end. Unlike many shows, *Dad's Army* was very conscious of the passing of what we might call "real time"—the progression of the war itself was painstakingly marked, with the show even signaling its own ending as it recognized the changing situation in which the Home Guard units found themselves.

The decision to allow women to enter the service, in 1941, was acknowledged (although not acted upon), while the arrival into the war of the USA at the end of that same year, and the spread across the country of their own bases, caused several problems during season six. Likewise, seasons seven and eight both reflected the diminishing danger of invasion (and, therefore, the increased redundancy of the Home Guard) by involving the gang instead in strictly local events—the building of a new aerodrome, village fetes and so forth.

By season nine, even Mainwaring's attempts to shake the town out of its growing complacency by disguising the platoon as enemy spies succeeds only in bringing down the wrath of his own superiors, and on November 13, 1977, at the end of that same season, we watch as Corporal Jones marries his longtime sweetheart, Mrs. Fox, and the entire cast turn to the camera to toast the memory of the "real" Home Guard.

Their war was over.

Dad's Army has been well served by the BBC's archive. Just three episodes are currently missing, all from season two (two more, hitherto believed lost, were recovered in 2001). Unfortunately, these include "The Loneliness of the Long Distance Walker," a fondly remembered episode in which Private Walker is called up to the regular army, much to the alarm of his Home

Guard comrades—to whom will they turn now for the generous supply of black market items that with which he hitherto supplied them?

A reprieve comes in the form of Walker's own constitution. Having passed all of the army's medical tests, he discovers on his first day as a soldier that he is allergic to corned beef, the single most prevalent meal in the army canteen. He is granted an honorable discharge and returns to Walmington-on-Sea to continue business as usual.

Those omissions notwithstanding, *Dad's Army* survives not only in its episodic form, but also via three Christmas specials, and a feature film, too, released in 1971 and effectively restaging the unit's creation. It was not, sad to say, a particularly brilliant effort, but few sitcoms of the era ever really made that transition successfully, and *Dad's Army* is no worse than any of the others.

The *Dad's Army* stage show was almost as popular as the TV series that spawned it.

For as long as the television series survives, though, there really is no reason to watch the movie. Either of them.

For You, Tommy, the War Is Never Over

Dad's Army was not British television's sole attempt to portray World War II in comedic terms; indeed, any examination of British culture through the 1960s, 1970s and 1980s will run up against the war again and again. It informed everything from popular fiction to TV mini-series, and on to children's comics—with some of the longest running of the latter being devoted wholly to the conflict.

Television dramas like *Piece of Cake*, *Wish Me Luck* and *We'll Meet Again* all sought to capture different aspects of the war, to varying degrees of success. In terms of popularity, however, and with *Dad's Army* indisputably king of the castle, few succeeded more thoroughly than the aforementioned *It Ain't Half Hot, Mum.*

Much of the show concentrated on the concert troupe's musical and thespian abilities and activities, with the majority of the characters likewise showing some dexterity in the required directions.

There was the diminutive "Lofty" Sugden (Don Estelle), with his trademark pith helmet and a voice to charm the birds from the trees (partnered by costar Windsor Davies, the platoon's bellowing Sergeant Major, Estelle would score a 1975 UK chart topper with "Whispering Grass").

There was "La-de-dah" Graham (John Clegg), a pianist; "Nobby" Clark (Kenneth MacDonald), with his talent for birdcall impersonations; and "Gloria" Beaumont (Melvyn Hayes), the troupe's resident female impersonator. (Cruel critics occasionally compared Beaumont's role to that of Corporal Clinger in *M*A*S*H*, and they were probably correct.) And there was a host of natives to add, as we have said before, some local color.

A musical troupe in a wartime setting, *It Ain't Half Hot, Mum* was, in many ways, as much a tribute to the entertainment corps of the war years as *Dad's Army* was intended to honor the Home Guard, and with so many of the postwar era's best-loved comedians having cut their teeth in such units, it was a well-placed tribute, too.

Reality and television, however, boasted one major difference—Sergeant Major Williams (Davies).

A ferocious fighting man, he despises the easy life that he sees all around him, and has no greater ambition than to see the concert party disbanded and the men sent off to fight. His constant insistence on drilling and parading the troops, and the troops' attempts to circumvent his schemes, is the basic premise of many of the episodes; the success and longevity (launched in 1974, it ran until 1981) of the show testifying to the skill with which the writers pulled it off.

At the same time, however, *It Ain't Half Hot, Mum* also reflects attitudes that modern viewers find discomforting, no matter how true-to-life they may have been during the era in which the show was set.

The treatment and the personalities of various native characters echoes all the prejudices that hallmarked the last years of Britain's presence in India, most notably Rumam, a lazy and resentful *punkah wallah* (the servant charged with ensuring the officers remained cool in the heat of the day, by manually fanning them); while Sergeant Major Williams's insult of choice was "poof," a derogatory term for homosexual.

Neither was out of place in the time and place depicted by the show, any more than an obstreperous air raid warden and a Cockney black marketeer were misplaced in *Dad's Army*, and the debate over whether light entertainment should whitewash history's darker aspects is one that will probably never be satisfactorily resolved.

Damned if they do, damned if they don't; a wartime comedy in which the Battle of Britain–era fighter pilots are all disabled females from minority backgrounds might tick all the correct boxes in terms of political inclusion, but would run into a host of other objections, too.

It Ain't Half Hot, Mum's critics were also, perhaps, a little too hasty when they condemned the heavily made-up appearance of white actor Michael Bates as one of the wallahs. Not only was Bates both Indian-born and a fluent Hindi speaker, he was hired only when it became apparent that no other high-profile Indian actors were available for the show. It's another drawback that critics frequently choose to ignore—the fact that you cannot *force* actors of a certain race or nationality to drop everything else to appear in your show. Sometimes, you have to choose from among those who actually want to do it.

Besides, nobody complained when *Dad's Army* hired a Welshman (Philip Madoc) to play a German.

Still, *It Ain't Half Hot, Mum* prospered. Entertained by the songs, amused by the script, entranced by the characters, the show may not receive the plaudits that its stablemate, *Dad's Army*, takes for granted (a consequence, perhaps, of the aforementioned criticisms), but it kept a large proportion of the country happy for six seasons, and in a medium that is all too often reliant on cheap laughter for its success, it engaged them as well.

A Sitcom with an Additional "H"

Which is more than can be said for the third "great" British wartime sitcom, *'Allo 'Allo*. Rated thirteenth in the 2004 TV series *Britain's Best Sitcom* poll; and running nine seasons across ten years of scheduling, *'Allo 'Allo* was focused on the staff and customers of a small cafe in a French town during the German occupation, most notably the small cadre of French Resistance fighters who were headquartered there.

Of course, there is a long and proud undercurrent to British comedy that finds foreign accents to be even funnier than the country's own local brogues, with that of the Frenchman probably top of the pile—although German, Indian (see *Curry and Chips*) and sundry Eastern European–sounding tones have all challenged it at different times.

'Allo 'Allo was onto a winner from the outset, then, affectionately toying with (if also reinforcing) stereotypes, even as it purportedly celebrated another of the war's lesser-sung bands of heroes and heroines. Furthermore, it was cowritten, once again, by David Croft, this time in partnership with Jeremy Lloyd, with whom he created *Are You Being Served?* There really was no way it could fail, and in terms of viewing figures, it didn't.

At the same time, however, it lacked the realism that had always been the essential premise of its predecessors, and with that absence a great deal of the sympathy and support that the average viewer might feel for the characters. It is hard to identify with a cipher, and too much of *'Allo 'Allo* relied upon just that.

Still, it was nowhere near as bad as Croft and Perry's next effort, *Hi-de-Hi!*, set in an English holiday camp in the 1950s and so absurdly popular throughout the bulk of the 1980s that *every* terrible thing you have ever heard about that decade's impact on popular culture is lit up in soul-charring neon.

Seriously, if this was what a vacation might turn out like, no wonder a lot of people choose to stay at home. Or join the military.

Goodie Goodie Yum Yum

Stuffing Gibbons with the Goodies

Brian Eno once said that writing about music is like dancing to architecture. By the same token, trying to describe *The Goodies* to someone who's never heard of them is like trying to sculpt a replica of our planet for a blind convention of the Flat Earth Society. You can list its cast, its premise, its shape. But it still won't really make sense.

The Goodies themselves were among the most familiar names in British comedy. Like the *Monty Python* crew, with whom Bill Oddie and Tim Brooke-Taylor had habitually worked through the sixties, their names and faces were common to a stream of shows: *I'm Sorry, I'll Read That Again, At Last the 1948 Show, Marty, Twice a Fortnight* and more, before they were united with Graeme Garden (whom they had known since university) in the short-lived *Broaden Your Mind*. In fact, one of the team's earliest ideas for their own show's title was *Narrow Your Mind*, while past experiences in broadcasting would perhaps spark a few of their more affectionate later jokes.

> Tim, outraged as he so often is: "I'm going to make a complaint to the very highest authority."
>
> Graeme: "Not . . ."
>
> Bill: ". . . David Frost!"
>
> Tim: "No, not that high . . . no . . . no . . . !"

Anytime, Anywhere

The Goodies launched in November 1970, in the aftermath of *Monty Python*, with which it was sometimes compared. Whereas the Pythons emphasized short, unconnected sketches, however, *The Goodies* strived toward single story lines, albeit viewed through a kaleidoscope of such unremitting surrealism that it was sometimes necessary to watch an episode several times, just to confirm how the plot got from A to Z. But be warned, B, C, D and the rest were rarely a part of the journey. *The Goons* had done the same thing, of course, but they took their journeys on radio. *The Goodies* did good in living color.

The Goodies themselves were a three-man operation whose motto was "any thing, any time"—they operated an agency that offered to solve any problem that could be thrust in their direction, and generally help out in any way they could. Graeme (Garden) was the computer genius, forever inventing new creations to aid them in their efforts. Bill (Oddie) was the ideas man, and Tim Brooke-Taylor was a bit of a wet fish, fiercely patriotic, prone to tears, a goody two-shoes through and through.

Their chosen method of transport was a three-seater tandem.

But somehow, everything gelled.

The first episode set the tone for the series. A call comes in from the Tower of London, whose traditional military guard of so-called Beefeaters is under attack from someone who keeps stealing their beef. And, because that is *all* that they will eat, they are now starving. Even the biggest Beefeater is just three foot tall now, and so the Goodies set to work, apprehending the thief and restoring the Beefeaters to their prior, towering glory.

The Goodies continue true to their motto, no matter how calamitous the risks. In one episode they set out to retrieve incriminating photographs of a government minister from the Playboy Club. In another, their search for a missing explorer sees them fall into the clutches of the cannibalistic Lost Tribe of the Orinoco. And in "The Baddies," they come up against the evil Dr. Petal, who has set out to discredit every competitor in the upcoming "Nicest Person in the World" contest.

The classic episode, however, was aired midway through the second season (and is still routinely trotted out when *The Goodies'* brilliance is questioned). "Kitten Kong" opens with the team opening a special clinic "for loony animals," and, to assure their guests' good health, Graeme invents a growth formula—which, perhaps inevitably, he hasn't thoroughly tested.

Most of the animals are fine—a bush baby, a goldfish, a vampire bat, a mongoose and so on. But the prize of their collection, the fluffiest, cutest little kitten you have ever seen, is not so fortunate. Twinkle starts to grow. And grow. And grow and grow and grow.

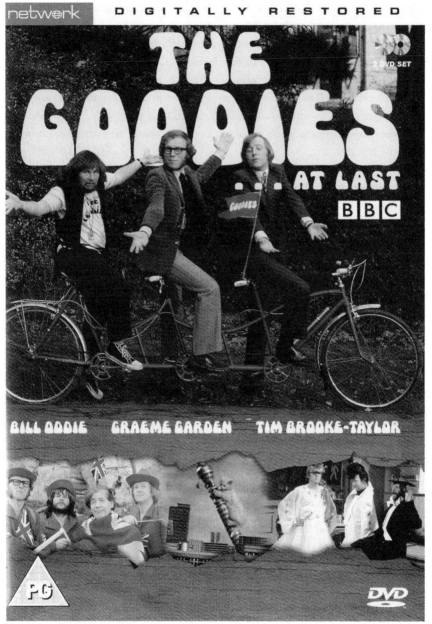

Bill, Graeme and Tim riding to the rescue.

Soon, the entire city of London cowers beneath the shadow of this monstrous kitten, and when it topples the Post Office Tower, five hundred feet of gleaming silver, destroys Saint Paul's Cathedral, and crushes (real-life) television host Michael Aspel beneath one outsized kitty paw, the Goodies know they have to do something.

First, Graeme develops an antidote to the growth formula. Then they equip their tandem with a hot air balloon, to enable it to fly. And then they disguise themselves as giant mice, in order to get close enough to administer the injection.

The operation is a success, Twinkle is back to normal. But returning home, another problem is discovered. During their absence, some mice have found the formula. And now they are starting to grow.

The stories themselves were not *The Goodies'* only attraction. Although the show was screened by the BBC, and therefore suffered no commercial break, the Goodies themselves chose to insert one, and then populate it with their own spoof advertisements. One in particular lives on in the memory, a parody of the Rice Crispies ad in which a little boy "listens" to his breakfast as it snaps, crackles and pops in the bowl.

Brooke-Taylor, gawky in his own school uniform, also listens. Only his cereal explodes violently.

Another ad promoted a new washing powder, somewhat suspiciously called Fairy Puff. Suspicious, because it permits Brooke-Taylor to dress up as the Fairy Puff Man, an unctuous, effeminate, Liberace-like creature, with a voice to match.

And a third retailed the Supermatic Camera, a fabulous device that "takes, develops and prints [photographs] in just ten seconds." Just like a regular Instamatic, then. Only Supermatic. For, when you peel the backing off the photograph, the person you photographed is revealed standing naked.

It is no criticism of *The Goodies* to acknowledge that not every episode was as enjoyable as "Kitten Kong" (which would be reedited for inclusion in the 1972 Montreux Festival, which it duly won, and would be nominated for a BAFTA too). Indeed, some offered very sparse gruel indeed, weak story lines peopled by weaker jokes, and a sense that this week, at least, the ideas had been a little thin on the ground.

If I Had a Gibbon Bow

But there was always next week, and the team constantly bounced back—episodes like "Winter Olympics," where the Goodies, representing Britain, decide to warm themselves up in the frigid conditions (the event is being staged at the North Pole that year). They succeed only in melting the ice, upsetting the training routines of every other competitor, but, because they themselves have no athletic abilities whatsoever, they suffer no hardships whatsoever. Result—Britain's greatest-ever medals sweep.

Or "Bunfight at the OK Tea Rooms," where Graeme visits an abandoned tin mine and discovers *not* tin but clotted cream—perhaps the greatest seam of the stuff ever found. The resultant riches go to his head; abandoning Bill and Tim, he strikes out on his own, a wealthy entrepreneur who is driven to distraction when he discovers that they, too, have now made a massive strike, a strawberry jam and scones mine a short distance away.

He challenges them to a poker game, winner takes all. But when they discover that he is cheating, guns . . . or, at least, plastic squeezable ketchup bottles . . . are drawn.

Or "Kung Fu Kapers," which introduces us to a vein of comedy that we will look at in greater detail in the next chapter, and the southern Briton's insistence that his northern cousins are Very Amusing Indeed. (Oddie himself was born in those parts.)

Martial arts mania was sweeping the country at the time, in the wake of the *Kung Fu* television series and Carl Douglas's "Kung Fu Fighting" hit single. Now Tim and Graeme, too, are learning the discipline, but Bill is not impressed. For he is already a master in the martial arts, a secret skill developed in Lancashire and named for the popular belief that the regional vocabulary comprises just one phrase, "Ecky Thump." Its exponents are then equipped with the solitary foodstuff that the locals are said to consume, black pudding.

It all sounds very foolish, but it is a lethal discipline. Martial arts experts from across the globe visit to test their skills against the Ecky Thump master. All are crushed, usually with a single blow from the black pudding.

Hollywood comes calling, and Bill is the star of a series of Ecky Thump–themed movies . . . *Enter with Drag On* and *Mary Poppins Meets Ecky Thump.* And out in the real world, one viewer laughed so hard at the episode that he died. Really. Twenty-five minutes of nonstop laughter placed such a strain on the fifty-year-old's heart that his heart gave out. Touchingly, his widow later wrote to the Goodies, thanking them for letting him go out with such a smile on his face.

Of course, *The Goodies* was a child of its time. Although it generally (but not altogether) avoided sequences that modern sensibilities would term racist, the gay community remained an open target, as the previously

mentioned Fairy Puff Man suggests. Another sequence that might raise hackles today is drawn from the episode "Hunting Pink."

> Graeme: "I know why he's all dressed up. He's after some bird."
>
> Bill: "Oh!"
>
> Tim : "If I was after some bird, I wouldn't need to dress up as a guardsman."
>
> Bill: "No, that's true. Must be after some fella." (Laughs hard)
>
> Tim: "As a matter of fact it's Butcher."
>
> Grame: "Butcher than what?"
>
> Tim: "My great uncle Butcher."
>
> Graeme: "Oh yes."

Religion, too, was frequently targeted, such as the time the team found itself transported back to ancient Rome. Tim was placed in charge of entertainments at the Colosseum, and is now explaining to the emperor why he is no longer booking the Christians to perform.

> Emperor: "It's a good family show!"
>
> Tim: "They're not doing it anymore. They said they got fed up with being thrown to the lions, so . . . they've all got much better jobs as fruit-growers. And what's more, there are no gladiators left, because they've all been eaten by the lions who were hungry because there were no Christians, and before you ask, there are no lions left, because they've been eaten by the Christians who have got sick of the sight of fruit."

The Goodies made no attempt to disguise their debt to *Monty Python*, for paving the way for their own brand of comedy, if not as a signal influence. John Cleese guested in one episode, the Christmas special *The Goodies and the Beanstalk*; Python's Gumbies were referenced a few times (and once named as John and Eric); and in the episode "Invasion of the Moon Creatures," Graeme is seen settling down to watch *Monty Python* itself.

Barely have the credits run, however, than Tim demands he change the channel, although ultimately neither will see what they want. For Graeme has just accepted a commission from the British space agency, and blasts two fluffy rabbits off into space. And then two more, when the first ones don't report back on their findings.

Unfortunately, Graeme may be a genius, but he has forgotten what happens when rabbits get together, and how quickly they can breed. Particularly, it seems, on the moon, where they have established a colony and developed a method of transforming humans into rabbits by performing random *Bugs Bunny* impressions. Now they are planning to conquer the world . . . .

Although it was, in many ways, a very British show, littered with cultural references that seldom translated once you left the island shores, the Goodies were never going to confine themselves to local television alone. Foreign sales saw the show become enormous in Australia; it was translated into a variety of languages for broadcast across Europe; it was picked up by PBS and given a sporadic, but memorable, American airing.

Beyond the box, too, *The Goodies* flourished. A series of books were published, following the Pythonic lead of littering the shelves with unabridged silliness and madcap humor. And then there were the records.

Oddie was already a proven songwriter, and in 1974, an LP was released of songs that he'd written for use in the show, joyous little ditties like "Winter Sportsman," "Mummy, I Don't Like My Meat" and, best of all, "Stuff That Gibbon"—a riotous assembly of grisly gibbon abuse, masquerading as an old-time hoedown.

Now there came a concerted assault on the pop charts: "The Inbetweenies," "Father Christmas, Do Not Touch Me," "Nappy Love," "Make a Daft Noise for Christmas; a rerun of the gibbon theme with the rambunctious "Funky Gibbon," and a return to northern English climes with "Black Pudding Bertha," an ode to the "Queen of Northern Soul," set to a contagious refrain of "eee bah gum."

They covered the classic "Wild Thing" and made it seem ridiculous ("come on, hold me tight. Uurggh, not *that* tight"). They delved into the deepest, darkest blues, with an ode to uncontrolled vomiting ("Sick Man Blues"—chorus "throwing up, throwing up, up up up"), and the more their critics complained that the whole thing was infantile, stupid and crass, the more infantile, stupid and crass they became, as evidenced by what we might describe as a typical Goodies joke, delivered as they prepare to investigate a coven of witches ("That Old Black Magic") by checking out a book on the subject.

Leafing through *Witches' Manual Volume 1—180 Dances to Do Around the Camp Fire*, they come across a photograph of a naked woman, shot from behind.

Bill: "Oh, what do you think that is? A Bum in the Coven!"

Bill and Tim together: "That's terrible! That's appalling! That's awful! You only get jokes like that in the . . .

Both: . . . Sunday papers!"

Or . . .

Bill: "Allow me to elucidate."

Graeme: "You do and you clean it up yourself."

The Goodies performing their hit "Funky Gibbon" on UK TV in 1975—(*left to right*) Bill Oddie, Graeme Garden, Tim Brooke-Taylor.   *Alamy*

Followed by a rare example of Oddie corpsing.

The BBC dropped the series in 1980 after eight seasons; the team simply transferred to the independent network and shot a ninth (unlike many other writers and creators, the Goodies retained ownership of their show throughout, merely licensing it to the broadcaster). And while we can again sing that old refrain of how it wasn't as good as it approached the end as it was when it first began, still . . . once a *Goodies* fan, always a *Goodies* fan, even when the lousy shows far outweighed the good ones.

From that final season, "Big Foot" documents the team's love of the Fortean documentary series *The Mysterious World of Arthur C. Clarke*, and the disbelief they feel when they learn that Clarke himself has been proven nonexistent. And so they set out in search of the fabled beast.

Several revivals have been accomplished, including 2005's *Return of the Goodies*, while of the seventy-six episodes that were originally broadcast, all but one exists in the BBC archive. Perhaps fittingly, that one is the original "Kitten Kong," *The Goodies'* finest half hour, and one of the greatest pieces of comedy television broadcast in the UK all decade long.

Thankfully, the cut screened at Montreux survived. If it hadn't . . . well, that wouldn't have been very goodie at all.

And though the show was gone, its spirit was not dead. It did take a while for it to be revivified, however; close to twenty years until the evening when Noel Fielding caught Julian Barratt's stand-up act at the Hellfire Comedy Club in High Wycombe, and birthed what became the Mighty Boosh.

Eels

They're a couple of shopkeepers. No, they're a couple of zookeepers. No, they're a two-man eighties synth band revival. No, they're free-form poetic pioneers. No, they're intrepid explorers, fearless crime fighters, friends of Old Greg and victims of the Cockney Hitcher.

They are Vince Noir (Fielding), supremely fashionable, an icon of style, the coolest dude on the planet; and Howard Moon (Barratt)—supremely *un*fashionable, the reeking armpit of style-lessness, the most unhip nerd in the universe. They are best friends, constant companions, and together they are the Mighty Boosh.

A double act since the late 1990s, the duo's stated and, more importantly, achieved goal was to become "the new Goodies"—that is, a pair (as opposed to a trio) of generally kindhearted misfits whose misadventures in a world of their own design plunges them into an unending sequence of absurd, surreal and most of all astonishingly funny situations.

A supporting cast built up around the duo's live act: Rich Fulcher, who became the maddeningly over-Americanized American Bob Fossil; Fielding's brother Michael, who was transformed into Naboo, an oddly ineffective shaman; and Dave Brown, as Naboo's familiar, a belligerent talking gorilla named Bollo. The name "mighty boosh" itself was derived from Michael Fielding's childhood description of his own hair.

Three stage shows, *The Mighty Boosh* (1998), *Arctic Boosh* (1999) and *Autoboosh* (2000), played the Edinburgh Fringe Festival, with the latter being followed by a BBC radio series in 2001; and, in 2004, the television series that, if the first decade of the twenty-first century had no other claim to cultural significance whatsoever, would still have rendered the span worthwhile.

There would ultimately be three seasons of *The Mighty Boosh*, broadcast in 2004, 2005 and 2007, plus two further nationwide tours, *The Mighty Bosh Live* (2006) and *Boosh Live: The Future Sailors Tour* (2008–2009), between them rounding up some genuinely inspired television characters—a band of Mod Wolves who are indeed both Mods and wolves; a sexually ambiguous underwater Lothario with a taste for Bailey's Irish Cream, named Old Greg; and, most chilling of all, the Hitcher, the archetypal nineteenth-century Cockney psychopath, all green skin and Dickensian patter, and blessed with a deep and abiding love of eels. And yes, that is "eels up inside ya, finding an entrance where they can . . . ."

And that's just three episodes. Add a rock star who is half-flamingo, a homicidal Betamax tape, a crack fox, a brigade of Naboo's fellow shamen (one of whom resembles a human posterior, with extra added tentacles), a talking moon that isn't Howard, a murderous boxing kangaroo, a demonically possessed grandmother and Bryan Ferry, and the true scope of the world of *The Mighty Boosh* is revealed among the least self-conscious, and indeed *Goodies*-esque, half hours in a long time.

Each of the three seasons took place in a new location; in the first, they are zookeepers, although caring for the animals is only a small part of what they wind up becoming involved with. In the second, they are sharing an apartment with Naboo and Bollo; in the third, they are employed in Naboo's east London antiques-and-oddities store, the suitably named Nabootique.

These more or less workaday settings, however, are little more than the jumping-off point for the story to come. But not always. On one occasion, Gary Numan is one day discovered living in a closet behind the shop's counter. On another, the Hitcher is delighted (well, that might not quite be the word; but he does pee in Howard's face) when he discovers that the Nabootique occupies the self-same premises as one of his own favorite childhood haunts, Elsie's Pie and Mash shop.

There, he used to be given free eels, "on account of me being an orphan n' that"; now, he offers the store his own brand of "protection," because terrible things can happen to people who don't accept his kind offers.

Worse than having a green Victorian Cockney pee in your face? Apparently so.

But our heroes are as likely to find themselves journeying to the Arctic tundra as they are trying to extricate Vince, disguised as a lady panda, from a hormonally thrusting male panda's enclosure; or recreating the micro-medicine of *The Fantastic Voyage*, deep inside Vince's diseased and comatose body, as they are bowing and scraping to Bob Fossil. Who himself is their

The Dance of the Sugar Plum Goodies: Graeme and Tim prepare to launch Bill into orbit. *Alamy*

boss at the zoo, and owner of the nightclub where Vince and Howard's musical aspirations are most commonly indulged.

Fossil himself is a phenomenon, if not precisely a law, unto himself. As a zoo manager, he has no idea what any of the animals are called, so he relies on his absolutely inept powers of description to identify them. As a fat, middle-aged nymphomaniac transvestite, he proves a sharp shooter par excellence. And as a man who answers the telephone . . . let's just say you do *not* want Bob Fossil answering the phone to you.

First, he will lay the receiver on the table.

Second, he will select a song from the realms of late 1970s/early 1980s top pop fodder.

Third, he will circle his nipples with a recently dampened finger, and embark upon the same kind of clumsy dance that polyester-clad middle-aged hipsters used to do to Rod Stewart songs, in the hope that the years would roll off them.

And then he would return to the phone and, depending on the song he just played, he would answer and then hang up. So, for Hall & Oates's "I Can't Go for That," you would hear him clump around to the chorus, before announcing "and that's why I can't go for that." For 10cc's "Dreadlock Holiday," you would hear the singers explain why they don't like cricket, and then Fossil would declare that he doesn't like it, either.

Nor were those the only musical interludes. Like the Goodies before them, the Boosh proved remarkable songsmiths, interspersing every episode with songs that, in another lifetime (say the mid-1970s), could have given even Bill Oddie a run for his chartbusting money.

The Hitcher's "Eels" is a sub-rave masterpiece, and a cogent commentary on the modern fashion for reviving the past in modern clothing too; Howard's brush with the sinister Old Gregg leads the Boosh into a fabulous funk number; while the duo's own attempts to form a synth band even titled their 2008–2009 UK tour, "Future Sailors." Nor should we forget that Bollo turned out to be a remarkably on-the-beat drummer . . . a funky gibbon indeed.

They had their own answer to Kitten Kong as well—Charlie, a hideous slug-like creature made of discarded bubblegum, escaping from a series of children's books written by Vince, to wreak a hideous revenge on mankind.

Or maybe that's nothing like Kitten Kong whatsoever.

Eeee Bah Gum, Thou Feckless Wassock

Trouble at Mill and Other Northern Clichés

Throughout the childhood years of British television, and on through its adolescence, early adulthood and into middle age as well, the Voice of the BBC was among the most distinct, and readily recognizable, tones in the broadcasting world—as comforting as the "beep beep beep" pips with which the top of every hour was announced when you listened into the radio; as familiar as the otherwise impossibly obscure place names that were related every night on the shipping weather forecast: "Viking, Forties, Cromarty, Dogger, German Bight."

The most avid geography student in class would be hard pressed to pinpoint them on the map, but everybody knew the names as well as they knew their own. Well, maybe not *quite* that well, but close. And because they, too, were read in the Voice of the BBC, we knew how to pronounce them all.

Because that's what the Voice of the BBC was. Indisputably male, irrefutably reassuring and unimpeachably correct. "Proper," as the average listener might put it, as in "oooh, don't he talk proper," and the images of what these men might look like danced before everybody's eyes, even when it was just a voice-over, announcing the evening's viewing schedule.

Oxbridge—that is, a graduate of Oxford or Cambridge University, at the very least. White. Early middle-aged at the very youngest, but probably older than that. He was fully besuited, with a bow tie. Army-short hair. Clean-shaven. Probably named Reginald. Or Sebastian. Or Percival.

His language was clear, concise, Queen's English, and you knew he would rather have impaled himself on a broadcasting tower than allow a solitary word of slang to creep out. And his diction was what was properly called "Received Pronunciation"—the measured, clear tones of the English southeast, the "Home Counties" as the locals refer to them.

It's dead posh.

Received Pronunciation ("RP") dominated the BBC's output. It was the sound of the evening news and the weather report that followed, in those days when both were over in twenty minutes, sandwiched between the last manic gasp of children's hour and a local magazine show.

It was the sound of the continuity announcers, and the man who turned up at the end of each evening to remind you to unplug your television before you went to sleep, for fear of whatever deadly calamity might erupt should you leave it connected to the power supply for a moment longer than it needed to be.

It was certainly the sound of children's programming, with one presenter in particular, Annette Mills, speaking with such icy cut-glass precision that she'd have made a magnificent Bond villain. Goodness knows what she would have made of the popular (but much later) insistence that the title of her best-known vehicle, the puppet show *Muffin the Mule*, really does sound like a heinous sex crime.

Light entertainment was the exception to this rule. There, regional accents were almost de rigueur, if only to introduce some local color to a given situation—or, if not the accent itself, at least some recognizable terms.

A Welshman, for example, would say "look you, boyo," because of course, that's what they do.

A Mancunian would call everyone "pet"; a west-country native would say "oo-arr"; and a Cockney, naturally, would deploy rhyming slang, the picturesque patter of days gone by that half of them make up as they go along. There's a great scene in *The Good Life* (as we stubbornly continue to call the show that American TV renamed *Good Neighbors*) in which Tony Selby appears as a rag-and-bone man, attempting to establish his credentials by unearthing arcane rhymes. It takes a while, but eventually Tom Good catches him out. It's a sales pitch, plain and simple.

Apples and pears—"stairs."

Harry Rag—"cigarette" (the British call them "fags").

Berkeley Hunt—"you stupid . . ." where were we? Oh yes, local color. And criminal underclasses. You could always tell a villain in an early British TV show from the way he spoke. A subtle mispronunciation, a slip into coarse vernacular. An utterly incomprehensible outburst of dialect scraped straight out of a particularly filthy gutter.

"It's a fair cop, guv, you've nailed me bang to rights."

Or words to that effect.

Up the Wooden 'ills to Bedfordshire

The tide turned but slowly. World War II films, of which an inordinate number were produced in the years following the war itself, made a virtue of the "chirpy Cockney," an ultimately heroic but also faintly untrustworthy chap who masked every emotion with a cheerful grin and an outburst of incomprehensible slang. This then eased its way onto the small screen most notably via the dubious charms of the most lovable rogue of them all, Tony Hancock's sidekick Sid.

Sid (Sid James) was both an unabashed Cockney and an unrepentant crook, but he was also among the first broadcast regulars to truly turn Received Pronunciation on its head, on both radio and TV. And audiences loved him for his daring.

Galton and Simpson's *Steptoe and Son* went even further, not only permitting its characters to speak in the tones of the common man (as befits another set of rag-and-bone men), but also portraying the younger of the duo, Harold (Harry H. Corbett) as a would-be social climber, desperately attempting to disguise his lowly origins by employing his own interpretation of RP. And doing it very, very, badly. Forever conscious of his habit of dropping his "aitches," he would remedy the situation by adding them to words that did not require them in the first place. What han habsolute himbecile 'e sounded.

Which was uproariously amusing to those people who didn't need to fake it.

Deeper into the sixties, *The Likely Lads* and *Till Death Us Do Part* both permitted the Queen's English to be mangled in terms and tones that defied convention; while *The Liver Birds* unleashed the language of Liverpool, the northern port town that brought us the Beatles, all bevied-up scallies blagging bifters off the divvies, upon an unsuspecting national ear.

The crucial element throughout, however, was not the creeping colonization of the broadcast waves by people who spoke the language through a mouthful of cigarettes. It was the unspoken reminder that, no matter how much we enjoyed these people dropping into our homes for thirty minutes once a week, they were not the kind of coves one would ordinarily want to be seen associating with. They were poor. They were usually rough. But, more than that, they were common.

Forget his racist views and his right-wing tendencies. Forget the fact he didn't know how to hold a teacup properly, and would probably butter his bread with a fish knife. Every time Alf Garnett (*Till Death Us Do Part*'s Warren

Mitchell) called his wife a "silly moo," a shiver of horror ran through the corridors of power and propriety. No decent person would ever use such a term.

Class structure, of course, has always been a focal point of English humor, with the differences between the classes themselves sufficient to provoke a belly laugh from one demographic or another. One's manner of

Sid James, poster boy for the joys of sport and exercise.   © *www.timeincukcontent.com*

speech was simply the most obvious manifestation of the gulfs that yawned across the landscape.

There was, however, another reason behind the unspoken reluctance to allow unfettered local accents to run riot across the screens.

No bugger could understand them.

Monty Python's Flying Circus, the axis around which so much of British humor has since been based, was also a ferociously observative onlooker as these traditions began to melt.

Leading into the maiden voyage of the legendary Spanish Inquisition sketch, we first are privy to a scene set in the mansion belonging to a mill owner in the northern county of Lancashire.

Graham Chapman: "Trouble at mill."

Carol Cleveland: "Oh no—what kind of trouble?"

Chapman: "One on't cross beams gone owt askew on treadle."

Cleveland: "Pardon?"

Chapman: "One on't cross beams gone owt askew on treadle."

Cleveland: "I don't understand what you're saying."

Chapman: [now speaking perfectly clearly] "One of the cross beams has gone out askew on the treadle."

Cleveland: "Well, what on earth does that mean?"

Chapman: "*I* don't know—Mr. Wentworth just told me to come in here and say that there was trouble at the mill, that's all—I didn't expect a kind of Spanish Inquisition."

Always the equal opportunity mocker, another Python sketch seizes upon the slang beloved of Royal Air Force fighter pilots during the Battle of Britain—at that time, merely thirty years old, and thus well within the memory of the majority of viewers.

The squadron leader (Eric Idle) has just returned from a mission, and is describing his exploits to one of the officers, Bovril (Terry Jones):

Squadron Leader: "Bally Jerry pranged his kite right in the how's your father. Hairy blighter, dicky-birdied, feathered back on his Sammy, took a waspy, flipped over on his Betty Harper's and caught his can in the Bertie."

Bovril: "Er, I'm afraid I don't quite follow you, squadron leader."

In puncturing such stereotypes, however, *Monty Python* also found itself perpetuating them, as great swathes of the viewing public not only took to learning the scripts, in order to vomit them verbatim to their more patient friends at every available opportunity, but also found themselves absorbing the very clichés that the show set out to mock.

John Cleese's television announcer, seated and suited at his desk to declare (in exquisite RP, of course) "and now for something completely different," would live on in the memory even of viewers too young to have witnessed the men he parodied; the phrase "Upper Class Twit of the Year" remained in vogue deep into the 1980s, and probably beyond. The parrot lives on deceased; Australian table wines continue to pack a bouquet like an Abo's armpit; and we still don't expect the Spanish Inquisition.

The Great Black Pudding Bloodbath

But *Monty Python*'s greatest contribution to Britain's twentieth-century political iconography dates from a decade after the show left the airwaves, when the team regrouped to make their final movie, *Monty Python's Meaning of Life.*

"Yorkshire," announces a caption at the dawn of a sketch, "The Third World."

Or perhaps it's the other way around. Either way, the point is made. If you know the map of England, Yorkshire is in the north. If you know the politics of England, the north is another world, a strange dark world peopled by semimythical harridans; put-upon husbands; flat-capped, whippet-walking, pigeon-fancying, clog-wearing, blood-pudding-devouring, pit-descending, loom-destroying, "ecky-thump" (pronounced "thooomp") declaiming troglodytes who will sup (pronounced "soop") thy ale as soon as look at thee, and who think a few choruses of "On Ilkla Moor Baht 'at" is the height of sophistication.

> Wheear 'ast tha bin sin' ah saw thee, ah saw thee?
>
> On Ilkla Mooar baht 'at
>
> Wheear 'ast tha bin sin' ah saw thee, ah saw thee?
>
> Wheear 'ast tha bin sin' ah saw thee?
>
> On Ilkla Mooar baht 'at

On Ilkla Mooar baht 'at

On Ilkla Mooar baht 'at

It's a traditional local folk song featuring love, death and the carnivorous habits of a range of local wildlife, and the perils of venturing into an exposed wilderness without wearing your hat. Wikipedia offers a translation into English. One presumes it's correct.

The point is, "the north" is as different from the rest of the country—meaning London and its soft-as-taters southeast environs—as a llama from an alpaca. They may look the same, and if you go by map references, you can drive from the center of London to the heart of Yorkshire in less time than it takes to get from Philadelphia to Pittsburgh.

The show was long off the air when this single of "The Lumberjack Song" returned the Pythons to the UK chart in 1976.

But oh, the differences you will perceive as you slip almost imperceptibly from the refined climes of the nation's capital to a land of rugged moors and clutching gorse, of colliery machines and clanking mills; to a region whose most stereotypical imagery was developed somewhere betwixt the dawn of the Industrial Revolution and the end of the Great Depression, and which has kept English (read southern) humorists in business since the dawn of mass entertainment.

Monty Python, again, accept some of the blame, with John Cleese and Graham Chapman joining the bug-eyed Marty Feldman and future *Goodie* Tim Brooke-Taylor in composing a sketch for *At Last the 1948 Show* in 1967, titled and featuring "Four Yorkshiremen," who sit supping wine and reflecting on the good old days.

Which means reflecting on the varying depths of deprivation in which each of them was brought up, and trying to outdo one another in terms of having it worst.

Subsequently reprised by the Python crew themselves (an excellent rendering appears on their *Live at Drury Lane* album), "The Four Yorkshiremen" was *not* the first piece of comedy to mock the average northerner's alleged capacity for wallowing in misery.

> "We had it tough: I used to 'ave to get out of shoebox at midnight, lick road clean w'tongue, eat a couple of bits of cold gravel, work twenty-three hours a day at mill for a penny every four years, and when we got 'ome, dad used to slice us in 'alf with a bread knife!"
>
> "Luxury."

But it spawned a lot of offspring regardless.

You Care?
I Didn't Know

Compo, Cleggie and Dear Old Uncle Stavely (He Heard That. Pardon?)

Didn't Know You Cared was the work of author Peter Tinniswood, himself a northerner (born in Liverpool, grew up in Manchester, first job in Sheffield). Starting life as a series of brilliantly realized novels, *A Touch of Daniel*, *I Didn't Know You Cared* and *Except You're a Bird*, it is the tale of a "typical" northern family—an overbearing mother, Annie (played by Liz Smith); her underachieving husband, Les (John Comer); her idle brother Mort (Robin Bailey) . . . none of whom, crucially, are in the prime of life; their son Carter (a young Stephen Rea) and his horrifyingly, but absurdly, upwardly mobile fiancée Pat (Anita Carey).

Into this basic unit is introduced a sordid succession of other friends and relations, grisly aunts and oddball uncles. There is the pneumatic blonde barmaid Linda Preston, who impresses all the menfolk with her taste for ale and her love of rugby.

There are the three aunts who descend like steampunk angels of a slow and meaningless death upon the first of the many funerals that occupy the Brandon family.

And there is Uncle Stavely, who bears a striking resemblance to a portly turtle; is forever accompanied by an old gasmask case, in which he carries the ashes of a late military associate; and whose catchphrase of "I heard that, pardon?" became something of a national craze throughout the show's late seventies run, and that despite scarcely being heard at all through the all-conquering debut season.

All of which is very interesting, but scarcely distinguishes *I Didn't Know You Cared* from any other working-class comedy in which the women rule the roost, the men go down the pub (or, in Mort and Mr. Brandon's case, to their precious allotments) and the humor derives as much from their personal interactions as it does from anything that might actually happen in the show.

Those interactions, however, are shaped almost wholly by location. It is a northern show, written by a northerner, starring northerners, and reveling in its northern-ness.

The grim scenery of an industrial town that is already in decline a decade before government mismanagement plunged the entire region into depression; a healthy disdain for anything southern (most frequently, but by no means only, London beer); and accents so thick you could black-lead the grate with them and still have enough left over for half a pound of monkey nuts; all of these things contributed to the sheer joy and ebullience of *I Didn't Know You Cared*.

The reasons for its success, however, were as regional as its language. In the north, in the regions where families like the Brandons might be said to have lived, the show's popularity genuinely could be ascribed to the sheer quality of Tinniswood's writing, and the virtuoso performances of its cast.

In the south, the show had all of those qualities and more—the confirmation, if such was needed, that everything *Monty Python* said was true. Northerners really *do* stand around complaining about how much better things were when they were worse. And saying "eee bah gum," as well.

Liz Smith, in particular, is brilliant. A forensically wielded battle-ax in dowdy housewife's clothing, she is so accustomed to getting her own way that her husband could point-blank refuse to do her bidding, and she wouldn't actually notice.

When we first join the family at the outset of season one, and sidestepping the funeral that lies at the heart of the episode, Mrs. Brandon has decided that she and her husband should have a second honeymoon, and it matters naught how loudly, bitterly and even overtly he objects. A second honeymoon they will have, and the resignation with which he accepts his fate is itself a thing of comedic genius.

Mort is crimson-nosedly laconic and so incapable of looking on the bright side of life that even the prospect of the grave depresses him . . . because it probably won't be as quiet as he hopes. How, after all, can you have eternal rest when you know your late wife will be waiting there for you, probably with a long list of things she wants you to fix.

He fought in World War I, lodges with his sister's family and keeps a disused railroad carriage on his allotment, his last refuge from the outside world. Les grows vegetables on his allotment. Mort hunts for junk, and unearths what he believes to be a discarded jockstrap. One scarcely needs to guess which pursuit he finds more rewarding.

I Didn't Know You Cared ran for four seasons, bowing out in 1979 and retaining sufficient affection that creator Tinniswood would subsequently return to the Brandon household for three further twelve-episode radio comedies during the late 1980s: *Uncle Mort's North Country*, *Uncle Mort's South Country* and *Uncle Mort's Celtic Fringe*.

But if a little piece of the north had left British television, British television was certainly not about to leave the north. For, running concurrently with *I Didn't Know You Cared* (debuting, in fact, two years earlier, but only hitting its stride when its much-delayed second season got under way in March 1975—five months before *I Didn't Know You Cared* took off) was *Last of the Summer Wine*.

Old Age—The Playground of the Young at Heart

Like Peter Tinniswood, *Last of the Summer Wine* writer Roy Clarke essentially forged a double-edged sword, a show that allowed southern viewers to relax into the accepted notion of northerners as somehow quaint and old-fashioned, while northerners could enjoy a gentle (and gently idealized) examination of their own culture fighting back against the creeping modernity radiating up from the nation's capital.

Again, the focus of the show was on characters some way removed from the first bloom of life. Compo Simmonite (Bill Owen), Norman "Cleggy" Clegg (Peter Salis) and Cyril Blamire (Michael Bates) are all retired (although there appeared to be some dispute as to whether Compo ever had a career to retire from).

Together, they band about, exploring the nooks and crannies of the small town in which they have lived most of their lives—only Blamire was at all worldly, but in the worst possible way; a frightful snob, a social climber, an authoritarian know-it-all, he was essentially the straight man to Compo's anarchic plebeian, forever locked in a losing battle to prevent his generally sensible ideas from being reduced to absolute chaos by Compo's refusal to take anything seriously.

In the midst of this, Cleggy is mild-mannered, gentle, cautious and shy; as averse, in many ways, to Blamire's grandiose schemes as he is to Compo's lawless disregard for even the most basic good manners, social graces or personal safety.

It is a potent brew, even if there is a hint of *The Goodies* in the characterization, with Compo as Bill and Cleggy as Tim, Graeme, of course, is he sensible one.

Self-contained though they are, the three cannot help but interact with their neighbors: Nora Batty (Kathy Staff), a dragon of a woman for whom Compo has carried the torch of unrequited love (or at least lust) since childhood; Sid (John Comer—again! Les Brandon certainly gets around) and Ivy (Jane Freedman), who run the local cafe in which the trio spend much of their leisure time, dawdling over a cup of tea while Ivy keeps a nervous eye on them; Howard (Robert Fyfe) and Pearl (Juliette Kaplan), the archetypal henpecked husband and his pecking hen of a wife; Marina (Jean Ferguson), the brassy blonde with whom Howard is having an affair; Auntie Wainwright (*Coronation Street*'s Jean Alexander), the conniving owner of the local junk store; and more.

Encounters with these effectively followed two courses; the menfolk as unwitting victims, or at least participants, in Compo's latest harebrained scheme; and the womenfolk as the inevitable scourge of all fun and games. Almost without exception, the wives of *The Last of the Summer Wine* are women you would not want to cross under any circumstances; whereas the husbands are the kind of guys you could readily imagine sharing a pint and a war story with, down at the local hostelry.

Originally commissioned as a single piece within the BBC's long-running *Comedy Playhouse* series, and broadcast on January 4, 1973, *The Last of the Summer Wine* laid out its intentions from the outset—the permanently penniless Compo arguing against his television being repossessed due to nonpayment of the rental fee.

Unsuccessful in his efforts, he joins Blamire and Cleggy at a funeral . . . a common occurrence at their time of life, of course; stop off at the library to taunt the head librarian and his assistant, as they flirt their way through a secret romance that the whole town knows about; drop by the cafe to watch Sid and Ivy argue; have a quick drink at the pub; and then take a walk by the stream, where they catch a very small fish, what the British call a "tiddler," in a jam jar.

Conversations among viewers the following day must have been gripping.

"Did you watch that show last night?"

"No. What's it about?"

"Three old guys."

"What do they do?"

"Not much."

"What happened?"

"Very little."

"So why did you keep watching?"

"Because it was hilarious."

Ferrets in a Boardinghouse

It's the characters, and the characterization, that made *The Last of the Summer Wine* work, even when it felt like it might not work at all. A six-episode series was ordered up for the end of the year, but viewing figures were low, reviews were cautious and even the studio audience was uncommonly silent. Although a second season had already been commissioned, it really did feel like a one-off, just another of those shows that passes a few weekday nights on the television schedule, never to be heard of again.

Even the title, which the BBC apparently hated, confused people. Also airing at this time was *Spring and Autumn*, veteran comedy actor Jimmy Jewel as a retired railroad worker who strikes up a friendship with a spirited youngster and finds his entire outlook on life being rejuvenated.

It, too, was set in the north, and the seasonal similarity of the two shows' titles, not to mention the essential childishness of the lead characters, might have suggested a sequel, a spin-off or even a knockoff. *The Last of the Summer Wine* ran for those six scheduled episodes, and then vanished.

The summer of 1974, after all, saw industrial action bring much of the BBC to a halt, with many of the scheduled productions either cancelled or delayed. Even audience favorites like the pop music chart show *Top of the Pops* were forced off the air for the duration. Had *The Last of the Summer Wine* been among the permanent casualties of the strike, few outsiders would either have noticed or cared.

As it happened, a seven-episode season two was shot, for broadcast in early spring 1975, and a most peculiar thing then happened. A program that so many people had not even heard of suddenly became one of the most watched shows of the week. Over eighteen million viewers tuned in for the first episode, and not too many of them drifted away again.

Once again, anybody asking what the show was about would have been left scratching their head. In that all-conquering first episode, Cleggy tries to get his bicycle fixed. In the second, Compo gets stuck up a tree while attempting to move a piano. In the third, Blamire gets a job as a door-to-door salesman. In another, they buy a canoe, and in the season finale, they discover that motorcycles are no easier to repair than bicycles.

Of such pleasures were Wednesday nights in the spring of 1975 comprised.

Behind the scenes, however, all was not well. Or, at least, Michael Bates was not well. Already starring in another sitcom, *It Ain't Half Hot, Mum*, Bates's health was simply not up to the more physical demands of *The Last of the Summer Wine*. He departed at the end of season two (he passed away three years later, in 1978), and season three, in fall 1976, opened with the arrival of Foggy Dewhurst (Brian Wilde), a former resident of the town returning to live out his retirement, but excited to meet up with some old friends again.

Old friends, incidentally, who best remember him for his resemblance to a pencil with an eraser on the end.

Like Blamire, Foggy is a stickler for doing things properly—a former military man (he was a sign writer in the army), he lives a life dictated by discipline and rules, standards that he expects . . . nay, *insists* . . . his companions also follow. He is insufferably pompous, inexcusably self-righteous, and the foil that Compo and Clrggi had been waiting for. With Foggy on board, *The Last of the Summer Wine* commenced its ascent not simply to the realms of the country's best-loved sitcoms, but also its most enduring.

Holmfirth, the Yorkshire village where the series was filmed, became a major tourism destination. Three Christmas specials were massive hits; two movie-length specials, *Getting Sam Home* and *Uncle of the Bride*, were similarly successful.

Bill Owen and Peter Sallis were stars of a mid-eighties theatrical adaptation that still undergoes revivals today; a couple of spin-off series appeared (although the less said about either, the better); a daily comic strip appeared in the national *Daily Star* newspaper and writer Roy Clarke created several novels around his characters.

And while the show certainly had its detractors, it was also unstoppable. In 2003, a poll in the BBC's own television listings magazine *Radio Times* revealed that *The Last of the Summer Wine* was the program readers most wanted to see canceled. But a mere 12,000 people took part in the poll. Twelve million and more watched the show, still going strong *thirty years* after its debut.

It would be 2010, following a staggering thirty-one seasons, before *The Last of the Summer Wine* finally departed the schedules, by which time Peter Sallis alone remained of the cast.

Much had changed. Foggy left in 1985 (to take over his family's egg-painting business), to be replaced by a harebrained inventor named Seymour Utterthwaite (Michael Aldridge), and then returned until illness forced him to leave again in 1998.

Compo departed when Bill Owen passed away in 1999; and a slew of new characters had passed down the winding cobblestoned streets of the town, to either fall prey to, or get the better of, the three childishly irrepressible characters at the heart of the action.

But even at the end, *The Last of the Summer Wine* retained all of the qualities for which it had become so beloved, its denizens steadfastly refusing to move with the times, even as time itself sped away from them.

When Foggy was forced to leave for the second time, Frank Thornton (of *Are You Being Served?*) became Compo's worst nightmare, in the form of a former police officer. Likewise, Compo's successors, who included Bill Owen's real-life son, Tom, as Compo's offspring Tom Simmonite, and Brian Murphy (*Man About the House*'s George Roper as-was) as the infuriating Alvin Smedley, each retained the essential spirit of their predecessor.

In fact, the only misstep that *The Last of the Summer Wine* truly made came at the very end of its lifetime, when an entire new ensemble was introduced across the penultimate season, and given the focus for the last two stories.

Comprising Alvin, "Electrical" Entwistle (Burt Kwouk) and Luther "Hobbo" Hobdyke (Russ Abbot), the motivation behind this development was wholly understandable—both Sallis and Thornton were getting on in years, and the outside work that the show's format demanded simply was no longer practical.

But viewers were never going to take to a wholesale change, even if more established characters remained on show, and many doubted that the show would even return following its landmark thirtieth season. It did, but the new format remained in force; Cleggy disappeared even deeper into the periphery, and the main thrust of the six episodes was to bring some form of closure to Howard and Pearl's so stormy marriage.

At least Cleggy had the last word, though. After so many years caught in the middle of the raging extremes of his companions, that was a very rare occurrence indeed.

Kids in the Hall, and the Other Rooms, Too

Likely Lads, Lively Birds and a Man About the House

Although the concept of the "teenager" as a living, breathing and, most of all, marketable creature had been around since the early 1950s, it was a decade later before British broadcasting came to at least the latter conclusion.

Hitherto, light entertainment had effectively been divided into just two categories—shows for children and shows for everyone else. It took the advent, and subsequent consolidation, of rock 'n' roll to prompt the first dedicated pop music shows, and even longer . . . 1964, and the birth of Beatlemania . . . before teens, or at least people who looked like they could remember their teens, were deemed a suitable topic for a sitcom.

That was *The Likely Lads*, a show whose own debt to the Beatles was illustrated by it being set in northeastern England (Newcastle-upon-Tyne . . . the other side of the country to Liverpool, but hey, they all have funny accents up there), and focusing on all the things that young men ought to focus on. Girls, pubs, soccer. Girls in pubs on the way to the soccer. And girls in pubs on the way home from the soccer.

The setting was essential. London was the epicenter of what the media was already terming the Swinging Sixties; other major cities, Liverpool included, had vibrant youth scenes that had likewise risen to national attention.

Newcastle would later become renowned as the birthplace of the Animals, who had a UK #1 that same year with "The House of the Rising Sun." But beyond that, outsiders considered it to be more or less a cultural wasteland—the perfect location for a pair of twenty-year-olds, stuck in a dead-end factory job and dreaming of the bright lights of other big cities.

Well regarded at the time, and certainly amusing across the eight episodes (and four audio recordings) that have survived from the twenty that spread across three seasons of the show, *The Likely Lads'* modern renown is ironically based not on the original series but on its successor a decade later, *Whatever Happened to the Likely Lads?*

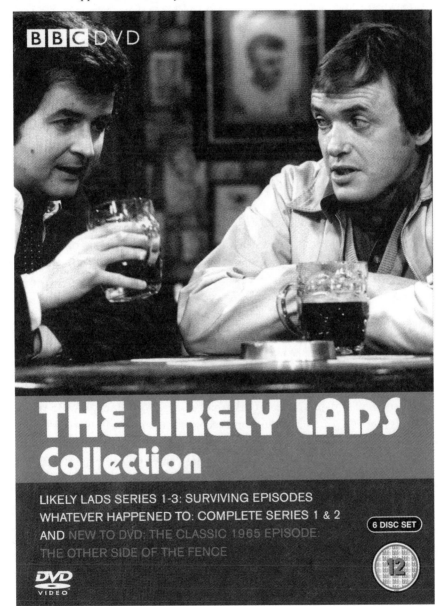

Rodney Bewes and James Bolam—the likeliest lads of them all.

Original cast members Rodney Bewes (Bob) and James Bolam (Terry) returned, older but not necessarily wiser—Terry, as in his youth, remains a stoic working-class man, his feet planted firmly on the ground; Bob, on the other hand, has clung to his dream of "making something of himself." Now he not only has an office job at a local building company, he is also looking to climb even higher, by marrying the owner's daughter Thelma (Brigit Forsyth).

The comedy, then, is twofold—Terry's attempts to haul Bob away from the boring straight and narrow, and Bob's occasional lapses of judgment; and, once again, the faithful standby of the working class striving to better themselves by putting on airs and graces that fool nobody but themselves.

These echoes of Hancock, Harry Steptoe (and sundry other characters, too) are then offset by a soft-focus variation on the nostalgia that fired Alf Garnett—the belief that, for all the conveniences that the modern world has given us, somehow the old world was better.

The earlier show, where that latter concern had still to be manifest, and Bob's pretensions were far more risible when he was still at the bottom of the ladder (as opposed to a few rungs higher, as he was in the sequel), had another function, however. It proved to broadcasters that a younger audience demanded younger casts—characters who would share (but not necessarily succeed in) the same aspirations as the viewer.

Girls and Boys

So, where *The Likely Lads* went between 1964–1966, *The Liver Birds* would travel in 1969—and with such success that they were still traveling a full decade later.

By then, of course, the lives of flatmates Beryl (Polly James) and Sandra (Nerys Hughes) had changed beyond recognition, although the early premise would remain constant—a pair of "dolly birds" living in Liverpool and making the most of whatever opportunities came their way. (Technically, mention should also be made of Beryl's original best friend Dawn, played by Pauline Collins, who appeared in the show's pilot and first season. Unfortunately, all these episodes were lost long ago and have yet to be rediscovered.)

The earliest seasons were the best, before the girls became too knowing and the scripts (by Carla Lane, following the departure of her original partner Myra Taylor) became more focused on long-term relationships, than the earlier "thrill of the chase." The sheer longevity of the show, of course, testifies to its quality—as does the involvement of Lane. But *The Liver*

Girls were *Liver Ladies* now; and by the time the show ended, both Hughes and James were *Liver Pushing Forty*.

Again, the search for a sitcom that attempted to depict the kind of life that the average college-age viewer might expect to be living switched elsewhere, toward a show that American audiences may (or may not) recognize as *Three's Company* but which, in its original UK form, was called *Man About the House*.

Paula Wilcox (*left*) and Sally Thomsett (*right*) gather round the Man About the House, Richard O'Sullivan.   © *www.timeincukcontent.com*

The show that transformed Richard O'Sullivan into a household name, at least until he edged out of the spotlight in the mid-1990s, *Man About the House* was the story of two girls, Chrissie (Paula Wilcox) and Jo (Sally Thomsett), sharing an apartment and recruiting a third roommate, Robin Tripp (O'Sullivan).

It would be a startlingly dull, not to mention commonplace topic today, but in 1973, it was something of a daring one—the idea that a single man and two single girls could live together in harmony without *something* wicked this way coming was one that few people found believable, and which many denounced as being positively shocking. Particularly as the girls, feisty brunette Chrissie and daffy blonde Jo, were eminently adorable, and Robin was something of a stud-muffin himself.

Neither was this disapproval merely a societal quirk. Four years on, preparing the spin-off series *Robin's Nest*, writers Brian Cooke and Johnnie Mortimer needed to apply for special permission from the IBA (the Independent Broadcasting Authority Watchdog) before they could portray an unmarried couple "living in sin." It was granted, and the floodgates opened thereafter for all manner of shows and situations. But still Robin Tripp (O'Sullivan) was a pioneering creation in British entertainment's long battle to overturn petty censorship.

Of the earlier show's main cast, Thomsett already had a small film career behind her, with very opposing roles in *The Railway Children* and Peckinpah's *Straw Dogs*; while O'Sullivan had risen from a child actor in the 1950s to becoming a familiar face in a variety of TV shows and movies.

Wilcox was probably the most immediately recognizable of the trio, however—during 1970–1971, she starred alongside the young and equally unknown Richard Beckinsale in *The Lovers*, a delightful sitcom that revolved around Beckinsale's character, Geoffrey, trying to lure his girlfriend Beryl into bed, while Beryl fought back with every verbal weapon at her disposal. Which, being a somewhat dreamy, girlish character, usually involved coining ever more absurd nicknames for her boyfriend and his peccadillos, and refusing point-blank to allow him to introduce her to Percy Filth.

Popular enough to spawn a movie, but unable to flourish beyond two short seasons, *The Lovers* nevertheless launched both stars' careers.

The marquee name on *Man About the House*, however, was Yootha Joyce, a sitcom veteran via appearances in *Steptoe and Son*, *On the Buses*, Milo O'Shea's (admittedly tiresome) *Me Mammy*, *Open All Hours* and more.

She was cast as Mildred Roper, landlady of the house that the kids were renting—a kindhearted forty-something housewife whose greatest regret was that she'd married her husband George (Brian Murphy), an ineffective, undersexed, shabby little man whose greatest love was his pet budgerigar, and whose sole purpose in life was to have as little purpose as possible.

Unless, of course, his ire was fired. In which case, he was still ineffective, but he *was* the landlord, so his tenants needed to at least pay him some heed. Indeed, the only way the girls were even able to take a male flatmate was by convincing Mr. Roper that Robin was gay, and therefore there'd be no "funny business" going on beneath his roof. Which, as his wife regularly, ruefully, commented, was just how George liked it. (In fact, O'Sullivan and Thomsett were dating in real life for much of the show's run.)

It was a gentle show; and, at the start, maybe too gentle. There was innuendo, of course—how could there not be, with Robin trying to get the girls in bed upstairs, while Mildred was hoping for some action downstairs?

But humor was also drawn from circumstance, misunderstanding and accident—such as the time Jo invited her boyfriend for dinner and convinced Robin (who is a cookery student, and already a skilled chef) to make the dinner. He prepares a delicious pork dish, which Jo passes off as her own handiwork. Unfortunately, the boyfriend is Jewish.

It sounds so unfunny on paper. Let's try again.

Having accepted that he will get nowhere with his flatmates, Robin brings a new girlfriend, Liz, home, and is clearly intending to have her stay the night. Until Chrissie, suddenly feeling irrationally jealous, blurts out that she is expecting Robin's baby. Exit Liz in a fury, and exit Chrissie in an embarrassed muddle. Robin spends another night alone.

Or then there was the evening that, in the hands of John Cleese, caused a generation to demand "don't mention the war," when a party of Germans visited Fawlty Towers. Months before that memorable encounter, however, George Roper had his own moment of anti-German fervor when Robin invited a fellow student, a German lad, to a party at the house. The episode's title sets the tone for what transpires: "Did You Ever Meet Rommel?"

The first season-and-a-half was uniformly excellent. Unfortunately, change was on the way. Viewers of American sitcoms will recall, probably painfully, how some of the finest sitcoms on the small screen are derailed by the introduction of a newborn baby, or at least a precocious child: *Mad About You* did it, *Murphy Brown* did it. And both *Robin's Nest* and *George and Mildred*, the Ropers' subsequent spin-off series, would do it.

But British shows, in the main, eschewed this approach, preferring to add to the adult cast instead. Enter Larry (Doug Fisher), Robin's best friend, and as scruffy, rough-cut and coarse-minded a character as any comedy writer could create.

Why? The show had meandered quite happily along without the need for Larry's lewd and crudeness, but he upped the belly-laugh quotient a little, and maybe that was the goal. Either way, he brought a new dynamic to the show, and it was obviously successful at the time.

Other recurring characters followed—Mr. Roper's friend Jerry (Roy Kinnear), for one. Percival Strapp. Mrs. Plummer. Sometimes for good, sometimes for bad. People kept on watching, anyway, and *Man About the House* ultimately ran for a total of six seasons, plus the inevitable movie—the last production ever made by the once legendary Hammer Studios, home of British horror for the past two decades, but now struggling to keep its head above water.

The series ended with Chrissie getting married to Robin's brother Norman (Norman Eshley), while Robin—who everyone knew had loved her all along—watched on in dismay. Their final kiss, for "goodbye and good luck," certainly took Chrissie by surprise. But she responded in a manner that makes one certain that she knew she'd wed the wrong brother, and so one of prime-time comedy's least challenging (but still enjoyable) shows wrapped up with a finale straight out of Shaw's *Pygmalion*. Eliza married the wrong man as well.

Robin on the Nest

Man About the House finished its run in spring 1976 (a year before the format was revamped for America's *Three's Company*); it was followed that fall by *George and Mildred*, five seasons and a movie that traced not only the Ropers' subsequent ups and downs, but also those of the respectable young family—a real estate agent, his wife and child—who had the misfortune of living next to them.

It might even have lasted longer (at least one further season was planned); sadly, shortly before the movie's release, Yootha Joyce passed away, victim of a chronic alcoholism whose reality shocked even her fellow professionals. (*George and Mildred*, too, would be reinvented as a US production, *The Ropers*.)

Wilcox, too, swiftly resurfaced in *Miss Jones and Son*, a short-lived comedy about a single mother (and this also went stateside, as *Miss Winslow and Son*), but largely left the screen thereafter; while Thomsett likewise disappeared into private life. O'Sullivan, however, would be back on-screen in the best of all the original show's successors, *Robin's Nest*.

Overcoming the loss of Chrissie, Robin is now living with Vicky (his latest real-life partner, Tessa Wyatt), and preparing to open a small, intimate bistro, financed by Vicky's ill-tempered father (Tony Britton), who hates Robin with a passion and loathes their lack of marital status, but will do anything to keep his beloved daughter happy.

On their way to Robin's Nest—Tessa Wyatt and Richard O'Sullivan.   *Alamy*

The couple would eventually marry, but of course the resentment lingered. Cue, therefore, six seasons, over four years, of father-in-law jokes, cookery jokes and, thanks to the presence of a one-armed Irish dishwasher named Albert Riddle (David Kelly), one-armed Irish dishwasher jokes.

But it worked, in part because of its pioneering approach to sexual relations of the day (even with the IBA's approval for the couple to be abed

Robin's Nest actress Tessa Wyatt with first husband Tony Blackburn, the popular BBC disc jockey.   © *www.timeincukcontent.com*

unmarried, censorious eyebrows were raised when one scene depicted them not only in bed, but also probably not altogether clothed); partly because the writing was sharp, the dialogue witty and the core ensemble worked together with such unalloyed glee.

Wyatt, in particular, was revelatory, and that despite being best known at the time as the former wife of BBC radio disc jockey Tony Blackburn—the breakdown of their marriage, which a tearful Blackburn revealed live on air, had kept the tabloid press impressively enthralled for far longer than such celebrity shenanigans normally should.

But she also had a long, if low-key, acting career behind her, including roles in the espionage drama *Callan*, the police series *Z-Cars* and *The Goodies*. Nobody, then, should have been surprised at how adept she proved in *Robin's Nest*, but (again, thanks to her tabloid coverage) they were.

As with so many shows, the great and the good alike, *Robin's Nest* went downhill in the end, and unless you're on a serious binge, you probably won't watch the last season or so more than once. But you will watch them because it was still better than a lot of the nonsense that was floating around then.

A Fool and His Roller Skates

Frank Spencer, Sid Abbott and Mrs. Slocombe's Pussy

Spearheaded by *Monty Python*, and followed up by its spin-off series, cutting-edge comedy has habitually grabbed the headlines. But the ratings (and, today, the classic repeats) have always belonged to more conventional fare—the retail hijinks of *Are You Being Served?* and *Open All Hours*; the prison farce *Porridge*; the domestic sometimes-bliss of *Bless This House*, *Some Mothers Do 'Ave 'Em* and *My Family*.

None of these shows expressly set out to break down barriers or make special social points. With no particular axe to grind, they were regarded as entertainment, pure and simple, the meat and potatoes of the TV industry.

Some were originally envisaged as vehicles for established stars (Ronnie Barker, Sid James, Robert Lindsay); others emerged as launching pads for future favorites (Michael Crawford, Wendy Richard, Daniela Denby-Ashe). All, however, had just one aim. To make people laugh.

Are You Being Served?, created by the same team of David Croft and Jeremy Lloyd that delivered *'Allo 'Allo* (and, therefore, half of *Dad's* Army too), was not Britain's first retail comedy, but it was the most successful, and the longest lived—ten seasons across a thirteen-year span (1972–1985) established Grace Brothers department store as one of the best-known retail outlets in the country (and beyond—Canada, Australia and the US all fell for it); and its staff among the best-loved actors.

No less than *Dad's Army*, this new show was based on its writers' own experiences in retail, and as with so many other Britcoms of the era, it was originally written in 1972, as a one-off presentation within *Comedy Playhouse*.

Unfortunately, the BBC didn't especially care for it, effectively rejecting it out of hand. The single episode's scheduled berth was filled with another show, and *Are You Being Served?* was left on a shelf—until the massacre of the Israeli athletes at the Munich Olympics brought the games to an awful halt, and the corporation was left scrambling for material to fill the now empty schedules.

Anything and everything was hauled from the archives, and on the principle that beggars cannot afford to be choosers, *Are You Being Served?* was among the hitherto mothballed shows that were dragged into view.

People loved it.

The characters were instantly recognizable—every store employed people like this. The situations were familiar; the humor was spot-on. Within a very short period, a full season had been commissioned, and while the schedulers were obviously still a little uncertain about it (they put the new show on at 7:30 on Wednesdays, directly opposite *Coronation Street*, a leviathan of a soap whose audience was both fiercely loyal and utterly enormous), *Are You Being Served?* debuted (with a rerun of the pilot) on March 14, 1973.

The basic cast in that pilot episode remained the same for much of the show's run—Mollie Sugden as Mrs. Slocombe, head of the women's clothing department; Frank Thornton as the ex-military Captain Peacock, a pompous floorwalker; his immediate superior, floor manager Mr. Rumbold (Nicholas Smith); and then the regular counter clerks, John Inman, playing the so-deliciously camp Mr. Humphries; and Wendy Richard as the sexy young Miss Brahms. This same quintet would also appear in the subsequent sitcom, *Grace & Favour.*

Elsewhere in the early series, Trevor Bannister played the cocky Mr. Lucas, another counter clerk; Arthur Brough was Mr. Grainger, the doddering head of the men's department; Larry Martin was maintenance man Mr. Mash; and, finally, there were the Grace Brothers themselves, Young Mr. Grace (Harold Bennett) and Old Mr. Grace, an unseen presence until as late as season eight (when Kenneth Waller took the role)—the joke being that both men were already so ancient that, when anyone questioned Young Mr. Grace's right to bear that epithet, the only possible response was "Old Mr. Grace doesn't get about much these days."

The store was decidedly old-fashioned, even by 1973 standards. It had been opened by one of the Grace brothers' uncles, probably before World War 1; they inherited it in 1926 and, though they attempted to move with the times in terms of technology and merchandise, still their staff were expected to adhere to certain old-world standards, and most of them had been there long enough that that was second nature to them.

Cue one of the show's longest-running conflicts, then (and, of course, a theme with which we should now be very familiar)—the disparity in outlook between the younger staff members and their superiors. Another clash, brought about by a reorganization of the store in the pilot episode, was the rivalry between the men's and women's departments, hitherto placed on separate floors, but now forced to share one between them.

That other faithful comedic standby of class, or an individual character's perception of it, was rife, with Captain Peacock in particular compensating for a less than stellar military career (another common feature—to wit, Captain Mainwaring and *Last of the Summer Wine*'s Foggy) by living out all his frustrated dreams of officer-hood by regarding his domain as an army parade ground.

There were the sexual tensions—Mr. Lucas's pursuit of Miss Brahms, whom he insists on referring to as "Miss Sexy Knickers"; Mrs. Slocombe's constant references to her pussy (cat); Mr. Humphries's undisguisedly ambiguous sexuality; and an absolute riot of double entendres. Even something as simple as moving a display rack could be transformed into a knowing snigger, as trousers are taken down and knickers put on in their stead.

Mr. Grainger: "Mrs. Slocombe. I suggest you take your underwear down at once."

Mr. Lucas: "Same goes for Miss Brahms."

Or . . .

Mr. Rumbold: "Let's try to keep [things] light and gay."

Mr. Lucas, to Mr. Humphries: "I'll handle the 'light' part."

Then there were the catchphrases. "Are you free, Mr. Humphries?" Mr. Grainger might ask; and without fail, Mr. Humphries would trill "I'm free." The staff would behave in an exemplary manner, and Young Mr. Grace would always tell them, "You've all done very well!"—to which Mr. Lucas would reply "Can we all go home then?"

And, of course, Mrs. Slocombe's pesky cat, which was not quite a catchphrase, but certainly became a repeated motif. Once, the city was shrouded in such thick, choking fog that even closed doors and windows were no barrier against it. "My pussy's been gasping all night," Mrs. Slocombe blandly announces.

Sid James and Diana Coupland framed on the DVD of *Bless This House*.

She even calls the animal on the phone, while she's on the floor. "Why don't you open your little flap and play with your ball?", she asks it. "and when I come home I'll tickle your tummy all over."

The critics were never too sure about *Are You Being Served?*, with the reliance on risqué jokes and double entendre in particular coming in for some flack. But, naturally, that's one of the reasons the public loved it.

Censorship, in some form, is part and parcel of broadcasting, and of public performance in general. Every age has had its prohibitions, both stated and unwritten; those topics that cannot be broached, those words that cannot be spoken.

These rules are strictly policed, too. Until as late as 1968, any stage show intended for public consumption in Great Britain needed first to be approved by the Lord Chancellor, a ruling that not only kept any overt "filth" off the stage, but also blocked such classic performances as *Cat on a Hot Tin Roof* and Arthur Miller's *A View from a Bridge* on the grounds that they mentioned homosexuality.

The arts responded with subterfuge, a comedic vernacular built entirely on crude double entendres. Flourishing first through the golden age of the Victorian music halls; broadened by vaudeville and such mid-century performers as Max Miller and George Formby, by the 1950s it was so firmly entrenched that an entire school of moviemaking was built around "pushing the envelope" as far as it could go.

It would be the early 1980s before this spirit of schoolboy smut, lavatorial humor and unsubtle innuendo finally began to fall out of favor (although it was by no means extinct), when a new wave of so-called "alternative" comics began seeking humor in other directions. Usually violence. Prior to that, ribaldry ruled, and there was nothing the censors could do about it.

After all, only the dirtiest mind could find anything amiss in Mrs. Slocombe recounting a recent shock. Even her pussy's hairs were standing on end.

Besides, the fact that writers, cast and audience were still finding new things to laugh about after *thirteen years* proves that *Are You Being Served?* was doing something right.

Opening Every Minute

There were further store-borne hijinks to be found in *Open All Hours*, a vehicle for longtime favorite Ronnie Barker, and set (because we all now know that the north of England is hysterically funny—particularly when writer Roy Clarke is on the scene) in the South Yorkshire town of Balby.

There, Mr. Arkwright (Barker) owns a grocery store, where he's helped out by his shiftless nephew Granville (David Jason), while a host of other characters pass through.

Its broadcast lifetime was sporadic; following a first season in 1976, it would be five years before the store reopened for two successive seasons in 1981–1982, and three years more before its final run. A sequel, *Still Open All Hours*, then arrived in 2013, with Granville having now inherited the shop.

Like *Are You Being Served?*, at least some of the humor derives from the fact that the shop is so old-fashioned—even the cash register is a temperamental old thing that should probably have gone out with hula hoops, while miserly Mr. Arkwright was as much a throwback as Captain Peacock, only nowhere near as pompous.

Ronnie Barker, however, was rarely anything less than comedic gold, whatever he turned his attention to, while Jason's portrayal of Granville, so far removed from the cocky Del Boy of *Only Fools and Horses* (surely his most sainted role), was a masterclass in surly youth as it spreads into resentful adulthood. The revamped show's continued popularity is simply an extension of those performances.

If Ronnie Barker was one of British television's most established, and beloved, comedians, Sid James was his equivalent in movieland. Though he was never a stranger to the small screen, even his best-remembered role as Tony Hancock's half-hourly sidekick was arrived at only after James had established himself in movies, usually playing what we might call a lovable rogue, with the most fantastic dirty laugh and a lecherous air that was almost palpable.

Citizen Sid

By 1971, James's best known roles were in the aforementioned *Carry On* movies, a long-running sequence of thirty-one comedies linked by the similarities in their titles (*Carry On Girls*, *Carry On Doctor*, *Carry On Up the Khyber*, *Carry On Nurse*, etc.), and by the development of a "Carry On team"—performers the caliber of Barbara Windsor, Joan Sims, Bernard Bresslaw, Hattie Jacques, Kenneth Williams, Charles Hawtrey and James, who appeared in no less than nineteen of the films.

Sid James and Amanda Barrie in 1964's *Carry On Cleo*.   *Photofest*

A crucial element in the perpetuation and development of smut as a standard element in British humor, the *Carry On*s were box-office gold for more than two decades, and the cast members were favorites as well. The advent, then, of *Bless This House* was one of those television events that a lot of folk looked forward to.

On paper, it doesn't sound especially exciting—just another set of ups and downs in the life of an average family. There was the grumpy dad, Sid Abbott (James), who believes he is the master of his own household; the understanding mum, Jean (the marvelous Diana Coupland), who knows he isn't; the gorgeous dolly bird daughter Sally (Sally Geeson) and the wannabe artist son, Mike (Robin Stewart).

But how "average" could any family be with a household made up of those four? James was worth a laugh track in his own right, needing only to look at the camera or emit *that* laugh to have the studio audience rolling around, but the remainder of the ensemble were equally sharp.

Add Anthony Jackson and Patsy Rowlands as the Abbott family's neighbors and closest friends, Trevor and Betty; and the *Liver Birds* duo of Carla

Lane and Myra Taylor as *Bless This House*'s primary writers, and six seasons raced by in no time at all.

They didn't even need babies, or new friends, or guest stars. Beautifully self-contained, mellow and madcap in more or less equal doses, and even the regular "obvious" plots, usually focusing either on daft misunderstandings or Sid's inability to "understand" his kids, could turn up something to raise them above the norm.

Neither was the show ever in danger of cancellation; it ended only when Sid James passed away, aged sixty-two, on April 26, 1976 (just four days after the final episode of season six was aired), after suffering a heart attack onstage in a production of *The Mating Game*. His costar, Olga Lane, later revealed that she initially thought he was fooling around when he suddenly stopped responding to her dialogue; it was only when he didn't react to her ad libs either that anyone realized that something had happened.

The tragedy of James's death was only compounded by its aftermath; with the entire nation, it seemed, in mourning, Sally Geeson—who had grown especially close to James over the past five years—abandoned her acting career altogether, so hard did his passing hit her. She moved instead into teaching and has been seen on television only once since then, in a TV commercial in 2013. A beautiful, instinctive and exquisitely gifted actress, her loss to her original profession was almost as tragic as James's.

They Certainly Do

If the Abbott family contended with the crises of everyday life, and pulled through via sheer strength of purpose (usually mom's), the Spencer household of *Some Mothers Do 'Ave 'Em* created the crises and then, generally, kept on making them worse.

It's hard to say exactly *what* Frank Spencer's (Michael Crawford) problem was. Politely, one would call him accident prone, naive and, perhaps, one sandwich short of a picnic basket. Impolitely, and in the eyes of almost everyone who came into contact with him, he was a borderline imbecile (with the border itself being so imprecise that it may as well not have existed), potentially retarded and certainly a menace to all around.

Generally good-natured, his appearance, mannerisms, speech and clumsiness all point toward there being something "funny" about him, and several times in the series we learn that his mother was equally cursed. Why Betty (Michele Dotrice), a relatively normal young lady, should even have considered marrying him is likewise questioned on occasion, particularly as she is no more capable of curbing his excesses than anyone else. Love, too, can be a "funny" thing.

So that's *Some Mothers Do 'Ave 'Em*. Every week, Frank would find himself in a calm, normal, everyday situation and, via a combination of all the personality faults at his disposal, transform it into a disaster area. Attempts to remedy the unfolding situation, both on his part and others', would only make matters worse, and while the expression "a bull in a china shop" might be deemed applicable on occasion, there is one major difference. People know what to expect from a bull. So, presumably, does the bull. Frank is surprised every time, and the people around him are left aghast.

How hard it is to believe that any other actor was considered for the role, and yet Ronnie Barker and Norman Wisdom were both preferred ahead of Crawford when the show was first conceived. It is to our (and possibly their) advantage that neither was eventually chosen.

With almost every show across three seasons (1973–1978) effectively following this same basic format, it would have been easy for it to become stale. That it didn't is a testament to Crawford's performance. Fearless in his stunt work, flawless in his timing, he is in equal parts a slapstick genius and a tragic fool, a Dostoevsky hero on an endless caffeine binge.

Even if one hates the show, loathes the characters and cannot believe anyone could ever react with anything but mortification at its portrayal of a clearly damaged young man undergoing crisis after crisis, it is all but impossible not to marvel at the breathtaking majesty with which Crawford plays his part.

It is more or less compulsory for admirers of the show to single out the season two episode "Father's Clinic" as *Some Mothers Do 'Ave 'Em*'s finest hour, by virtue of the breathtaking stunts that Crawford undertakes at the conclusion of the episode, roller skating at the local rink, being propelled out of a side door and into a crowded shopping center and bus lane.

Desperately he clings to the back of a speeding bus; frantically he loses his grip and hurtles down a side street; ultimately he crashes through the window of a luckless store, causing untold damage before coming to rest.

That, however, *is* the conclusion of the episode. The remainder of the show is considerably less memorable, with Frank's misunderstanding-filled visit to a class for expectant parents more or less playing out precisely as you'd expect it to.

Funnier by far are those stories in which it's difficult to see quite how he could mess up, only to stare aghast as he finds a way—going for a job in a hardware store . . . or a public relations office . . . or a window-cleaning firm . . .

Michael Crawford and Michelle Dotrice prove that Some Mothers Do 'Ave 'Em, and so do some wives.

or any of the myriad other professions, or even day-to-day mundanities, for which he ultimately proved so unsuited. Moving house. Buying a tube of Superglue. Having a baby.

Or, best of all, house-sitting Betty's brother's gadget-filled home. All right, that one was already a recipe for disaster, but only Frank could start a fire simply by losing his slippers down the toilet. Only Frank could lose his slippers down the toilet in the first place.

The series ends with Frank and Betty preparing to emigrate to Australia. Of course, their interview does not go well. But, for once, that works to their advantage. The poor clerk charged with overseeing their application is so overwhelmed by Frank's madness that he clears them for departure, simply to get the man out of his office.

A Dentist's Job Is Never Done

The spirit of *Bless This House* (and, in fairness, its domestic predecessors) was not, however, overwhelmed by a stream of *Some Mothers* look-alikes. Homely happiness continued to proliferate, and homely unhappiness too. But no show better captured the ups, downs and round-and-rounds of the typical family than *My Family*, launched in 2000 and destined for eleven annual seasons, with a wealth of Christmas specials besides.

The cast was stellar: Robert Lindsay and Zoë Wanamaker starred as dentist Ben and control freak Susan Harper—he a misanthropic revision of Sid Abbott, she the psychotic twin of Jean. Their eldest son Nick (Kris Marshall) makes Mike Abbott look like an overachiever, daughter Janey (Daniela Denby-Ashe) is the kind of girl that Sally tried hard to hide from her parents, and youngest child Michael (Gabriel Thomson) doesn't have an equivalent, but the analogies hold true regardless.

No matter how bad the Abbott family had things, the Harpers have them worse—not in an "oh dear, Frank Spencer's coming for tea" kind of way, but usually of their (read Susan's, because she made all the big decisions) own making.

No sooner do their own oldest children leave home, for instance, than she is filling the house with other people's—Abi (Siobhan Hayes), the suddenly homeless daughter of Ben's disreputable cousin (and something of a clone of *Friends'* Phoebe until the writers decided what else they could do with her); a guitar-playing Welshman named Alfie (Rhodri Meilir), who turned up to visit Nick one day and wound up staying when he learned that

Robert Lindsay and Zoe Wanamaker grimace and grin at the thought of *their* family.

Nick had already moved out; and Roger, one of Ben's coworkers, who never actually moved in but might as well have, so often did he call.

The fact that Ben really doesn't seem to like him does not phase Roger in the slightest—partially because nothing phases Roger (he's one of the world's "nice" guys, and believes everyone else is similarly disposed), and partially because Ben does not like anyone. Or anything.

He hates his job, he hates his friends, he hates his neighbors, he hates his dental assistants (and seems to sack one every week) and he hates his life. Half the time one wonders whether he hates his family as well, but unlike most of TV's best curmudgeons, his mean-spiritedness rarely gets him anywhere. The kids outsmart him through natural teenage guile; Roger outsmarts him through absolute naïveté; and Susan outsmarts him because, like Mrs. Brandon in *I Didn't Know You Cared*, she doesn't merely refuse to take "no" for an answer, she doesn't ever hear anyone say "no" to begin with. What she wants, she gets, whether it's control of a given situation or control over her husband's entire existence.

When the show first started, it was Nick who was the focus—more or less a total idiot, his entire outlook on life was predicated on a succession of harebrained get-rich-quick schemes, most of which wound up costing his father money.

Later, with him having left the house, Janey became the problem child, particularly after she left to attend college and wound up getting pregnant. (Enter, incidentally, one of the few TV children who did not then drag the show into a morass of stinky nappies and cute baby jokes.)

And through all this, the youngest son, Michael, watched and learned and connived and confounded, and had everyone wrapped around his finger while scarcely seeming to be there half the time. But he was.

Abi, who was as forgetful and scatty as Nick was—well, frankly, Nick was dangerous—remained delightfully entertaining, particularly once she and Roger started dating (although one dreads to imagine how *their* kids would turn out); and Alfie was such a bizarre and unnecessary addition to the cast that one couldn't help but enjoy him.

So, eleven seasons of grumpiness, mania, appalling children and dreadful friends. It sounds delightful and it was, not only because the writing and the acting excelled, but also because the overall vision of a truly and freakish dysfunctional family was always underpinned by the knowledge that the reality was even worse than that.

In traditional sitcom style, situations were woven out of unlikely coincidences (or another of Nick's daft ideas), and the cast would struggle to get out of them. Unlike many traditional sitcoms, however, the show presented the problem from each character's viewpoint, so while Ben might be verging on utter despair, Susan would already be looking on the bright side. And the kids wouldn't care because it was just mom-and-dad stuff, and made no difference to them.

Exactly like real life, then. *My Family* wasn't a show. It was a sodding mirror.

I Didn't Get Where I Am Today Without . . .

Self-Sufficiency, Suburbia and Suicide

You always knew when you met a fellow Reggie Perrin fan.

They might react to a situation by insisting "I didn't get where I am today by [doing, saying or tolerating some particular thing]."

They might be prone to wild, exuberant outbursts of "great" and/or "super."

They might have detailed their enthusiasms . . . say for Australian table wines . . . by announcing "I'm an Australian table wine kind of person." Or, if they didn't like Australian table wines, by saying "I'm *not* an Australian table wine kind of person."

Maybe it was the doctor you were consulting, asking him or her what your ailment may be and marveling as he (or she) was able to parrot back all your symptoms before you've even begun. "That's it exactly," you will excitedly proclaim, at which point the doctor will inform you he has exactly the same complaint. "I wonder what it is."

Or maybe you yourself have awakened one morning to realize that you are sick, sick, sick of the daily grind of modern life; of the same monotonous commute with the same monotonous people, the changeless office and the drone-like coworkers, the mindless drudgery of doing the same stupid job for the same stupid rewards, and saying the exact same things to the exact same people, who say the exact same things back to you, day in and day out for the rest of your life, until you finally die and they plant you beneath a tombstone that doesn't even get your middle initial right.

In which case, you could unnerve your wife by constantly referring to her mother as a hippopotamus; undertake a doomed affair with your secretary; compare every exotic ice cream you have ever tasted with a Bolivian unicyclist's jockstrap; and then steal a truck from the company parking lot (preferably a nondescript vehicle in the shape of a giant jello mould, for example), drive to a deserted strip of coastland, leave your clothes in an orderly pile on the beach and disappear forever.

Or, if that all seems a little too extreme, perhaps you could merely abandon your job as a reasonably well-paid draftsman for a company that designs plastic animals to give away with packets of breakfast cereals; replace your household electric supply with a generator that runs off pig's droppings; obtain a loom, on which you will create all your own clothing; replace your entire wardrobe with overalls; and reinvent your home in a wealthy, quiet, suburban street as a self-sufficient farm.

In which case you're less a Reggie Perrin fan than a *Good Life* fan. Which in turn, if you're in the United States, means you're a *Good Neighbors* fan, because *The Good Life* was something else entirely.

Either way . . . .

The Best Life

Either way, we all get sick of the way things are sometimes, and we wish there was a button we could push that would realign our lives completely.

Enjoying *The Good Life*—(*left to right*) Penelope Keith (Margo Leadbetter), Richard Briers (Tom Good), Paul Eddington (Jerry Leadbetter) and Felicity Kendal (Barbara Good).   *Photofest*

It's why politicians go to war (well, not personally . . . they have people to do that kind of thing for them), and why parents pack their kids off to college, so they can catch all the exotic social diseases that mom and dad missed out on when they were that age. "And don't forget your Morning After pills; you don't want to make the same mistake I made nine months before you were born."

And it's why college, and indeed education itself, is today so devoted to turning out obedient little automatons, who learn only the words that the teachers tell them, and only the facts that are in the right books.

To prevent this kind of thing ever happening again.

Turning your back on society and doing something different?

How dare you.

Was it coincidence that these two shows, David Nobbs's *The Fall and Rise of Reginald Perrin* and Bob Larbey and John Esmonde's *The Good Life*, should debut within just a few months of one another during 1975–1976, each with its own unique slant on the need to escape the modern dystopia and actually live like a human being for once?

No more than it's coincidental that, in the midst of that same time span, the British charts should be topped by a reissue of David Bowie's song "Space Oddity," in which an astronaut cuts off all communications with Planet Earth, preferring to drift in the endless void of space than face another day back on boring *terra firma*, doing the same dull things every same dull day, and really . . . if astronauts feel that way, with all the amazing gadgets and tech that they have, imagine what it's like for the rest of us.

The stories themselves, those of Reggie Perrin and Tom and Barbara Good, are effectively very similar. In *The Good Life*, we follow Tom (Richard Briars) and Barbara (Felicity Kendal) as they struggle to overcome the manifold hardships that automatically follow the decision to abandon the comforts of modernity, at the same time as continuing to live in the heart of suburbia; in *Reginald Perrin*, we are shocked witnesses to the titular Reggie's (Leonard Rossiter) slow but utterly inexorable decline, as he cuts himself off from that same society while continuing to function within it.

Debuting in April 1975, and ultimately running to four seasons, *The Good Life* begins with the ties being cut. By the end of episode one, we know exactly what the Goods are planning, and the only question is, how will they cope with the challenges ahead—and how will Margo (Penelope Keith) and Jerry (Paul Eddington), their super-snobbish neighbors and closest friends, react to . . . for example . . . finding pigs snuffling across their manicured lawns, and the sound of a diesel-powered muck spreader being fired up at the crack of dawn?

Launched in September 1976, and likewise set for four seasons (albeit under modified titles, and with a long wait for the fourth), *Reginald Perrin* might have signposted its hero's intentions with opening credits that see him rush into the sea (and then rush just as hurriedly out again), but it is only toward the end that we finally see him reach that point.

The Good Life was nice. Very, very nice. In one episode, Tom infuriates Barbara when she discovers he's been doing some freelance work for his former employer, only to relent when she learns that he only did it so he could take her to a luxury hotel for one night of luxury. In another, he confronts a passerby who keeps stealing produce from the garden, but they make up when Tom discovers that the thief likes cricket. In a third, one of the pigs has piglets, and a kindhearted policeman helps them get oxygen from the hospital for the runt.

The Fall and Rise of Reginald Perrin, on the other hand, was not very nice at all. Think of it as *The Good Life*'s evil twin.

Eleven Minutes Late. Signal Failure at Clapham Junction

The Perrin saga was based on a series of novels written by David Nobbs, a gloriously anarchically minded humorist whose television writing credits stretched back to *TW3*, but also embraced *The Two Ronnies*, and shows featuring the likes of Kenneth Williams and Frankie Howerd.

His first novel, *The Itinerant Lodger*, was published in 1965; *Ostrich Country* (1968) and *A Piece of the Sky Is Missing* (1969) followed, and then Reggie in 1975. It was the first book, *The Death of Reginald Perrin*, that was adapted for the TV series; its successors, *The Return of Reginald Perrin* in 1977 and *The Better World of Reginald Perrin* (1978), were purposefully written as successors to the original show, but both appeared in novel form first.

By virtue of being the first, and therefore the one least susceptible to audience expectation, *The Fall and Rise of Reginald Perrin* is the most enduring, both at the time and in terms of repeat viewings.

We really do not know what is going on with Reggie, any more than his family and coworkers do—wife Elizabeth (Pauline Yates); actor son Mark (David Warwick); daughter Linda (Sally-Jane Spencer) and pompous son-in-law, the real estate agent Tom (Tim Preece); boss CJ (John Barron, who didn't get where he is today by having employees go crazy on him); secretary

Joan (Sue Nicholls); and coworkers Tony Webster (who thinks everything is "great") and David Harris Jones (the "super" Bruce Boulds).

However, watching these people through Reggie's eyes, we begin to suspect what is on his mind.

It's a funny thing. Comedians have catchphrases, and how we howl whenever they deploy them! *The Fast Show*, the quick-fire comedy sketch show that was a big hit in the 1990s, offers a succinct commentary on entertainment's historical reliance on the things by depicting characters as far removed as a music hall comedian and a foreign language weather girl, each armed with their own signature statement—respectively, "oooh, where's me washboard" and "scorchio."

And watch your local news tonight. Notice how the people who now do the job that the anchor used to . . . the grinning buffoons who front the show . . . always have their little stock phrases, even if it's as affectedly innocuous as the way they say their own names. (Which, of course, they love doing. Best part of the job, that is.)

Catchphrases. They make us comfortable. They let us know that, in an ever-changing world, some things remain the same. Even if they do make you want to put a chair leg through your head.

Now take that same comfort out into the real world. To the people with whom you live, work, play and travel. The way they, too, have words and terms that they always use. Always. Every time they open their mouths.

"What a lovely day we're having," regardless of how many shades of shit it has passed through.

"Don't you look well today," as the fourth plague pustule in an hour breaks out on your forehead.

"Paper or plastic?" as the supermarket checkout clerk drops your newly purchased eggs on the floor and says "oops" with a cheerful grin.

"Have a nice day" in general.

These are not catchphrases. At best, they're verbal ticks; at worse, they're a sign that whoever you're talking to is so disengaged from reality that their brain is effectively on autopilot. They are "making" conversation, without having an inkling what the conversation is about, or whether you even want to be having one.

In later years, *The Office* (like *The Fast Show*) would turn this torment into a fine art. In earlier times, *Monty Python* made it a point of honor to mock the monotony, while Andy Warhol made a similar point in the stage show *Pork* (1971), the cast reduced to reciting dialogue from Warhol's old telephone conversations, while heedlessly indulging in sundry acts of sexual and chemical depravity.

Of course, in an age when television still couldn't show an unmarried couple in bed together before a certain time of night, it certainly wasn't going to get away with a bunch of people pooping on one another. But *Reginald Perrin*, while innocuous on a visual level, was just as disturbing as *Pork*, a brutal denunciation of the sheer redundancy of most of what passes as everyday speech.

In a way, Reggie's an attention seeker in a room full of deaf and blind people. We know after just a few moments in his company that he's heading toward a breakdown of some sort.

But while a few people might ask if he's feeling okay, and the company doctor (John Horsley) readily dispenses a couple of Aspirin, their own agendas are really the only things that they care about—Elizabeth, bent on remaining the ideal suburban housewife; Tom and Linda, concerned only that Grandpa doesn't say anything that might impact negatively on their frankly revolting children; Tony Webster, caring only to out-yesman coworker David Harris-Jones ("great" is far more forceful than "super"); and CJ, who only wants the company to prosper, and who didn't get where is today by worrying about whether Reggie is losing his drive. True, he once asks point-blank whether that might be the case, but he is carelessly satisfied with Reggie's denial.

And so Reggie lurches from one crisis to another; from one cry for help to a louder scream of anguish, and not a single soul notices. Until the day when his clothes are found on the beach, and they have to bury him. Except there's no body to bury, so they have a memorial service instead, and how nice of his long lost friend Martin Wellbourne, who really looks a bit like Reggie, to come all the way from South America to pay respects to his old chum.

He and Elizabeth begin shyly courting. Well, he's shy, because he's just realized how much he really loves her. And she's just playing along because she knows exactly who he is, and has a good idea why he did what he did.

That was season one. The following year, *The Return of Reginald Perrin* saw Reggie indeed return as his old self, and opens a store called Grot, retailing . . . rubbish. With Reggie still accompanied by all our favorite characters from season one, his mind is now a hive of activity, conjuring up new commodities that have absolutely no purpose whatsoever. Square hoops. Board games with no rules. Furniture that cannot be used. Pre-popped balloons. His son-in-law's home-made wine.

We are seriously approaching *The Good Life* territory here. While Tom and Barbara, in their show, are challenging "normalcy" by despising its trappings and turning other people's waste and rubbish into usable items, Reggie is doing the precise opposite, but for the same reasons—bucking

Poor Reginald Perrin (Leonard Rossiter). Even color-coding his phones didn't make life any easier.   *Photofest*

the system by convincing people that his waste and rubbish are exactly what they need.

The consumer society takes a kicking, of course, and it is dispiriting to realize just how accurately Grot echoes many of the stores on the modern high street. Think of that, next time you take a walk and discover your favorite newsstand has been replaced by a snack bar selling mustard flavored sushi cupcakes, or you take a turn through New York City and discover an entire city block of stores selling cellphone cases.

But the key now is that while Tom and Barbara's lifestyle continues a success, at least by their own standards (Margo and Jerry still don't understand), Reggie's unravels again.

He fought the system from within and the system gobbled him up. Grot is a huge success; he is a huge success; and again, the outside world of musical entertainment peeped in to Reggie's world. In 1977, the year this season ran, British pop was consumed by Punk Rock, a fiercely anti-establishment force that claimed to be snatching music back from the record labels, and giving it back to the people.

Which they seemed to think they could do by joining those very same record labels, who are charging the same amount of money for the punk bands' records, as they did for everyone else's. Maybe a little bit more. The overpriced colored vinyl and shaped picture discs that became such popular items in the late 1970s really were no more useless than anything Grot might have sold.

Reggie tries to destroy Grot; it becomes more successful. He sacks his staff and hires the most unsuitable, unqualified, people he can. They turn out to be retail and marketing geniuses. Finally, shattered and disillusioned, Reggie does the only thing he can. He fakes his own suicide again, only this time there's two piles of clothes on the beach. Elizabeth comes with him.

And so to season three in late 1978, *The Better World of Reginald Perrin*. He forms a commune, an away-from-it-all retreat for the middle-aged middle class, in the heart of suburbia. Maybe even the same suburbia that Tom and Barbara's farm has already blighted.

He is not shy of using his status as the founder of Grot as promotion; nor is he wise enough to avoid hiring the same crowd of regulars to work for him. And once again, the venture is a success—until it is raided at the end of the season by a group of vandals, who trash the place. Maybe the same ones who, in the guise of burglars, trashed Tom and Barbara's home at the end of *their* third season.

The difference is, Tom and Barbara dismiss Jerry's insistence that they should end the experiment, and Tom return to the office, by vowing to carry on. Reggie, on the other hand, takes a job with CJ's brother and climbs back onto the same wagon he was riding in the very first episode. And contemplating yet another staged suicide.

There would be a fourth season, but we'd have to hang around for it. In 1996, *The Legacy of Reginald Perrin* overlooked the death, a decade previous, of Leonard Rossiter himself, by regrouping the rest of the cast to live out the conditions of Reggie's will. Everyone will inherit a million pounds, but only if they do something quite absurd and utterly out of character.

It was . . . vaguely entertaining. But the script and action missed Reggie almost as much as the viewers did. There was also an attempted remake featuring Martin Clunes in 2009–2010, in which the familiar story missed Leonard Rossiter; and there was even an American remake in 1983, unpromisingly titled *Reggie*, and that just missed the mark altogether.

Sadly, for all of these, Reggie didn't get where he was today by having other people try to go where he'd been.

The Pythonic Legacy

Manuel in Rutland by Frog

W ithout actually acknowledging a split (because there had not, of course been one; the final television series at an end, they immediately set to work on their second movie), the Pythons would spend the remainder of the 1970s spinning off on their own projects.

John Cleese and Connie Booth's *Fawlty Towers* is the legend, the everyday story of a manic hotelier that is routinely voted among the best British comedies of all time. But Palin and Jones's riotous recapturing of old-fashioned boys' adventures stories, *Ripping Yarns*, is almost as good (if not quite so consistent); Gilliam's *Jabberwocky* movie remains spellbinding; and Eric Idle and former Bonzo Dog Band/occasional Python Neil Innes's *Rutland Weekend Television* was so ambitious that a mere half-hour comedy seemed genuinely to believe itself to be an entire broadcasting network.

No matter that it was forced to constrict even its most popular shows down to a mere minute or two, to compensate for its lack of airtime. *Rutland Weekend Television* gave the world the Rutles, and a great deal more besides.

Fawlty Towers made its broadcast debut on September 19, 1975, ultimately running to two seasons of half a dozen episodes apiece, each of them focusing on the lives of the staff and residents of a fictional hotel in the English town of Torquay, Devon.

Basil Fawlty (Cleese) is the owner, a tense, neurotic and pretentious beanpole, whose principal weapons, as the Spanish Inquisition would put it, were sarcasm, violence and rudeness. Sybil (Prunella Scales) is his wife, and effectively his owner, too—nothing is done, and even less achieved, without this monstrous harridan making certain of it, because left to his own devices, Basil will surely mess it up.

Chambermaid Polly (Connie Booth) is the buffer between the two, patiently trying to reason with one or the other; and Manuel (Andrew Sachs) is the waiter-cum-bellboy who arrived in England from Spain with very little English, and seems to have lost even more since he got there. In other hands, his constant repetition of the plaintive question "que?" would be considered a catchphrase. In Manuel's, it is his sole form of defense against Basil's rage, and often the reason for that rage in the first place.

With staff like that, who needs weird guests?

But they descend regardless; the two dotty ladies and a blustering colonel who constitute the hotel's permanent residents, and a string of hapless vacationers who booked because the place looked nice in the brochure, but came very swiftly to regret their decision.

The Germans, who are berated throughout their stay by Basil's inability to refrain from mentioning World War II for a moment.

The young man and woman whom Fawlty assumed were conducting an affair, when it was apparent to all that they weren't.

The guest who died.

The Rudest Man in Christendom

The initial concept for *Fawlty Towers* was born out of the Python team's visit to Torquay in spring 1970; the hotel where they stayed, the Gleneagles, was apparently operated by what Cleese described as the rudest man he had ever met, albeit one who blamed all his failings on staffing difficulties.

Fascinated by the experience, Cleese and wife-to-be Connie Booth would remain at the hotel even after filming was complete, just to experience more of its so-unique service, and Cleese quick-blueprinted Basil Fawlty in an episode of *Doctor in the House*, a medical comedy he was then writing for.

But his first attempt at creating a series, or even a one-off show, from the idea met with failure. Not only did the BBC reject it as cliché-ridden and built on stereotypes, the hotel setting itself was dismissed as unworkable.

Still Cleese and Booth persevered, and while the Head of Light Entertainment, Bill Cotton, also expressed reservations (he admitted he did not find the scripts remotely amusing), the BBC's trust in Cleese's instincts eventually led to a green light.

In many ways, accusations that *Fawlty Towers* relied on cliché and stereotype were very accurate. What those critics failed to see was, it was supposed to.

By now, it should be apparent to most readers that a great deal of British comedy (when it's not mistaking melons for mammaries) is predicated on class—the "little" man trying to transform himself into a "big" one, the rag-and-bone man who wants to run a high-end antiques store. Basil Fawlty, while he is content with the hotel itself, is no exception, and many of the humorous situations revolved around his attempts to "raise the tone" of the establishment's clientele.

Of course, there are ways of doing this, and there are ways of not doing it, and Fawlty was a master of the latter. His attempts at policing the guests' behavior were doomed to failure; his attempts to curry the favor of those he perceived as upper class likewise. He could not even put a stuffed animal head on the wall without the entire affair descending into debacle.

His efforts were further hamstrung by his penny-pinching ways. Planning a redesign of the hotel lobby, he ignores wife Sybil's insistence that they employ a reputable handyman, by sticking with a cheaper crew. Once again, disaster ensues.

Fawlty's relationship with Sybil, too, steps out of any number of earlier sitcoms—his defiance of her domineering ways echoes George Roper's reactions to Mildred's demands in *Man About the House* (that show's fifth season had just got under way when Fawlty Towers debuted on September 19, 1975), and so did the manner in which she completely ignored him.

Fawlty's repertoire of unpleasant names for her . . . "my little piranha fish," "my nest of vipers" . . . simply brought some variety to Alf Garnett's constant references to Else as a "silly old moo" (*Till Death Us Do Part*).

In other comedies, it was quite commonplace for a husband to be caught with his hand inadvertently clutching a strange woman's breast. Only Fawlty would leave a dirty handprint there, though.

And Manuel is simply the ultimate realization of a trait that George Orwell had assigned to the British psyche almost forty years before. That foreigners are funny. He even published what amounts to a user's guide to national stereotyping, in the 1940 essay "Boys' Weeklies":

- Frenchman: Excitable. Wears beard, gesticulates wildly.
- Spaniard, Mexican, etc.: Sinister, treacherous.
- Arab, Afghan, etc.: Sinister, treacherous.
- Chinese: Sinister, treacherous. Wears pigtail.
- Italian: Excitable. Grinds barrel-organ or carries stiletto.
- Swede, Dane, etc.: Kindhearted, stupid.
- Negro: Comic, very faithful.

Manuel is not, in this case, particularly sinister, although Fawlty certainly sees him as treacherous, as another of his schemes is waylaid by the waiter's inability to understand what is required of him. Manuel's apparent refusal to learn the language of the land where he is now employed, meanwhile, could also be seen as an act of rebellion.

There again, maybe it's Fawlty's fault for employing him. A non-English-speaking waiter was probably cheaper than a competent one.

So yes, the stereotypes abound. But that was the point—taking everything that people traditionally found funny and then exaggerating it to the point of absurdity, and then compounding the absurdity by dropping a raging madman into the center of things.

No less than *Some Mothers Do 'Ave 'Em*, with its transplanting of a (be polite) well-meaning incompetent into the midst of a daily situation, just to see how other people would react, so *Fawlty Towers* went for the opposite character extreme, by placing a mouth-frothing, fist-waving, insult-catapulting, screaming lunatic at the heart of what might otherwise have been a serene, if slightly shabby, environment.

Thus we watched *Fawlty Towers* not to see what would happen, as is the case with most other sitcoms, but to see how Fawlty would react to what happened, and if those events were clichéd, that was to the show's advantage. It meant less time had to be spent on setting up Fawlty's response. (Again, the spirit of *Some Mothers Do 'Ave 'Em* is writ large on the walls of the hotel.)

None of which is to decry, or deny, the show's brilliance. The cast could not have been improved upon, the timing is impeccable, and the show's basic format of piling misunderstanding upon coincidence and then setting everybody at cross-purposes to one another ensured that no viewer could ever second-guess the action.

It's a device, albeit one that is employed to more dramatic ends, that has long sustained soap operas. One character catches another in a situation and immediately jumps to a conclusion. The other, rather than simply explain, takes offense and goes off a deep end of his own. A third enters, selects a side to support, and so on. Soon, the entire cast is at loggerheads, and, as fans of the British soap *EastEnders* will instinctively understand, it's going to be another perfect Christmas in Walford.

Fawlty Towers does this a lot. The difference is Basil Fawlty, who could transform even the most conciliatory peace conference into a battleground and then single-handedly lead an army to war. Other comic characters have tantrums. Fawlty goes into total nuclear meltdown, and only one thing can stop him: a sharp, shrill command of "Basil" from his wife. Beyond humiliation, embarrassment, and making an utter ass of himself, she is the only thing he fears.

And, most viewers would agree, with good reason.

Fawlty Towers ran for just two seasons of six episodes, in 1975 and 1979 (by which time Cleese and Booth had ended their marriage). Calls for more were immediate and remain constant, but in truth, it was enough. More than perhaps any other show in this book, the sheer intensity of *Fawlty Towers*, and the genius of its creation, was not born for the long run.

It was short, sharp and shocking, a maniacal novelty over the course of a dozen episodes, but how quickly would that novelty have faded? And how long, living on such an edge of anger, stress and frustration, would Fawlty himself have lived? Anyone else would probably have had a heart attack long before. Probably around the same time as Manuel's pet rat got loose in the hotel, just as a health inspector came to check out the premises.

Maybe there's a reason why that was the very last episode.

Or perhaps they just ran out of anagrams for the hotel's name. Across the two series, as the opening sequence unfolded, the sign outside the building (which doubled as the show's own title) went from boasting the occasional misaligned letter . . . a slipshod "S," a leaning "L," a wobbly "W" (each of which would then be missing the following week) . . . to some most unfortunate misplaced corrections. And so "Fawlty Towers" became "Fawlty Tower," which in turn was rendered "Fawty Tower" and then "Fawty Toer."

Somebody scooped up the lost letters and replaced them. Badly: "Warty Towels." Somebody else attempted to correct it in time for the launch of season two: "Fawlty Tower." And then all hell broke loose: "Watery Fowls"; "Flay Otters"; "Fatty Owls"; "Flowery Twats" and, finally, "Farty Towels."

Another reason for the show to end. The Hotel Inspector would have noticed that immediately.

Rutled in Rutland

While John Cleese was single-handedly destroying the tourist trade (at the same time as boosting Torquay's appeal as a vacation destination), his fellow former Pythons Eric Idle and Neil Innes were operating their own commercial television channel from within the heart of the BBC's headquarters.

Rutland Weekend Television (*RWT*) represented the output of the country's smallest television station, as located in its smallest county—Rutland, an eighteen-by-seventeen-mile slither, with two towns, a reservoir . . . and now a TV station. Which was born, with becoming irony, around the same time as Rutland itself was absorbed into the neighboring country of Leicestershire, as part of the government's latest attempt to rearrange the country's electoral boundaries in time for the next election. (It has since been restored to life.)

If there had been a Free Rutland protest movement, *RWT* would have been its flagship program. There wasn't, really, so it showed other stuff instead.

It didn't last long, fourteen episodes during 1975 and 1976, including a Christmas special. But it was the acorn from which the mighty oak of Rutlesmania would grow, and no better parody of local television could have been devised than the very circumstances of the show's birth.

Rather than receiving the kind of budget that a half-hour comedy usually would, the standard entertaining budget, *RWT* received the considerably smaller presentation budget. As Idle told the *Radio Times* magazine at the time, "it was made on a shoestring budget, and someone else was wearing the shoe."

Still they muddled on, and what a magnificent muddle it was. Pursuing *Monty Python*'s old fascination with lampooning "typical" television shows, *RWT* devoted itself to such jewels as "Gibberish," in which the cast do indeed speak gibberish, in the form of a classic television interview program:

"Plugged rabbit emulsion, zinc custard without sustenance in kipling-duff geriatric scenery, maximises press insulating government grunting sapphire-clubs incidentally. But tonight. . . ."

As much as any but the most pernicious Python sketches, this particular sequence became a legend among those folk who enjoy going round spouting lengthy quotes from their favorite television shows. Except most people couldn't even keep up with the verbiage and contented themselves with walking around declaiming "saddlebags, saddlebags" all day.

Yeah, it did get annoying, after a bit.

With Innes handling the show's musical content, which included (beyond the Rutles' Beatles parody) pastiches of both different forms of music and other music TV shows, other regular cast members included the permanent hangdog expressions of David Battley, the suave elegance of Henry Woolf, Gwen Taylor, and Terence Bayler, so memorable as a brightly colored Nazi officer known as the Pink Panzer.

The humor was quick-fire, irreverent and delightfully stupid, the Python notion of continuity between sketches allowing for scenes to spin on a dime. The documentary "Being Normal," in which we are told the sad tale of a man who grew up with every advantage—madmen for parents and an utterly horrific childhood—and steadfastly refused to be anything but very ordinary; "Expose," in which the team investigate the failure of the British public to believe in the existence of former Secretary of State for Social Services, Sir Keith Joseph; an Ill Health Food Store, in which you could purchase such delicious snacks as Diarrhoea Delight; and a report on a new government initiative under which the running of maximum security prisons would be handled by suburban housewives. One of several *RWT* scoops that, under modern privatization policies, have come within a whisper of coming true.

Across the Andes by Frog

Truth, or an approximation thereof, was also the goal of *Ripping Yarns*, a Michael Palin–led serial that reflected back on the golden age of the very same "Boys' Weeklies" that George Orwell was speaking of in the essay of the same name. The ones with the helpful list of foreigners in it.

There was a veritable sea of such publications existing before World War II, all of them telling, indeed, "ripping yarns" (or breathtakingly exciting stories, for the colloquially challenged among us) of heroism, excitement, derring-do and danger.

Murder at Moorstones Manor! Roger of the Raj! The Curse of the Claw! The Testing of Eric Olthwaite! Whinfrey's Last Case! Certainly paving the way for *The Comic Strip*'s later demolition of beloved English children's author Enid Blyton's *Famous Five*, *Ripping Yarns* was a word-and-deed-perfect encapsulation of the kind of tales that once held a generation enraptured.

"Tomkinson's Schooldays," the pilot episode (broadcast as a one-off on January 7, 1976, eighteen months before the series got under way), took its tale, as well as its title, from the classic novel *Tom Brown's Schooldays*, a reflection of the life and times of an English Public Schoolboy during the early nineteenth century—an era in which upperclassmen were encouraged to knock some spirit into their inferiors via the infamous "fagging" system. At which point we should clarify that being a "fag" at Eton did not mean you were a cigarette or homosexual. It meant an older lad could do pretty much whatever he wanted to you, just short of murder.

Which isn't necessarily the case in "Tomkinson's Schooldays."

"Escape from Stalag Luft 112B," an extraordinarily lifelike, if utterly absurd, recounting of life in a German prisoner of war camp was another classic, but perhaps *Ripping Yarns'* finest hour arrived with "Golden Gordon," the penultimate episode of the show's second season in October 1979.

It was a story of devotion; the tale of one man's all-consuming love for his local soccer team. But the team has fallen on hard times; having lost every game they have played all season, the club's owner decides that one more defeat would leave him with no option but to wind up the club.

Yet the current lineup of players was simply not up to the task of winning a game. Neither was there money in the kitty to buy in a new squad.

There was just one alternative. Loyal supporter Gordon Ottershaw scours the town, seeking out all the legends of Barnestoneworth history, regardless of how old and infirm they might be. It is they who will play in the crucial game. and they who will carry the day.

As a piece of humor, it is hilarious; but it is more than that. More than any other of the words and scripts that have been written about what it means to be a true sports fan, "Golden Gordon" captures every last nuance; and when the day is finally won, the viewer feels as tearfully triumphant as Gordon Ottershaw himself.

Tony Hancock's theater of the common man remained alive and well.

Five Go Mad in Student Accommodation

The Birth of the Comic Strip

By the end of the 1970s, the fringes of British comedy had not really changed since the heyday of the Pythons, and its heart was essentially the same as it had been since *Life with the Lyons*—one cockles-warming half hour after another, occasionally rising to the occasion with a well-chosen star, or a well-designed premise, but more likely to saunter unconcernedly along, raising laughs in the same way that it always had.

Certainly as the decade ended, any roundup of the decade's best comedies did seem to rely on the same faces, even beyond those already mentioned here. Ronnie Barker, who preceded *Open All Hours* with *Porridge*, the first sitcom ever to be set in a prison ("doing porridge" is a slang term for a jail sentence), in which the guile of the inmates is set against the discipline of the guards.

Leonard Rossiter, whose stint as Reginald Perrin succeeded an equally memorable role as Rigsby, the griping, gruesome landlord of the rundown apartment building at the center of *Rising Damp*.

Richard Beckinsale, who followed *The Lovers* by appearing in both of those shows, and who would surely have been destined for even greater heights had he not passed away aged just thirty-one on March 19, 1979. (His two daughters, Samantha and Kate Beckinsale, both followed him into acting.)

Robert Lindsay, an impossibly youthful-looking twenty-something who rose from a regular role in *Get Some In*, a comedy set during the 1950s era of conscription into the British military; to starring in *Citizen Smith*, an aspiring Marxist revolutionary attempting to foment an uprising in a south London suburb.

Hywel Bennett, a familiar face from smaller roles throughout the sixties and seventies, snagging the national consciousness as the archetypal layabout in 1979's *Shelley*.

Wendy Craig, the eternal mother of *Not in Front of the Children* (1967), *And Mother Makes Three/Five* (1971) and *Butterflies* (1978).

John Alderton, star of the high school comedy *Please Sir!*, whose subsequent double act with wife Pauline Collins traveled from the period drama of *Upstairs Downstairs* to the periodic humor of the sitcom *No, Honestly*.

There were others, of course. Everyone who could claim to name a best show from the seventies can also name a best actor or actress.

But one thing was not so open to conjecture. The fact that a new generation of comic stars was demanded, before we all sank into a morass of mildly mirthful mediocrity. We'd had enough of the old ones. It was time we got some Young Ones.

Oh Timmy, You're So Licky

A few new faces had already appeared, beyond those traditional comics unearthed by the talent show *New Faces*. In October 1979, the BBC began airing *Not the Nine O'Clock News*, a six-episode series of occasionally current-affairs-related sketches and anarchic routines fronted by the remarkably rubber-faced Rowan Atkinson, an Oxford graduate fresh from his own *The Atkinson People* show on BBC Radio.

A gifted impersonator, he also proved to be an extraordinarily physical performer, at least from the neck up. He was certainly the star of this new show, whose cast was almost completely revised before the second season— Atkinson and Chris Langham alone were retained from the original six-man cast; in now came Pamela Stephenson and Mel Smith, with Griff Rhys Jones then replacing Langham for the third season in late 1980. A fourth season then ran in 1982, but with the cast all now scheming fresh programs of their own, a new troupe emerged in their groundbreaking wake.

Like the *Not the Nine O'Clock News* crew, the four embers that flared into *The Young Ones* were new only to the majority of viewers; unlike them, they were not a product of the Oxbridge machine (only New Zealand-born Stephenson had not attended either Oxford or Cambridge). Ade Edmondson and Rik Mayall met at the University of Manchester; Nigel Planer attended university in Edinburgh; and Christopher Ryan emerged from the East 15 Acting School in London.

Before *Spinal Tap* (but after *The Rutles*), the greatest nonexistent band in the world bring Bad News to fans of *The Comic Strip*.

Ryan was also the only cast member not to have already impacted the underground comedy scene—or, indeed, to have any kind of comedy background at all, establishing him as the ideal straight man in a show that otherwise overflowed with zaniness. (The towering genius of stand-up comic Alexei Sayle was also a regular.) The remainder of the cast were all drawn from the ranks of comedian Peter Richardson's Comic Strip, a London nightclub that prided itself on birthing new and revolutionary humor.

Half the team already had something of a televisual reputation. Shortly before *The Young Ones* took to air, the Comic Strip empire was invited to formulate a new series for Channel 4, as it became (as its name suggests), Britain's fourth television channel, almost two decades after the third commenced transmission.

Touted as the home to alternative entertainment, and an antidote to the sometimes bland, but equally, oftentimes, bizarre fare that was increasingly creeping onto the other networks' schedules (live snooker and sheep-dog trials were inexplicably popular at the time), Channel 4 launched on November 2, 1982, with a lineup that included the game show *Countdown*, a new soap called *Brookside*, Australian comic Paul Hogan and—the longest title of the night—*The Comic Strip Presents: Five Go Mad in Dorset*.

Edmondson, Richardson, Robbie Coltrane, Dawn French and Jennifer Saunders were all drawn from the Comic Strip stage to perform, but not in their usual guise of stand-up comedians. *Five Go Mad* was, instead, an affectionate parody of a series of children's books written between 1942 and 1963 by Enid Blyton, one of the most prolific authors in the world.

"The Famous Five," one of her most bewitching creations, were four children—siblings Julian, Dick and Anne; their cousin George (short for Georgina) and her faithful hound, Timmy. And together they would get into the most hair-raising adventures, usually involving criminals who mumble, doors that creak, secret passages that echo . . . oh, all manner of stuff, and there are more than a few generations of young British (and beyond) children who could rhapsodize all night about the stories' many sterling qualities.

Yes, they had what we might call their "problems": a certain difficulty with not stereotyping all foreigners as somehow suspicious; all Americans as brash and obnoxious; all sibling-less children (George included) as somewhat peculiar; all adopted children as downright weird; all poor people as potential mass-murderers. In fact, they were suspicious of everything. And obnoxious to everyone.

Or is that only how we remember them, through a prism that has been utterly warped by exposure to *Five Go Mad in Dorset* and its sequel, *Five Go Mad on Mescaline?*

The parody was merciless, brutal and spot-on. Every reservation that has ever been raised about Blyton's (and, by extension, her era's) attitudes toward race, class, the sexes, politics and family was incisively slit open, from the cry of "I say, that chap looks foreign, let's call the police," as an Asian railroad porter struggles with the children's luggage; to the rather unconventional manner in which Georgina (French) allows Timmy to show how licky he is.

Every line of dialog, every piece of action, every character trait the cast calls up, seems to reach deep into the heart of the original stories, to haul an original Blyton-ian quirk out of one context and into another. Watch the shows and then read one of the books (there's more than twenty to choose from). The entire story will feel like it was written in code, and the Comic Strip were the lexicographers who finally cracked it after decades of study.

Five Go Mad in Dorset was an immediate hit, all the more so once it was revealed that the show also received a barrel load of complaints from people who hadn't always thought Dick (Edmondson) was a closet homosexual, and Julian (Richardson) was a bit of a dick, Anne (Saunders) a simpering goody-goody, and George an aspiring lesbian. It was also the opening salvo in a whole series of further *Comic Strip Presents* episodes.

Alternative comedy, as it was portrayed to the masses in the early 1980s, basically meant abandoning the most common devices of traditional humor, and replacing them with equally effective but less well-worn devices. In many ways, too, it was a reversion to the current-affairs heavy spirit of the early sixties satire movement, but with the intellectual subtlety of that replaced by a more sledgehammer approach.

Pythonic imagery was exaggerated, as though cartoonist Terry Gilliam's most surreal drawings were suddenly put into words and deeds, while Derek and Clive provided the soundtrack.

Of course, this effect was diluted by its transition to television, which is why a lot of the Comic Strip productions felt as though they were missing something; as with the early days of Python (and, indeed, *TW3*), wet-nursing a new form of humor into the mainstream was as experimental a process as it was exciting, and just as prone to failure.

This meant a lot of material got tried out simply to see if it worked, and some of it didn't. The highs that the Comic Strip team reached on their two incursions into the Famous Five were only sporadically revisited elsewhere in the five seasons to which the show eventually ran, although when they did get it right, they were brilliant.

From season one, "The Bad News Tour" (which more or less blueprinted *Spinal Tap* several years before anyone smelled that particular glove) was a classic tale of rock 'n' roll madness, and (again like *Spinal Tap*) spun off music, a tour and a sequel. "Eddie Monsoon—A Life?" highlighted season two during 1983–1984; further seasons followed later in the eighties and into the early nineties, with specials appearing into the new century too.

By which time, of course, "alternative" comedy was as long in the tooth as the laughs it once set out to supersede, and entire new ways of making people laugh had been developed.

The Best Time to Sing

In its prime, however, and at its best, it boldly went where no broadcast comics had gone before, with *The Young Ones* forever at the forefront of the action.

> Vyvyan: "I'm entering a contest to win a Ford Tippex. You have to say what Cornflakes mean to you in ten words. So I said: "Cornflakes. Cornflakes. Cornflakes, Cornflakes. Cornflakes, Cornflakes, Cornflakes, Cornflakes, Cornflakes."
>
> Rick: "Pathetic! You'll never win, Vyvyan."
>
> Vyvyan: "Why not?"
>
> Rick: "It's only nine words."

The quartet are college kids, sharing a house (Alexi Sayle plays their dubiously Eastern European landlord) and wallowing in the kind of filth and squalor that the Sunday papers always used to insist was the natural habitat of any student.

Indeed, that was the show's basic premise—rounding up every existing stereotype of students as dirty, loud, scruffy layabouts, for whom Britain's then (but no more) policy of free further education was simply an invitation to lay around the house all day, taking drugs, breaking things and playing obnoxious music.

Education, or at least the creatures that required it, had long been a staple of the sitcom milieu, ever since the great, and remarkably moustached, Jimmy Edwards first flexed a cane in *Whack-O*, initially between 1956 and 1960 and then again during 1971–1972. There, however, it was Edwards himself, in the role of the formidably dissolute Professor James Edwards, headmaster of Chiselbury public school, who was the greatest menace, as he stalked the corridors in cape and tweeds, lashing out at anything that dared to cross his path.

Later, in *Please Sir!* (1968–1972) and the spin-off *Fenn Street Gang*, it was the kids who were the focal point, a bunch of high-spirited lads and lasses who went out of their way to distract and bedevil their mild-mannered teacher, Bernard Hedges (John Alderton).

Now, any hint of authority whatsoever had been removed. Yes, *The Young Ones* were college students. But they rarely mentioned college itself, and never seemed to actually attend it.

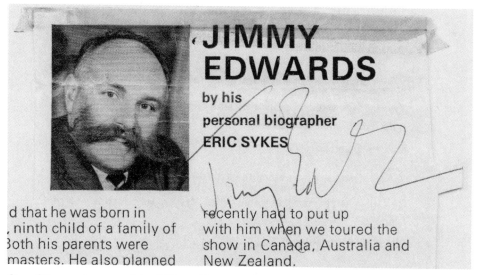

One of the comic giants of the fifties and beyond, Jimmy Edwards signed this theater playbill for a young fan in 1971.

They just rattled around the house, arguing, fighting, smashing things and bullying the meekest of their number, the hippy Neil (Planer), and when it came time to drown out Rick's (Mayall) constant whining, there was usually a live band to be found somewhere, living in a bathroom or camped out beneath the floorboards . . . anyplace where a rapacious landlord might decide you could cram another four or five tenants, and up the rent accordingly. After all, if you could fit five people in the closet, then you rented it to five people, and they could sort out whose bed went where between them.

Unlike *The Comic Strip Presents*, *The Young Ones* was wholly devoted to the misadventures that devoured the quartet—or at least those who, unlike Mike (Ryan), were not cool and smart enough to spend as much time out of the house as possible.

It's hard to say which of the remaining trio was the most archetypal. Rick was supercilious, smarmy, smug and obnoxious, with a face and manner that made a lot of people just want to punch him. He worships Cliff Richard, which was period English shorthand for being about as unhip as it was possible to be, and writes appalling poetry about "the kids."

Even at school, we discover, when some unnamed miscreant scrawled "Prick is a wonker—signed, the rest of the class" in Rick's history textbook, it was appended by the words "I agree with the rest of the class—signed teacher."

So it's a good job the punk-rocking Vyvyan (Edmondson) was around, because at some point during his latest crazed orgy of destruction, Rick would inevitably end up getting hurt. Which was no less than he deserved.

Vyvyan's Mum: "Well aren't you going to introduce me to your friends?"

Vyvyan: "Oh yeah. Uh, this is a friend of mine called Mike . . . uh . . . this is a friend of mine called Neil . . ."

Neil: "Hello."

Vyvyan: "And that's a complete bastard I know called Rick."

Rick: [laughing] "He's just joshing, Mrs. Vyvyan, we're actually terrific friends."

Vyvyan's Mum: "Ooh-ah. He is a bastard, isn't he?"

Impervious to pain, or most other types of feeling, Vyvyan (Edmondson) is responsible for much of the damage that has been done to the house. He is also the owner of a talking hamster with a pronounced Glaswegian accent, that he has named Special Patrol Group—after one of the then-less-respected branches of the British police force. It is, after all, instructive to remember that *The Young Ones* aired in an era when police violence was a major cause for concern in the UK, and the SPG was widely regarded as the most violent police of them all.

SPG the hamster is no better. When Vyvyan swallows a television set, it's SPG who plugs it in. Which does at least amuse Rick, who normally despises the hamster with every breath he takes.

Rick: "I think Special Patrol Group is a stupid name for a hamster!"

Vyvyan: "Ok, I'll change it, then! Hello, Cliff Richard!"

Rick: "Bastard!"

The quietest of the three is Nigel, a supremely paranoid, but generally good-natured hippy who would much rather be living in a treehouse eating lentils and mushrooms than getting dragged again and again into the absurd situations that haunt Vyvyan and Rick. He is also the most bullied member of the household, with Rick and Vyvyan frequently calling a brief truce in their own endless warfare to make Nigel suffer for his sins. Most of which revolve around him being boring.

Nigel is the group's housekeeper (because they force him to be), cook (ditto), and he does the shopping too (ditto once more). He is also prone to savage bouts of hypochondria, including the deeply seated belief that sleeping causes cancer—which does make sense, because he has never met a cancer sufferer who didn't also sleep on occasion. And neither have you.

It was with this cast of characters that *The Young Ones* set sail. It ran for two seasons of six episodes apiece (the second was in 1984), and it remains a tumultuous experience, even after thirty years.

Across both seasons, one-word episode titles offer only the merest hint of what is to come, although it's often more obvious afterwards. In "Demolition," the quartet learn that their house is scheduled for demolition, and concoct a wealth of elaborate schemes and threats to prevent that from taking place. Their efforts are in vain. Even if the local council had listened to their entreaties, an aircraft crashes into the house before the bulldozers even arrive.

In "Oil," Vyvyan claims to have struck oil in the basement, while Mike discovers Buddy Holly in his bedroom; in "Bomb," they find a thermonuclear device propped up next to the fridge; in "Nasty," they encounter a vampire; and in "Sick," they are unwell.

But that is always only a fragment of the overall plot, scripts so overflowing with ideas and idiocy that the shows could easily have stretched to an hour piece, if only every notion had been explored. Which, of course, would have completely spoiled everything.

It was the fact that, a lot of the time, you didn't know what was going on that gave *The Young Ones* so much of its appeal, at least with other young ones. Old Ones, on the other hand, gave the show a very wide berth, and turned over to watch something more to their tastes.

Like live snooker and sheepdog trials.

Like the Python crew, both *The Young Ones* and the *Comic Strip Presents* gangs would go on to a wealth of other shows—Edmondson and Mayall starred in their own *Bottom*, and revisited their Comic Strip double act as the Dangerous Brothers, while Mayall also impressed by portraying possibly the most obnoxious politician outside of the real thing in the comedy *The New Statesman*. (Mayall passed away aged fifty-six on June 9, 2014.)

French and Saunders, too, remained a double act, headlining with their own eponymous show before Saunders took off for *Absolutely Fabulous* and French became the star of *Murder Most Horrid* and *The Vicar of Dibley*. Robbie Coltrane seems to turn up every time you switch on the TV, although a lot of people recall him best for playing Hagrid in the Harry Potter movies;

and Alexei Sayle's one-fat-bald-man TV series *Alexei Sayle's Stuff* (1988–1991) somehow defies the passage of time's every attempt to date it.

Other names, too, arose from the rubble that surrounded *The Young Ones*: Hugh Laurie and Stephen Fry were guests in one episode, and when Rowan Atkinson formulated the historical sitcom *Blackadder* in 1983, both became integral characters. As indeed, on occasion, did Edmondson and Mayall.

Not everything that *The Young Ones* touched, however, turned to gold. With the original episodes an MTV hit in the mid-1980s, the perhaps inevitable attempt was made to concoct an American version of the show, featuring Nigel Planer alone of the UK cast and titled *Oh, No! Not THEM!*

A pilot was shot and it crashed. A full series never materialized.

But *The Young Ones* did top the British chart when they teamed up with none other than Cliff Richard to rerecord the show's title song (with which he had already scored a hit, back in the early 1960s), and while the team's overall influence on the future can never truly be compared to the impact of *Monty Python*, still it ushered in both a cultural sea change and a new wave of stars that changed the British comedy landscape forever.

An entire older generation of stand-ups, for a start, became old news more or less overnight, a happenstance that reinforces Mayall's description of his art as "punk rock comedy"; and an entire generation of jokes, too, fell into disrepute.

From mothers-in-law to actresses-and-bishops; from fat wives to a variety of foreign characters, there ensued a mass extinction so profound that many comics stopped tickling even their own supporters. Indeed, the ease with which the British public adapted to the change was so pronounced that only one can conclusion can really be drawn.

Even audiences were sick of hearing the same old jokes. Now they could get bored with hearing the same new ones.

An Utter Bastard, Elizabethan Style

Blackadder and the Bean

Rowan Atkinson is another of those comedians who one either loves or hates. Catch his performance as an oily schoolmaster performing roll call in the first *Secret Policeman's Ball* movie, and he is one of the funniest and most expressive creatures alive. Sit through a few episodes of *Mr. Bean*, featuring one more in a long line of classic English simpletons, and you should easily be able to excuse those viewers who found it almost frighteningly unfunny.

But then you encounter *Blackadder*, and the past will never be the same again.

With its breathtakingly callous disregard for the niceties of history, *Blackadder* very much harks back to a pair of comedies featuring the veteran Frankie Howerd and dating back to the early 1970s: the television series *Up Pompeii!* and no less than three associated movies (*Up Pompeii!*, *Up the Chastity Belt*, and *Up the Front*).

It was a debt that *Blackadder* emphasized via the introduction of Ivor "Jest Ye Not Madam" Biggun (Geoffrey McGivern), a minor character laboring beneath a name that encapsulated both a typical Howerd pun and one of his catchphrases, too. But it was also one that the show acknowledged every time another supposedly proven historical fact was burned on a pyre of discarded textbooks.

Originally an installment of *Comedy Playhouse* in 1969, *Up Pompeii!* was set in Roman times, in the town of Pompeii (prior to its destruction by the volcano Vesuvius), with Howerd as a slave, Lurcio, and a script that was so riddled with double entendres that it is astonishing it didn't meet itself coming around the corner. In both senses of the word.

Howerd himself was as verbally expressive as Atkinson was facially; like Sid James's laugh and Kenneth Williams's sneer, his very tone of voice

Mr. Bean contemplating his holiday. *Photofest*

conveyed all manner of innuendo, while he too was the master of his own physical features. A single raised eyebrow from Howerd was worth a thousand "I'm free"'s from John Inman.

Playing hard and loose with anything that might be construed as historically accurate (a failing that Howerd, in his asides to the camera, would blame on the BBC misleading him), *Up Pompeii!* reveled in its own smuttiness; a quality that would not be reiterated in *Blackadder*. Prince Edmund Blackadder reveled in his own smugness.

An Antihero in Hose and Codpiece

A fourteenth-century princeling with no hope whatsoever of ascending to the throne, Blackadder cavorted cavalierly through the first six-part series, *The Black Adder*, abusing his servant Baldrick (Tony Robinson); insulting his mild-mannered and faintly stupid friend, Percy, Duke of Northumberland (Tim McInnerny); infuriating his father, the king (Brian Blessed), and generally being the most obnoxious four-letter-word one could imagine. And, while that first season ended, mercilessly, with the entire rotten crew being cruelly slaughtered, it was clear that the family tree still stood. Not only that, but it would also soon be bearing further foul fruit.

Across four seasons, broadcast between 1983 and 1989, *Blackadder* was set in four different eras. The first, and the least "true to life," takes place during the reign of a fictional King Richard IV, which places it around the fifteenth century. Here, the young Edmund is already fully formed as a vile little creature, but has yet to develop into the utter, craven beast that he will become.

That process takes a major step forward in season two, *Blackadder II.* Popular though it was, neither Atkinson nor the BBC were especially happy with the way the first season panned out—it was neither as funny as Atkinson (cowriting with Richard Curtis) hoped nor as cost-effective as the BBC wished.

A second season was commissioned on the condition that some radical improvements were made to the premise, the characters and the budget. Atkinson agreed, but stepped back from continuing as a cowriter; henceforth Blackadder's adventures would be told by Curtis and Ben Elton, another member of the Comic Strip team, as he transitioned between a mouthy, and somewhat irritating, stand-up with fiery left-wing political views, to the author of a West End musical about the pop group Queen.

Blackadder II is where we meet the medieval Blackadder's Tudor descendant, another Edmund, who is attended both by another young and utterly ineffective aristocrat Lord Percy Percy and another Baldrick. This would, in fact, be the case throughout the entire series, and we will leave aside what this says about the supposed randomness of fate. In the world of *Blackadder,* it seems, there are certain people whom your bloodline will never shake off.

The trio's relationship remains the same. Baldrick is stupid, squalid and generally disgusting, and absolutely devoted to his master. Percy is what an earlier generation of comics might have termed "a big girl's blouse," and even slower than last time. And Blackadder is dismissive, rude, violent, abrupt, and so convinced of his own superiority over the world that even when Baldrick has a good idea (usually preluded by the announcement "I have a cunning plan"), Blackadder's immediate response is to hurt him.

"Am I jumping the gun, Baldrick, or are the words 'I have a cunning plan' marching with ill-deserved confidence in the direction of this conversation?"

We pause again to consider how the so-called alternative comedy scene's greatest contribution to the field was to replace innuendo with cruelty and smut with pain—a stance, peculiarly, that would often be justified by dismissing the comedies of the past as sexist, racist and homophobic, which of course they were. Whereas the new wave was an equal opportunity abuser.

The same jokes would continue to be told, and the same situations arrived at. Some things are funny no matter what the prevalent attitudes might be. But the perpetrators of those jokes were now generally depicted in varying shades of hatefulness, allowing the audience to laugh *at*, as opposed to *with*, them. Apparently.

It's all rather disingenuous if you consider it at length. A larger woman can still be described as fat, but only if the person doing the calling is himself ridded with character defects. A homosexual can still be mocked, but only if the mocker himself is a laughable buffoon. Unwanted sexual advances can still be made, but only if it's obvious that they have no hope of being reciprocated.

Needless to say, Blackadder excelled at all of these.

That said, the scripting itself was often dangerously close to self-conscious cleverness, a school that can maybe be traced back to Reginald Perrin's occasionally labored way with words, and reached an apogee in the maw of Douglas Adams's *The Hitchhiker's Guide to the Galaxy*—televised in early 1981 and generally held in low esteem by fans of both the earlier book and radio series.

For its time, however, it was a remarkable production, relatively true to the glorious madness of its predecessors, but with the added incentive of an excellent cast (Sandra Dickinson, wife of the then incumbent Doctor Who, Peter Davison, was truly effervescent), endearingly clunky visuals and dialogue that tied itself in knots in its drive to be as arrestingly absurd, and cripplingly convoluted, as possible.

And that became its legacy, to TV humor in general, but to *Blackadder* in particular. Humorous remarks that might once have flowed naturally within their surroundings were out; sharp, smart-arse one-liners were in, usually punctuated by multiple exclamation marks, and more likely to be a complicatedly constructed insult, loaded with pungent imagery, than anything a real person was likely to say.

For example, in the words of Blackadder:

"You ride a horse rather less well than another horse would. Your brain would make a grain of sand look large and ungainly and the part of you that can't be mentioned, I am reliably informed by women around the Court, wouldn't be worth mentioning even if it could be."

Or:

"I couldn't be more petrified if a wild Rhinoceros had just come home from a hard day at the swamp and found me wearing his pyjamas, smoking his cigars and in bed with his wife."

Seven years before she appeared as Trillian in the BBC's adaptation of *The Hitch Hiker's Guide to the Galaxy*, Sandra Dickinson was Marilyn Monroe in the stage play *Legend*—here backstage at the Bournemouth Winter Gardens.

Or even:

> "I'm as poor as a church mouse, that's just had an enormous tax bill on the very day his wife ran off with another mouse, taking all the cheese."

My Genitalia Is Stuck up in a Tree Somewhere in Rutland

Despite (or maybe because of) these shortcomings, *Blackadder II* might well be the series's crowning glory. Set in the court of Queen Elizabeth I,

Blackadder is one of Her Majesty's three most trusted advisors, the others being the smarmy, oily, sycophant Lord Melchett (Stephen Fry), and Nursie (Patsy Byrne), who was Elizabeth's nurse back in childhood, and who believes she is still her nurse today.

The Queen herself is riveting. Played by Miranda Richardson, she is flighty, childish, impulsive and even crueler than Blackadder. Especially *to* Blackadder. She delights in nothing so much as ordering him to perform one unpleasant task or another; is constantly demanding he give her money (a fate he admittedly deserves, by feigning great wealth when he is usually close to penniless); and, even when she is apparently on his side, she can normally contrive to cause him some consternation.

Situations arise, and become the focus of each episode. In one, the Queen sends Blackadder and Co. to discover new lands and treasures for her; he winds up hiring the cheapest ship he can, and is trapped in absolute squalor and misery with a magnificently demented Tom Baker, as Captain Redbeard Rum.

In another, Blackadder hopes to inherit money from some wealthy but fiercely Puritan relatives, only for the Queen and Melchett to stage a wild drinking party at his home on the same night they are visiting.

Much fun is had with a turnip, by the way.

For the third season, *Blackadder the Third*, we are introduced to a Regency-era descendant at the court of the future King George IV, the Prince of Wales (Hugh Laurie). Again, Blackadder is poor, Baldrick is put-upon and sundry other favorites reappear in new roles—Percy is absent, but Tim McInnerny is a positively dashing Scarlet Pimpernel; Stephen Fry emerges as the Duke of Wellington; and Miranda Richardson shimmers as a highwaywoman with a pathological hatred of squirrels. And in *Blackadder Goes Forth*, we find him in the trenches of World War I, in the weeks prior to one of the Allies' big pushes into German-held territory.

Of the four, it is the most affecting season—Blackadder remains as hateful as he ever was, but we see him, too, through the prism of our own knowledge of that particular war.

The vast majority of those pushes were little more than an excuse for absolute slaughter, and no matter how much we dislike Blackadder, we cannot help but feel sorry for him too. Particularly as one of Lord Melchett's descendants is now among the generals who are planning his fate. The British troops will walk very slowly toward the German lines, because "it'll be the last thing Fritz will expect."

Hugh Laurie as the foppish Prince Regent, Tony Robinson as the mistreated Baldrick and Rowan Atkinson as the scheming Edmund in the third season of *Blackadder*. *Photofest*

There was no room on the western front for sinister foreign villains, executing their convoluted and elaborate schemes. Just bombs, bullets and gas, and milk made from Baldrick's spittle. The series ends with Blackadder and Co. going "over the top" for the final time.

It would not be the end of the family line. Blackadder, Baldrick and Percy would return in three specials, one set in Victorian times, living out a Christmas special; one for the Comic Relief charity, during the English Civil War; and one to mark the turn of the millennium, in modern times, with the added twist of Blackadder having invented a time machine. Which means he can have further misadventures in all the eras that his ancestors neglected to blight.

If you want to know the real reason why dinosaurs became extinct, this is the show for you. (Spoiler alert: it involved Baldrick's underpants.)

Rowan and the Mr. Beanstalk

Rowan Atkinson's next major television role was as Mr. Bean, a character who could scarcely have been further from Edmund Blackadder or, indeed, many of the other, similarly supercilious characters he had played.

Where Blackadder was rude, Bean was simpering; where Blackadder was driven (if only by greed), Bean was bumbling; and where Blackadder lashed out, Bean fell over.

Not always. Bean had a temper, and was capable of exhibiting a ruthlessly petulant pettiness when his own schemes were thwarted. In the main, however, Bean was little more than a latter-day redirection of one of Michael Crawford's descriptions of Frank Spencer, that he was a child in a man's body, wreaking havoc through the simple process of trying to be helpful.

There was also a fond reflection, however, on the comedy greats of the silent film era, with Bean himself rarely speaking and the majority of the action directed by slapstick—an intriguing idea that, by 1991, was attracting British TV audiences in excess of eighteen million.

Just fifteen episodes were shot, broadcast in the main between 1990 and 1995; Bean lived on, however, in an animated series (in which the original title credits' suggestion that he is actually an alien is explored in a little more depth); and also in a variety of spin-offs—two movies, a couple of books, a hit record and guest appearances as far afield as a Hale and Pace music video, and the opening ceremony for the 2012 London Olympics.

His name has also become one of that select few whose mark on popular culture is only amplified whenever it is invoked as an insult—"you're a right Mr. Bean," for example.

Even Homer Simpson knew who he was, as he proved when a picture of then British Prime Minister Tony Blair appeared on the television screen. He mistook the honorable gentleman for Mr. Bean.

An easy mistake to make.

Only Fools and Aristocrats

Would You Buy a Used Stately Home from This Man?

Not all eighties-era British comedy fell under the thrall of the alternatives, of course—just the ones that the hip people watched and then recited back and forth to one another. For all the seventies stars whose reputation was irrevocably affixed to the now-dead decade, there were many who prospered in the new age. And for all the old shows that lingered on, there were new ones that looked capable of lingering just as long.

'Allo 'Allo and *Hi-di-Hi* have already been cringed at; *Shelley* and Simon Callow's *Chance in a Million* cannot be regarded too highly. Few shows of the era, however, were as beloved as *To the Manor Born*, with Penelope Keith enlarging on the character of Margo Leadbetter (in *The Good Life*) by embracing the world of a high-born aristocrat, Audrey fforbes-Hamilton.

Critically, one can point out that it certainly followed in the cozy manner that one would have expected from Keith—albeit with a twist. She appears as a widow battling to keep the family standards alive in the face of mounting odds, while also growing increasingly (if extremely unwillingly) fond of the self-made millionaire, Richard DeVere (Peter Bowles), who bought her family home when she could no longer afford to run it.

Airing between 1979 and 1981, across three seasons, *To the Manor Born* never lost sight of these two angles: the loss of status and the birth of romance. What was remarkable was that it never needed to.

Margo had firmly established Keith as Britain's favorite snob, with all the foolishness, pride and attendant airs and graces that go with the role. Audrey fforbes-Hamilton simply provided her with a certain amount of justification for her attitudes, while subtly noting that she didn't actually possess many of them—a reminder that it's the people who weren't "to the manor born" who are most likely to behave like they were. Welcome, Tony Hancock, Harold Steptoe and, a little later in the decade, Del Boy Trotter.

Bowles, on the other hand, plays the role of the newly minted millionaire with consummate grace, desperately trying to be accepted in his new role as lord of the manor, but well aware of his failings in that department.

He is not helped, of course, by his elderly Czechoslovak mother, Mrs. Polouvicka (Daphne Heard), who has moved in with him, and is certainly

Penelope Keith—from *The Good Life* to *To the Manor Born*.   *Photofest*

not aided by Audrey's patent refusal to accept his friendship as anything but another display of social climbing.

The first glimmering of what would become the show was bound up in a radio pilot in 1976, in which the character of Audrey, still played by Keith, was displaced by a vulgar American (Bernard Braden), who only belatedly discovers that he is in fact descended from the fforbes-Hamiltons.

However, before the show could be broadcast, it became apparent that there was interest in taking the idea to television, too. The pilot was archived; the American became a Czech; and on September 30, 1979, just a year on from the end of *The Good Life*, *To the Manor Born* was born. (Further continuity, albeit obscure, was delivered by the fact that Bowles had been the first choice to play Margo's husband Jerry in *The Good Life*. Other commitments prevented that from happening, and that was probably to the show's advantage—Paul Eddington was the perfect Jerry, just as Bowles became the perfect Richard. Whether Margo and Audrey saw either of them in that light or not.)

In and around the principal story arcs, village affairs went on as usual, with Audrey a constant presence, and occasional thorn, in every aspect of local life. Throughout the episodes in which she most opposes De Vere, it is Audrey who sets about undermining his attempts to ingratiate himself with the villagers, and it's not until the third season that it truly become apparent that a happy ending is imminent, particularly as Richard's business interests begin to cause him concern.

Owner of a major food company, he wants to purchase a refrigerated plant in Argentina. His board of directors oppose it, and he is now planning to sell the manor to finance the purchase out of his own money.

Aghast at the prospect of her old home changing hands again, Audrey asks a wealthy uncle to loan him the money; unfortunately, the uncle passes away just before the deals are signed, and all looks black again. Until his will is read. Audrey inherits the old man's fortune, just in time to purchase the manor herself. Then, unable to bear the thought of living there alone, she asks Richard to marry her. He accepts.

The popularity of *To the Manor Born* was never in doubt; an immediate ratings hit, it spawned a couple of books, and a successful radio sequel after all, in 1997. Then, in 2007, the twenty-fifth anniversary of the show's ending was celebrated with Richard and Audrey's silver wedding anniversary party. Of course, it is not a carefree day, and the pair almost end their married life instead. But all comes right in the end.

Rodney, You Plonker

While *To the Manor Born* focused, at least in part, on the idea of the wealthy adjusting to a less palatial life, *Only Fools and Horses* adopted the everyman (and ever popular) notion of the working class aspiring toward the upper, with Del "Del Boy" Trotter (David Jason) a smart, sharp wheeler-dealer reincarnation of Harold Steptoe, whose greatest dream is to be accepted as the "yuppy" he already believes he is; Rodney (Nicholas Lyndhurst) as his younger brother and not always willing sidekick, and the reasonably steady cast of friends, relations and associates with whom the pair habitually consorts.

Such a large ensemble certainly fuels the notion that, with a few less laughs, *Only Fools and Horses* could have been a soap opera; so does the almost real-time continuity between episodes. But make no mistake. More than one poll has adjudged *Only Fools and Horses* the greatest British sitcom ever, while its longevity (seven seasons plus close to another decade's worth of Christmas specials) likewise testifies to its popularity. One episode, 1996's "Time on Our Hands," was viewed by over one-third of the British population.

The show is set in Peckham, a downmarket corner of south London where, at the time, a great deal of local trading was done either in the pub, from a market stall or out of a suitcase on the street corner, with a lookout constantly alert for any approaching policeman.

And what did they sell? Well, whereas the Steptoes legitimately purchased their stock, touring the streets collecting people's castoffs, Del Boy was a little less cautious. Items "fall off the back of a lorry." Light-fingered colleagues offer unrepeatable bargains on unopened boxes of consumer goods. Military surplus material comes their way, without necessarily being strictly surplus.

The day of the average sidewalk salesman might be spent in perpetual motion, as he hustles from one deal to another, then dodges the law as he tries to offload his wares. But his nights are spent circumnavigating the boxes, crates and cases full of merchandise that occupy every empty space in the home. And *Only Fools and Horses* captured every nuance of that existence.

The show was created by BBC scriptwriter John Sullivan, at that time the brains behind Robert Lindsay's *Citizen Smith*. With that show coming to an end, Sullivan initially proposed a new sitcom set in the world of soccer—*not* a bad idea in theory, but one that has never been done with any measure of success. The BBC certainly didn't think it had, and the proposal was rejected.

Another idea, however, did seem to have legs, all the more so as the BBC jealously watched the independent networks' latest hit, *Minder*—a drama set among the working-class folk of the London suburbs, starring George Cole and Dennis Waterman.

A similarly serious approach to that premise, of course, was not acceptable. TV stations were less prone to copying one another's best ideas back then than they maybe are today. ("Oh look! Another celebrity zombie show! That's a good idea.")

But taking the same culture and placing it into a comedy landscape, without allowing the characters themselves to slip into the Cockney stereotyping that might have been expected; that was a fresh notion.

A series was commissioned, and *Only Fools and Horses* debuted in September 1981. It was a slow burner to begin with, poor viewing figures and weak critical reactions that left many people doubting that it would ever survive. A second season, too, fared poorly, and cancellation appeared to be looming.

But a series of repeats in mid-1983 saw the numbers pick up, and by the time of the show's fourth season, its future was assured.

When we first meet them, the Trotters live with their grandfather (Lennard Pearce), who has raised them since their mother died, in what the Brits call a tower block—a fifteen-, twenty-story apartment building, traditionally cast from the most unappealing concrete and steel design that the guilty architect could muster. The lifts smell of pee, the walls are caked in graffiti, and there's usually one family on every floor with either a screaming baby or a barking dog.

They're rarely an especially pleasant place to live, and that environment alone is sufficient to foster dreams of escape. Especially when the street market seems to offer an easy route to riches.

Who, after all, would not want to purchase a beautiful, realistic sex doll, even if she is filled with propane gas? So long as you refrain from smoking while she's in the room, you're fine.

Obsolete electronics are a popular line; Betamax videos in the VHS age, 8-track tapes for the CD crowd, and so on. Tins of paint that may or may not have been "lost" from a council lorry always come in handy if you need to touch up the yellow lines outside your home; more tins of bright white that turn out to be battleship gray; telescopic Christmas trees, mislabeled men's hairpieces . . . .

Del Boy (David Jason) and cohorts. Would you buy a used *anything* from these men?

Because that's the other trick of the trade. It's not only a matter of having things to sell. You also need to believe in them, and make your potential customers share that faith.

There's an element of Reginald Perrin's Grot stores at play here, the purposeful unloading of more or less useless junk on an unsuspecting public. The difference is, Grot was honest about what it sold. Everything was rubbish, and that's why people wanted it. Del Boy's stock was the opposite. People thought they wanted it, then only discovered its true nature later. By which time, the funny little man in the raincoat and cap who sold it to them from a suitcase on the sidewalk will have long since moved to a different pitch.

Trigger's Broom

Such shenanigans could not, alone, have sustained a show for any particular amount of time. Enter, then, *Only Fools and Horses*' trump card, the love-hate-and mutual-mocking partnership of Del Boy and Rodney. Siblings for whom (to deploy a common British euphemism for rank stupidity) blood is even thicker than they are.

Del Boy has various methods of crushing his younger brother, mostly involving tragic tales of what their mother told him on her deathbed. Unfortunately, after a while, the stories have mounted up so high that even the extraordinarily gullible Rodney can no longer believe in them.

> "Whatever the subject is, Mum had something to say about it on her deathbed. She must've spent her final few hours in this mortal realm doing nothing but rabbiting."

There is also the growing conviction that, despite Del Boy's insistence that the brothers are an equal partnership, it may not be quite so balanced as it could be. It's just little things, of course; the fact that Del Boy always has much more money than Rodney; the fact that he dresses smarter and flashier. That, and his reassurance that "everything between you and me [is] split straight down the middle. Sixty-forty."

Spectacular, too, was the supporting cast: the roadsweeper Trigger (Roger Lloyd-Pack), who still proudly employs the same broom he has used his entire career. Occasionally he's had to replace the head or the handle—and, if you think about it, that rather stymies his boast. But so far as he is concerned, it is still the same broom. Yes, he's maybe a little thick, as well.

There's Boycie (John Challis), a used car salesman who has learned how to turn rags into riches by overselling the vehicles on his lot, and who never misses an opportunity to belittle Del Boy's dreams.

> "Did you know, 500 years ago this was a green and peaceful area?" he announces one day. "The old Earl of Peckham had a castle where the Kwik-Fit exhaust centre now stands. Flaxen-haired maidens used to dance round the village maypole of an evening. And then one fateful medieval day, the Trotter clan arrived in a stolen Zephyr.
>
> "Before you knew it, the flaxen-haired maiden was up the spout, the old Earl had been sold some hooky armor and someone nicked the maypole."

Boyce's wife, Marlene (Sue Holderness), has a softer spot for the elder Trotter, and does little to curb rumors that she and Del were once lovers. She remains a vivacious flirt, too, who loves nothing so much as the chance to flaunt her husband's money.

There's Mickey Pearce (Patrick Murray), a youngster who has already set his eyes on becoming a big wheel just like Boycie. For now he's content to indulge in petty larceny.

There's the Nag's Head pub landlord Mike (Kenneth MacDonald) and the lorry driver Denzil (Paul Barber); and, following the death of actor Lennard Pearce, the Trotters' Uncle Albert (Buster Merryfield), who moves into the tower block with them, a former naval man who has had more than his share of bad luck.

"Do you remember your cousin Audrey?" he once asks. "I went to stay with her and her husband Kevin for a year. One day, he sent me down to Sainsbury's with a shopping list. When I got back, they'd emigrated."

Or, as Rodney puts it, "Every single ship he ever sailed on either got torpedoed or dive-bombed . . . two of 'em in peace time. "

It was a funny old show, really. Funny odd, as well as funny ha-ha. Particularly later in its life span, even comics the strength of Jason and Lyndhurst stopped playing their roles for the laughs, and allowed *Only Fools and Horses* to address more dramatic issues—nothing too heavy, just the usual domestic stuff, but they played it relatively straight regardless.

Flashes of the old sibling rivalry remained, of course; in Del Boy's eyes, Rodney would forever merit being described as "a plonker," but he always looked out for his easily led kid brother, even as Rodney embraced full adulthood. Likewise, Rodney never stopped casting a worried, and usually correctly so, eye over his elder brother's latest scheme—looking out for him, too, in other words.

But if life itself is filled with ups and downs, so was *Only Fools and Horses*, and maybe that is why it was so popular. At last, a sitcom that did not close every story line with the punch line you'd been expecting for the past ten minutes; or transform any situation into a feel-good finale. Ultimately, at the end of the show's life the Trotters would indeed become millionaires. But they needed to suffer a lot of uncertainty, hardship and ill luck first.

It was an effective device, as their characters (and those of the supporting cast) stepped wholly out of the sometimes two-dimensional world of mere sitcom life to become fully fledged "people" in their own right, all with their own crowd of vociferous fans—particularly Trigger, whose haunted, put-upon expression, and uncertain eye for reality, established him as one of the most sympathetic characters of the age.

Likewise, the saga of Rodney's courtship of the middle-class Cassandra (Gwyneth Strong) took on all the ramifications of, indeed, a soap opera, as they overcame parental opposition (her parents, of course), familial cynicism (courtesy of Del Boy) and their own up-and-down relations, to marry, separate, reunite, suffer a miscarriage and finally have a son.

There were not too many laughs in that story arc.

The death of Uncle Albert was a killer, as well.

Likewise, Del Boy's pretensions to yuppyhood are extremely amusing, and often the key to some of the show's funniest moments. But they also paint a sad picture, too, as we see him cruising toward another disappointment, secretly mocked by the very people he is trying to impress.

He certainly is not the connoisseur he likes to think he is. "I'm a Ming fan myself," Del Boy announces once. "He made some wonderful stuff, that Ming. Pity he had to go and die when he did."

Having grown to admire his chutzpah over however many years you've been watching the show, it's always sad to see him being taken down a few pegs, whether or not his behavior merited it. Just once, it would be nice to see him successfully pull the wool over the eyes of a bunch of smirking snobs.

But the show's greatest humor comes from several sources. The interaction between Del and Rodney is key, with each an ideal comic foil for the other in both personality and appearance. Even as the show entered its semiserious phase, the rivalry between the brothers remained among the primary elements, with Rodney (always the better educated of the pair) growing ever more subtle in his attempts to add some mockery to Del Boy's life.

Usually, it would backfire, and if the saga of his attempts to start a family often verged on the tearjerking, those of Del Boy and his eventual wife, Raquel, ignited one of the show's most popular story lines.

Of course, Rodney was only joking when he suggested that Del Boy should name his son Damien, after the devil child in the movie *The Omen*. He certainly never expected them to take him seriously, and expected even less to then spend the remainder of the series in mortal terror of the child. Full marks to the musical department, too, for accompanying the baby's on-screen appearances with "O Fortuna" from *Carmina Burana*, an apocalyptic theme that is as much a part of *The Omen* as its original theme music.

Despite both the BBC and the public's enthusiasm, *Only Fools and Horses* was never secure in its life span. Indeed, when David Jason announced he was leaving during the fifth season, writer Sullivan set about devising what he believed would be the show's final episode.

He settled on Del Boy being offered the chance to go into business with a friend in Australia. Neither Rodney nor Albert would be accompanying him, and a spin-off series called *Hot-Rod* was in the works, with Rodney and Mickey Pearce attempting to follow in Del Boy's footsteps and establish themselves as Peckham's finest street traders.

Then Jason changed his mind. *Hot-Rod* was put on ice, the tearjerking ending to the episode, "Who Wants to be a Millionaire?", was reversed, and *Only Fools and Horses* not only galloped on for another two seasons, it also stepped out of conventional sitcom territory by being expanded to episodes of fifty minutes' duration. Time enough indeed for all of life's other little worries to descend upon the Trotters' heads. And when it did finally end, and the cast moved on to other projects, still they would reconvene for annual holiday specials, until the Trotters' boat at last came in, and they struck it mega-rich.

Nobody could say they hadn't worked for it, either.

The Lord Is My Scriptwriter

Faith, Hope and Father Ted

There is a place (or, at least, there was until the overcrowding became too much) where bad priests go. Some place between Hell and Limbo, less than jail but worse than exile. It is called Craggy Island, and it has no east. It was lost in a storm and never recovered.

Off the coast of Ireland lies this dank and dismal isle; off the church's radar, too, or so they like to think. Even seasoned television journalists cannot find it on the map, for the simple reason, they are told by one of the parish's leading figures, that it isn't on any.

> "Oh no, it wouldn't be on any maps. We're not exactly New York! No, the best way to find it is to head out from Galway and go slightly north until you see the English boats with the nuclear symbol. They go very close to the island when dumping the old 'glow-in-the-dark.'"

But there, in a barren, windswept parochial house, overseeing a village so tiny you could cloak it with a cassock, dwell three of the Catholic Church's best-kept secrets: Father Dougal McGuire (Ardal O'Hanlon), a feckless idiot so stupid that even his failure to understand the rudiments of his faith no longer raise eyebrows; Father Jack Hackett (Frank Kelly), a priest so dissolute, old and alcohol-drenched that his vocabulary—three words, "drink," "girls" and "feck"—makes more sense than he does; and Father Ted Crilly (Dermot Morgan), a man whose misappropriation of parish funds was so heinous, so hideous, so utterly unforgivable that there are some who believe even Craggy was too good for him.

But they are wrong.

Craggy Island makes Hades look like a holiday camp.

Girls Feck Drink

Religion and comedy make awkward bedfellows.

It is hard, after all, to make jokes out of something that so many people believe in and still expect them to laugh. That's why there's not many sitcoms about aardvarks. In essence, the concept could be described as faintly ridiculous, and it takes several suspensions of disbelief to comprehend that such a thing exists. But there they are, large as life, bristling with their aardvark hair, defying you to say there's no such thing.

So it is with religion, and many is the comic who has perished on the storm-tossed rocks of faith-based controversy; deafening is the outrage that drowns their petty mewling.

Father Ted was different. *Father Ted* was hysterically funny.

A degree of mockery was to be expected, but it was targeted at the priests, as opposed to their religion itself. True, you could say that the Catholic Church's very recruitment policies were under attack, but that's only if you believe men such as these would ever have been given a job in the first place.

No, these are bad 'uns so bad that even their fictional existence makes us thank the Lord for the good 'uns that are really out there. And so all of us can laugh at the night when Father Ted tries leading Father Dougal in prayer.

Father Dougal: "Our Father, who art in heaven . . ."

Father Ted: "Hallowed . . ."

Father Dougal: "Hallowed be thy . . ."

Father Ted: "Name!"

Father Dougal: "Papa don't preach . . ."

Father Ted: "Dougal, you know you can praise God in other ways."

Father Dougal: "Oh yeah, like that time you told me I could praise him just by leaving the room."

Father Ted: "Yes, that was a good one, all right."

Which is why *Father Ted* is no more about religion than *On the Buses* was about buses. It is about people. Strange, discomforting and oddly conflicted people, three of whom happen to be priests, and the fourth is a housekeeper, name of Mrs. Doyle (Pauline McLynn), whose entire existence is predicated on the creation of snacks and the offering of tea.

"Have a nice cup of tea," she'll say, and maybe she'll be turned down, politely but firmly. "No thank you, Mrs. Doyle."

"Oh go on, just a drop."

"No thank you."

"Oh go onnnnnnn. Go-on go-on go-on go-on go-on go-on go-on." Until all resistance has been sapped, all willpower erased, and she can bustle away triumphantly, ready to pour another one.

Only Father Jack has been known to succeed where other men have so abjectly failed.

"What would say to a nice cup?" asks Mrs. Doyle.

"Feck off, cup," replies the angry old man.

She is very much the voice of the three priests' conscience, however. Indeed, when Father Ted professed his admiration for an author named Polly Clark, Mrs. Doyle not only waxed lyrical on the faults of the woman's novels, she could repeat those faults verbatim.

"'Eff you! Eff your effing wife! I'll stick this effing pitchfork up your hole,' oh that was another one, oh yes! [. . .] 'Bastard this' and 'Bastard that,' you can't move for the bastards in her novels; it's wall-to-wall bastards! [. . .] You bastard, you fecker, you bollocks! Get your bollocks out of my face! [. . .] 'Ride me sideways' was another one!"

There again, literature of all kinds seems to cause problems on the island.

Father Dougal [answering an innocent question]: "I wouldn't know Ted, you big bollocks!"

Father Ted: "I'm sorry!?"

Father Dougal: "I said 'I wouldn't know Ted, you big bollocks!'"

Father Ted: "Have you been reading those Roddy Doyle books again, Dougal!?"

Father Dougal: "I have, yeah Ted, you big gobshite!"

Nuns Are People, Too

Written by Arthur Mathews and Graham Linehan, *Father Ted* lived three seasons on the island, beginning in spring 1995.

The inmates of Craggy Island—Ardal O'Hanlon (Dougal), Dermot Morgan (Father Ted), Frank Kelly (Father Jack) and Pauline McLynn (Mrs. Doyle).

We never truly learn the darkest details behind the three priests' banishment. True, Crilley will occasionally protest that the money was merely "resting" in his account, and maybe it was. For a long time. But we never discover the truth behind the infamous Blackrock Incident, in which the lives of several nuns were "irreparably damaged," and for which Father Dougal was held responsible. And while it really isn't hard to see why Father Jack should have been barred from further contact with the rest of the human race (particularly after he transforms into a werewolf), it might have been illuminating to discover more about that ill-fated wedding in Athlone . . . .

They are not telling, however, and neither is Bishop Len Brennan (Jim Norton), the man who arranged their exile in the first place, and who positively dreads the rare occasions when he needs to visit the island. And with good reason, too.

Once, his bedroom became mysteriously overrun by rabbits, and Bishop Brennan *hates* rabbits. Once, Father Ted kicked him "up the arse," and Bishop Brennan *hates* being kicked up the arse. Perhaps more than he hates Father Ted. And once, Father Jack got hold of an incriminating videotape, featuring the Bishop at play, and maybe Len would be a little kinder in future. Wouldn't he, *daddy*?

He did once consider sending Father Ted further afield. "There's a lovely little island, off the coast of Surinam, and they have a couple of tribes there—you're going to love this!—and they have been knocking the *shit* out of each other since 1907! And we have never found the right man to bring them together in the spirit of Christian harmony. But I think that you, Ted, are *the* man!"

It never happened. Maybe Brennan believed such a fate was too merciful.

They are exiled, then, but they are not alone. The village has its share of characters, even if the majority of them are quite insane; while there are also regular trips to the mainland, although they usually end in disaster—the need to bail Mrs. Doyle out of jail, for example, on a charge of brawling and public disorder (she and a friend were arguing over whose turn it was to pay for their lunch). Or the need to escape from an enraged Richard Wilson, star of the sitcom *One Foot in the Grave* and creator of the catchphrase "I don't belieeeeeeve it." Which he loathes and detests hearing people repeat whenever they happen to see him.

Or, the most terrifying ordeal of all, an entire bevy of priests getting trapped inside the largest women's lingerie department in Ireland. It was a cataclysm from which only Father Ted's leadership, calm and ingenuity could save them, and for which he received the Golden Cleric award.

It was one of the precious few honors Ted ever got. Although Crilley has vast and extravagant dreams (if only he can get off this godforsaken rock), the fates have not finished with him yet.

He is invited to take a parish in Los Angeles, only to discover, at the very last moment, that it's almost as bad (and much more violent) than the one he'd be leaving behind. He enters the Eurosong Contest (a parody of the real-life Eurovision Song Contest), representing Ireland with a song that has only one note, and finishes last.

He *does* win the All Priests Stars in Their Eyes Lookalike Competition, teaming up with Jack and Dougal as the three ages of Elvis, but he is also responsible for one of the judges falling off the wagon and reverting to rampant alcoholism. And, when an Irish TV crew come to visit him, a succession of minor mishaps sees them interview Father Dougal instead, while Ted is stuck on the big wheel at the Funland amusement park.

Those are the good days. The bad ones are worse, though, and all have one thing in common. The more Father Ted wishes someone would go away, the more likely they are to stay around.

There is that fateful night when Father Jack dies, decked by one bottle of furniture polish too many. (He survives.) There is that awful day when Father Stone (Michael Redmond), the most boring man in the world, is struck by lightning while visiting the island. (He survives, too.) And there are several encounters with Father Noel Furlong (Graham Norton), an impossibly irrepressible soul who believes his maniacal enthusiasm for dancing, singing and laughter has endeared him to everyone he meets. He gets crushed by a rock fall. (And survives.)

Only in his dreams is Father Ted likely to find happiness. A recurring image finds him living the life of a playboy, surrounded by cash and beautiful women. Or living the high life like other priests do.

In one of the most unexpected (and, for that, brilliant) scenes in the entire show, an episode opens with Ted declaring his love for a beautiful woman—Assumpta Fitzgerald (Dervla Kirwan), landlady of the pub in the drama *Ballykissangel*, where she is usually found embroiled within a steamy flirtation with the local priest Peter Clifford (Stephen Tompkinson).

Nor is the presence of Father Clifford, preparing to leave the village forever, able to forestall the lovebirds' canoodling. They just keep right on at it, leaving Clifford to depart alone and unnoticed.

Which is better than dreaming of being pursued by a band of angry peanuts, but Ted has had that one as well.

It was while season three was still before the cameras that Dermot Morgan suggested that it would be the final season; that he did not want to be typecast in the role of a faintly bumbling but generally pleasant priest forever. The tragedy was that he would not be. The day after shooting finished, he was dead, felled by a massive heart attack, at the age of forty-five.

The popularity of *Father Ted* was not confined to the UK, where (unlike its namesake) it would win many awards. Ireland and Australia both adored it, while its run on BBC America was not only a major hit for the then still-fledging network, it also spawned plans for an American version to be made, with Steve Martin as Father Ted and Graham Norton as Father Dougal. Neither it, nor any of several other rumored stateside successors, has yet seen the light of day.

They've probably been sent to Craggy Island instead.

That's Not a Lady, That's a Priest

If *Father Ted* depicted the religious life in one of the cruelest corners of God's Earth (although it looks quite attractive on the show), *The Vicar of Dibley* portrayed it at its most pastoral, in the tiny village of Dibley, Oxfordshire, in the aftermath of the Church of England's decision to allow the ordination of women.

It was a controversial theme, at least at the time, but the show was destined to prove a major success, with actress Dawn French, as the Reverend Geraldine Granger, credited for going some way toward accustoming people to the fact that five centuries of male domination had finally been shattered in the pulpit.

One-half of a comedy duo called the Menopause Sisters, accompanied by Jennifer Saunders, French arose from the Comic Strip on the same wave of talent that brought *The Young Ones* to fame.

A star of almost three-quarters of episodes of *The Comic Strip Presents*, French was then one-quarter of the *Girls on Top* team, a mid-1980s sitcom costarring Saunders, Ruby Wax and Tracey Ullman as four decidedly unconventional London housemates.

Two years later, French and Saunders launched their own eponymous comedy show, but both enjoyed their own careers too—Saunders with *Absolutely Fabulous* alongside Joanna Lumley, and French, prior to *The Vicar of Dibley*, with *Murder Most Horrid*, a series of spoof murder mysteries in which French appeared as victims, killers, school dinner ladies and grandmothers alike. She also delivered one of the daftest, yet most memorable, lines in nineties television history—at least if you enjoy atrocious puns.

Playing the Grim Reaper in the season-three episode "Dead on Time," French completes her assignment, then returns to her car, and wrestles for a moment with her music collection. "Death," she murmurs, "where is thy sting?" And then she finds his album. Grim no more, the Reaper smiles once again.

Written by *Blackadder* coauthor Richard Curtis, *The Vicar of Dibley* debuted in November 1994, running first as a short series, but then expanding its lifetime via special Christmas and holiday editions, and its charm is instantly apparent.

Certainly it bristles with gentle humor, even on those occasions when Curtis could be reflecting fondly on Blackadder himself. Discussing, for example, the change of seasons, the reverend is reminded, "why don't we just say that that was the autumn that was and let's just see what winter brings?" To which Geraldine responds, "Yeah. Either that or 'get out of my house you treacherous gigantic elongated bastard.' Ah, but no. Probably the autumny-wintry metaphor is much nicer. Much nicer for you."

No less than *Father Ted*, *The Vicar of Dibley* could not resist acknowledging the success of the aforementioned *Ballykissangel*, in an episode titled, naturally, "Ballykissdibley."

Father Peter visits St. Barnabas's as part of a cultural exchange, only to be soundly abused by one of Geraldine's more vociferously anti-papist parishioners. Further chaos ensues in the shape of the other villagers' particular eccentricities, and while Geraldine does eventually impose a certain calm, it won't last. Peter is selling kisses for charity, when suddenly Assumpta arrives.

Whimsical absurdity also abounded, such as the conversation between Geraldine and her friend Alice, regarding the efficacy of home pregnancy tests.

Alice: "Well the pregnancy test said I'm not pregnant. The hamster didn't turn blue."

Geraldine: "I'm sorry, I don't think I'm familiar with that particular test."

Alice: "Oh yes, it's very common in Dibley. You go out and you buy a hamster, and you wee on it. And if it turns blue, you're pregnant."

Despite such a comparatively short run, *The Vicar of Dibley* attracted some remarkable guest stars. Australian pop songstress Kylie Minogue, character actor (and future Doctor Who) Peter Capaldi, former Royal Sarah Ferguson, Sean Bean, Emma Watson and Johnny Depp all appeared, while that short run is itself disguised (particularly in the United States) by the sensation that *The Vicar of Dibley* (and many others besides) ran eternally.

The cause of this, of course, is down to the very different manner in which cable television operates, compared to the terrestrial networks—a difference that grew ever more marked as the 1990s went on.

In cable, once a show finds a time slot, it often stays there, day after day after day, through the span of all available episodes, and then through them all again. And sometimes even again. It's a practice that PBS perfected as far back as the 1970s, when an imported British show might well have been credited with perfecting perpetual motion.

It's a boon to viewers who are rarely in the same place at the same time every day; they can just tune in and out as circumstance allows, and if the chronology and continuity are a little skewed, that's what episode guides are for.

It's a curse, however, for those people who like a little variety with their viewing, which is why we should be thankful for *The Vicar of Dibley*. Even on the umpteenth viewing, the comedy is so fresh, the cast so appealing and the setting so attractive that there is always something new to marvel at. (Unlike the American remake, Kirstie Alley's *The Minister of Divine*. That was hard to sit through even once.)

And besides, Dawn French herself had come a long way since she was sitting in a tent with the Famous Five, telling Timmy the dog that he was "so licky."

22

And That's Why They Changed the Way You Say "Uranus"

Smegheads in Space

Space: the final frontier. These are the voyages of the mining vessel *Red Dwarf*, on a ten-and-counting season mission to float aimlessly in space, and try to prevent its one man, one cat, one droid and one hologram crew from going stark raving bonkers.

It's not going to be easy.

The story is set years into the future, and light years away from Earth. But the Jupiter Mining Corporation's *Red Dwarf* is far from the kind of gleaming high-tech spacecraft that we were raised to believe the space race demanded. In fact, it's rather sordid, dusty and dirty, and more like a six-mile-long, three-mile-wide and four-mile-high factory (with attendant canteen) than something out of *Star Trek*.

People, too, don't seem to have changed very much. Same hairstyles, same clothing, same slang, same attitudes, same boredom. Maybe there are exciting jobs available aboard the *Red Dwarf*, but we don't get to see them. Even the ship's captain looks like he's been at sea for a millennium too long, and can't wait to get home for pizza and beer.

And then, something *does* happen.

Born of a short series of radio plays, Rob Grant and Doug Naylor's *Dave Hollins: Space Cadet*, in 1984, and launched on television in 1988, *Red Dwarf*'s thirty-plus-year life span has not been continuous. Originally broadcast between 1988 and 1993, it would be four years before it returned to run until the end of the century; and then another decade before season nine. A tenth followed in 2012; seasons eleven and twelve (at the time of writing) are scheduled for 2016/2017.

Not much has changed in all that time, though. Not since the very first episode.

In the beginning there was a crew, among whose number was one Arnold Judas Rimmer (Chris Barrie), a lowly technician whose main function seemed to be supervising the refilling of the drink and food dispensers—until the day when he was working with a volatile form of radiation known as cadmium II. So volatile that it killed everybody on board, including the hapless Rimmer.

Just two life forms survived the catastrophe; Rimmer's bunkmate, Dave Lister (Craig Charles), serving eighteen months in the stasis, or suspended animation, cell at the time, as a punishment for bringing a pet cat on board the craft; and the cat itself.

The only other form of intelligence aboard was Holly (Norman Lovett), the ship's computer, and the first indication we are given that *Red Dwarf* is the product of futuristic technology. Capable of thought, logic, humor and independent action, Holly sets about repairing the ship as best he/it can and releases Lister from stasis. Aware, however that the desolation of the empty craft will surely drive the young man insane, Holly applies another piece of tech to the problem.

Death, in the world that *Red Dwarf* left behind, is no longer a permanent state. It can be sidestepped hologrammatically, with minds and personalities living on within a shell of pure light. Damage to the ship means only one hologram can now be sustained, so Holly does the only sensible thing; he revives the member of the crew with whom Lister has spent the most time—Rimmer.

He overlooks the fact that the two men loathe one another.

In fact, most people loathe Rimmer. He is a very loathe-able person. Pompous, arrogant, cowardly and smarmy, he is a space-aged mutation of *The Young One*'s Rick. The same high opinion of himself, the same self-defeating drive to be loved by all, the same ruthlessly fruitless ambition.

Only where Rick dreamed of becoming the People's Poet, Rimmer dreams of being a starship commander, a status that evades him because he has yet to pass even the most basic exams in any subject whatsoever. His sole qualifications for any meaningful role in life are a pair of swimming certificates (bronze and silver) awarded when he was young, and he wears their distinction like campaign medals. Address him formally, and the initials Bsc Ssc should always be appended to his name.

He is, in the slang of the *Red Dwarf* day, a total smeghead (a phrase popularized in our time by the poet Attila the Stockbroker). Or, as Captain

Todhunter put it, "There's a saying amongst the officers: If a job's worth doing, it's worth doing well. If it's not worth doing, give it to Rimmer. Astoundingly zealous, possibly mad; probably has more teeth than brain cells. Promotion prospects: comical."

That is the kind of person Rimmer is.

> Rimmer: "Last time [I sat an exam], I only failed by the narrowest of narrow margins."
>
> Lister: "You what? You walked in there, wrote 'I am a fish' four hundred times, did a funny little dance and fainted!"
>
> Rimmer: "That's a total lie."
>
> Lister: "No, it's not. Peterson told me."
>
> Rimmer (mockingly): "'No, it's not. Peterson told me.' Lister, if you must know, I submitted a discourse on porous circuitry that was too . . . radical, too unconventional, too mould-breaking for the examiners to accept."
>
> Lister: "Yeah. You said you were a fish!"

Oh Rimmer, You Are a Smeghead

Lister is the complete opposite. Liverpool born and bred, he is a carefree joker who takes very little seriously and who, prior to the accident, had just two goals in life. One was to make it with Kristine Kochanski, one of his fellow crew members, and the other was to return to Earth and live in Fiji. He drinks copiously and loves Indian food. He's scruffy, and fancies himself a burgeoning rock guitarist. He just finds it difficult to take orders from a smeghead, as he tells the ship's captain before any of this takes place.

Rimmer has had him brought up on a charge of insubordination, and Captain Todhunter is despairing of the pair.

> Lister: "I'm not an insubordinate man by nature. I try and respect Rimmer and everything, but it's not easy, 'cos he's such a smeghead!"
>
> Rimmer: "Did you hear that, sir? Lister, do you have any conception of the penalty for describing a superior technician as a 'smeghead'?
>
> Todhunter: "Oh, Rimmer, you are a smeghead!"

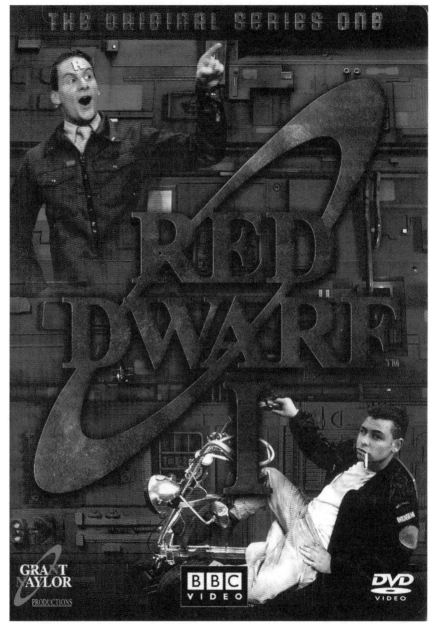

In space, nobody can hear you call Rimmer a smeghead. Except for Rimmer, of course.

The Captain doesn't really think much more of Lister, though, than he does his voyage-long nemesis. "Has requested sick leave due to diarrhea on no less than 500 occasions. Left his previous job as a supermarket trolley attendant after ten years because he didn't want to get tied down to a career. Promotion prospects: zero."

Rimmer considers Lister to be a waste of space. So, well done, Holly (as Lister constantly reminds him). From a crew of 169 people, the computer decides to bring Rimmer back to life.

Enter—the cat. Definitive article intended.

So far as Lister is concerned, no time whatsoever has passed since the day he was locked inside the stasis chamber. But Holly is not a fast worker. Three million years, in fact, have elapsed—time enough for evolution to take some very dramatic turns. Including the birth, development and existence of a whole new breed of domestic moggy.

It still eats fish, and it still spends an inordinate amount of time grooming itself to perfection and then reclining in comfortable places so we can all admire its beauty. It still chases shiny things, and runs from one place to another for absolutely no reason whatsoever. It still has six nipples. But it is also tall and handsome, with color-coordinated internal organs. It is capable of speech, and it walks on two legs.

Soon the Cat (Danny John-Jules) is as much a part of the crew as either Lister or Rimmer, and because cats are naturally intelligent beings, he hates Rimmer, too.

What a happy family this will be.

The early episodes are, as is so often the case, usually regarded as the best, in that both the show and the characters were still finding their space legs, which leaves Lister and Rimmer free to bicker like the oddest Odd Couple.

Nothing Lister does will ever please Rimmer; nothing Rimmer says will ever cause Lister to like him. But a friendship develops regardless, as the pair face the adversity engendered by their situation. Later in its life span, a certain self-conscious silliness would creep into the show (the talking toaster was an especially bad idea), but for now, *Red Dwarf* dwarfed the competition. Plus, it had the greatest theme song.

Much of the humor surrounds Lister's attempts to outmaneuver Rimmer, who now sees himself (accurately, as it happens) as the highest-ranking officer aboard ship. For example, when it is suggested that Rimmer allow himself to be turned off for an evening so Lister can have a date with

Kochanski's hologram, he is ordered not to try. So Lister takes the cookery exam, in a bid to gain an even higher rank.

Again, however, there are moments of tenderness. Celebrating the anniversary of Rimmer's death, Lister manipulates his companion's database to restore his memories of a former girlfriend. Actually, his *only* former girlfriend.

Still, loneliness takes its toll, despite Holly's precautions.

Lister: "Cat . . . Did you ever see the Flintstones?"

Cat: "Of course."

Lister: "Do you think Wilma's sexy?"

Cat: "Wilma Flintstone?"

Lister: "Maybe we've been alone in deep space for too long, but every time I see that show, her body drives me crazy. Is it just me?"

Cat: "I think in all probability, Wilma Flintstone is the most desirable woman who ever lived."

Lister: "That's good, I thought I was goin' strange."

Cat: "She's incredible!"

Lister: "What do you think of Betty?"

Cat: "Betty Rubble? Well, I would go with Betty . . . but I'd be thinkin' of Wilma."

Lister: "This is stupid. Why are we talking about going to bed with Wilma Flintstone?"

Cat: "You're right. We're nuts. This is an insane conversation."

Lister: "She'll never leave Fred and we know it."

In this mood, *Red Dwarf* is unassailable.

In fairness, much of the reasoning behind *Red Dwarf*'s occasional descents into less rewarding comedic territory was a by-product of its very premise. With few exceptions, it is difficult for any show with a small, self-contained cast to sustain the same level of originality across the course of a single season, let alone ten of the things. The Cat and Holly aside, Rimmer and Lister had nobody but one another, and while the latter at least was able to amuse himself in some delightfully foolish ways, still he would have welcomed someone else for company.

Hence, briefly in season two, but permanently the following year, the arrival of Kryten 2X4B-523P (originally David Ross; subsequently Robert Llewellyn), a Service Mechanoid whom the *Red Dwarf* team rescue from the crashed spaceship *Nova 5*. He, too, has been alone for thousands of years, but bound by his "behavioural protocols," he has continued to serve his function—that of a very tall housekeeper/cook, with a head shaped like an ice cube.

Much of season three is dedicated, like some bizarre twisted *Pygmalion*, to Lister's efforts to deprogram Kryten and teach him how to think and act for himself. Watching the robot attempt to call "Mr. Rimmer" a "smeghead" will forever be a treat.

Gradually other characters emerge, either for real, via flashback, or through sundry mysteries of time and space. We meet Rimmer's parents, and learn how he became such a smeghead to begin with; and we see into Lister's future. Kristine Kochanski (Clare Grogan, and later Chloë Annett) briefly reemerges to further haunt Lister's fevered dreams, and the rest of the crew as well.

We visit various aspects of Earth, including one where time is running backwards; another where the cast are visitors to the set of the soap *Coronation Street*; a third where they travel home to buy some curry, using Kryten's spare head, and wind up creating a parallel planet. And then there's the one where they discover their entire time together was the product of a virtual reality game, and that they've been on present-day Earth all along. Before subsequently finding out that they haven't.

Nonhumans abound. Rimmer, in life and in death, is obsessed with the notion that they might one day encounter a genuine alien race; that they might even be already aboard.

Lister: "Oh God, aliens . . . Your explanation for anything slightly peculiar is aliens, isn't it? You lose your keys—it's aliens. A picture falls off the wall—it's aliens. That time we used up a whole bog roll [toilet tissue] in a day, you thought that was aliens as well!"

Rimmer: "Well, we didn't use it all, Lister. Who did?"

Lister: "Rimmer, aliens used our bog roll?"

Rimmer: "Just 'cos they're aliens, doesn't mean they don't have to visit the little boys' room. Although they probably do something weird and alien-esque, like it comes out of the top of their heads or something."

Lister: "Well, I wouldn't like to be stuck behind one in a cinema!"

In fact, they never meet any actual aliens. But there are plenty of robots, androids, holograms, doppelgängers, simulants, GELF (genetically engineered life forms), future selves and a Curry Monster, most of whom seem rather hostile; and there's a magnificent encounter with a Despair Squid, which lives up to its name with morbid abandon. Unlike Rimmer's alter ego, Ace, who turns out to be quite a nice chap.

Holly undergoes a metamorphosis, changing his appearance from male to female (played by Hattie Hayridge), and his personality too; and in case anybody wonders where's the sci-fi in all of this, there are few genre staples that do not get explored at one time or another, from the paradox of time travel to the future of mankind (rather grim, if you need to know).

What does enthrall is the sheer hopelessness of it all. For all the laughter and humorous situations, for all the Cat's hijinks and Lister's curry burps, *Red Dwarf* is actually a very thoughtful show. And what it thinks is dark. Darker than dark. Darker, even, than space.

Bleaker, even, than Rimmer's knowledge of company law.

Rimmer: "We can remove him from duty as per Space Corps Directive 196156."

Kryten: "196156? Any officer caught sniffing the saddle of the exercise bicycle in the women's gym will be discharged without trial? Hmm. I'm sorry, sir, that doesn't quite get to the nub of the matter for me."

Again, it is human nature to look at the future as a glimmering, sparkling beast, bristling with possibility, hope and jet packs. *Red Dwarf*, however, paints one where life really isn't much different from what we have today, except it is now all but extinct.

With the exception of space travel itself, and the admittedly rather handy hologram technology, the greatest cultural advances appear to be confined to fresh linguistic constructs and mass-marketable sporting events ("smeg," and variations thereof, as an all-purpose expletive; "dollarpound" as a new form of currency; and Zero-Gee Football); while the relics of past human exploration that the crew find tend to be shattered, and more like disused present-day railroad cars than the latest in twenty-third-century luxury.

In many ways, there was no reason for Rimmer and Lister to have ever encountered the Despair Squid. Their lives were certainly drab enough before they joined the mining corps, and they only became drabber still. Could things really have seemed any worse?

Yes. There could have been an attempt at making an American version of the show. Which there was. Twice. The first pilot featured Craig Bierko as Lister, Chris Eigeman as Rimmer, Hinton Battle as Cat and Robert Llewellyn reappearing as Kryten; the second was partially recast, but fared no better than its predecessor.

Bootleg copies circulate. It is smegging unwatchable.

23

If Voting Could Change Things, They'd Make It Illegal

Yes Minister, No Minister . . . and Malcolm Tucker. The Spin Doctor Who . . .

O f all the headlines that accompanied actor Peter Capaldi's ascension to the role of the world's favorite time and space traveler, *Doctor Who*, few were louder than those that referenced the role for which he was most recently renowned, that of Malcolm Tucker in the political Britcom *The Thick of It*.

The foul-mouthed Malcolm Tucker. The super-sweary, ultra-aggressive and all-round unlikable Malcolm Tucker. What sort of role model, querulous journalists asked, would he be for a nation of kiddies, drawn to the show by their love of the Doctor?

Well . . . a rude one.

No less than religion, comedy and politics have always made querulous room-mates. Not because politics itself does not offer a thick seam of comic gold, to be mined by anyone with half an eye for the theater of the absolutely absurd; nor because it must be astonishingly difficult for any single writing team to ever capture the sheer ridiculousness of a week in modern politicking.

It's difficult because, in the case of the BBC, do you really want to piss off the people who ultimately control the purse strings—while the BBC is regarded as an independent operator, it remains beholden on the government to set both its state funding and the cost of the TV license that every viewer must purchase? Or, if you're not the BBC, those whose special interest lobbyists represent some of the most powerful potential advertisers?

Not that that has in any way halted, gagged or even swayed political commentary from being delivered. The raft of radical satire shows that gave the early sixties such a contemporary edge were the standard-bearers, of course, mocking government and opposition parties alike for the foibles and failings with which they purported to run the country. And the years since then had suffered no shortage of similar comment, whether it be Alf Garnett raging against the dying of the right or *Spitting Image* reducing the rich and powerful to ugly rubber puppets, and allowing us to pull their strings for once.

As it turned out (returning to Peter Capaldi and Doctor Who), there was no mass outbreak of uncontrolled swearing among the youth of the UK, or anyplace else. No more than there usually is, anyway. Nor did Capaldi transform the consul room of the Doctor's TARDIS into a graffiti-strewn den of Anglo-Saxon crudities. But still *The Thick of It* stands as a remarkable program, if only because—for the third time in a generation—it showed us politics as we like to believe they are. And you can construe that observation in whichever manner you choose.

Yes Minister, No Minister, Three Bands Full, Minister

Yes Minister dawned on UK television at a very propitious time for political satire. After a decade of increasing industrial, cultural, racial and political unrest, during which time three separate prime ministers had struggled to put the "Great" back into Great Britain, 1979 saw the country elect its first-ever female leader, Margaret Thatcher, on a platform that promised a lot of things (not all of them welcome), but all designed to stop the rot.

Even in opposition, and particularly throughout the election campaign itself, Thatcher revealed herself to be among the most divisive party leaders in British history—earlier in the decade, while serving as Secretary of State for Education and Science of Education, it was Thatcher who ended the long-standing policy of providing free milk to Britain's junior school children every morning; only a third of a pint per pupil, in tiny little bottles, but it was one of the highlights of the day. Now children as young as seven were rejoicing in condemning "Mrs. Thatcher, the Milk Snatcher," and it was a name that was to stick.

One of many names that would stick. At the Comic Strip comedy club in London, a night out wouldn't be a night out without at least a handful of laughs at this purportedly ghastly woman's expense, and while not all of her government's policies and plans came to fruition, still it was no coincidence that, when she died in 2013, the *Wizard of Oz* favorite "Ding Dong, the Witch Is Dead" became a massive UK hit.

Launched in 1980, and ultimately running until 1988, *Yes Minister* (which segued effortlessly into *Yes Prime Minister*) did not address the reign of Thatcher in any way. Indeed, it was careful to avoid any direct political affiliations whatsoever. Not one of Britain's leading political parties was mentioned by name, with the heart of both shows set not around the personalities of politics (although they were certainly a part of it), but on the behind-the-scenes clashes between government ministers, attempting to do what they had promised (or threatened) the electorate would be done, and the civil servants who seemed equally dead set on stopping them.

That was a battle that every incumbent government had faced; Britain's Civil Service, after all, was the apparatus that truly ran the country—an unelected bureaucracy whose stated purpose was to assist the government in keeping the machinery of state in operation, but which, over the centuries, had also formulated their own methods of doing so. Meaning, they would bend over backwards to appear obliging, helpful and, most of all, respectful to the ministers to whom they were attached, but if they didn't want to do what needed to be done, then they wouldn't.

Or, as it is more succinctly put in the show, "While it has been government policy to regard policy as a responsibility of Ministers and administration as a responsibility of Officials, the questions of administrative policy can cause confusion between the policy of administration and the administration of policy, especially when responsibility for the administration of the policy of administration conflicts, or overlaps with, responsibility for the policy of the administration of policy."

Jim Hacker (Paul Eddington, fresh from *The Good Life*) is the newly appointed Minister of Administrative Affairs (a fictional department, but a very believable one); a generally good-natured man who truly believes that his government's policies are exactly what the country needs.

Sir Humphrey Appleby (Nigel Hawthorne), on the other hand, is the obsequious, conniving and devious Permanent Secretary to that same department; and Bernard Woolley (Derek Fowlds) is the Principal Private Secretary whose basic niceness sees him try to serve two masters. Across a total of thirty-eight episodes, this trio rose from simply overseeing one small part of the government to running the entire country.

And Mrs. Thatcher, at least disproving the theory that she was utterly devoid of all human emotion, loved it. As did a lot of other people. In the aforementioned Britain's Best Sitcom poll in 2004, *Yes Minister/Prime Minister* was voted sixth.

The workings of British government revealed

The Lady's Not for Spurning

The behind-the-scenes verisimilitude of the show was applauded by those who are, presumably, in the know; and so did the essential truth that Sir Humphrey utters very early on into Hacker's career in government, that Ministers are effectively mayfly, flitting into the office for a finite period of time and then being swept out again the moment the country, or their own party, tires of them—forty years have passed since Thatcher's time as Secretary of State for Education and Science, for example, since when (at the time of writing), no less than nineteen fresh faces have passed through that office, an average of little more than one every two years.

But Permanent Secretaries are, indeed, permanent, and they have a lot more important things to do than bow and scrape to the whims of a succession of passing yes-men. A status quo was arrived at long, long ago, and their only concern is to ensure it remains in place.

As Sir Humphrey puts it, "I have served eleven governments in the past thirty years. If I'd believed in all their policies, I'd have been passionately committed to keeping out of the Common Market, and passionately committed to joining it. I'd have been utterly convinced of the rightness of nationalising steel and of denationalising it and renationalising it. Capital punishment? I'd have been a fervent retentionist and an ardent abolitionist. I'd have been a Keynesian and a Friedmanite, a grammar school preserver and destroyer, a nationalisation freak and a privatisation maniac, but above all, I would have been a stark-staring raving schizophrenic!"

We learn, very early on, the true machinations of diplomacy, on this occasion following a hostile speech by a visiting head of state.

Sir Humphrey: "Well, Minister, in practical terms we have the usual six options:
>   One: do nothing.
>   Two: issue a statement deploring the speech.
>   Three: lodge an official protest.
>   Four: cut off aid.
>   Five: break off diplomatic relations.
>   And six: declare war."

Hacker: "Which should be it?"

Sir Humphrey: "Well:
>   If we do nothing, that means we implicitly agree with the speech.
>   If we issue a statement, we'll just look foolish.

If we lodge a protest, it'll be ignored.

We can't cut off aid, because we don't give them any.

If we break off diplomatic relations, then we can't negotiate the oil rig contracts.

And if we declare war, it might just look as though we were over-reacting!"

Or, on what is still, even following the Brexit vote in 2016, the thorny subject of Britain's membership of the European Union:

Sir Humphrey: "We 'had' to break the whole thing up, so we had to get inside. We tried to break it up from the outside, but that wouldn't work. Now that we're inside, we can make a complete pig's breakfast of the whole thing: set the Germans against the French, the French against the Italians, the Italians against the Dutch. The Foreign Office is terribly pleased; it's just like old times."

Hacker: "But surely we're all committed to the European ideal?"

Sir Humphrey: "Really, Minister."

Hacker: "If not, why are we pushing for an increase in the membership?"

Sir Humphrey: "Well, for the same reason. It's just like the United Nations, in fact; the more members it has, the more arguments it can stir up, the more futile and impotent it becomes."

Hacker: "What appalling cynicism."

Sir Humphrey: "Yes . . . We call it diplomacy, Minister."

Sir Humphrey will not have it all his own way, of course. He, too, has pet projects and designs that he has to get past Jim Hacker. The ingenuity with which the two men face off was one of *Yes Minister*'s key assets; that, and the public's realization that, no matter where one turns in society, one will always encounter an Odd Couple in the end. It is for the viewer to then decide which side to support, the conscientious and idealistic Hacker, or the cynical, underhand Sir Humphrey.

It was, in many ways, a poisoned chalice. The Thatcher years marked the first age during which an incumbent British government appeared wholeheartedly to side with big business against the unions and the people, privatizing essential services that had hitherto been held in the national interest (gas, electricity, the railroad and so forth); igniting the piecemeal dismantlement of the National Health Service; scrapping entire industries that no longer turned vast profits, but which provided employment for thousands of workers (mining, shipbuilding, etc.); transforming what had once been an ailing but sustainable manufacturing base into little more than a glorified service economy.

How hard it was, under such circumstances, to sympathize with any man who represented "modern" government, but how easy it became to understand that what we, the people, see as government policy is rarely the single-minded dictate of one power-crazed (at that time) harridan, but the consequence of any amount of debate, negotiation and compromise, not only among the ruling party but across the entire political spectrum—not just the party that "other people" voted for, but the party that we supported as well. And men like Jim Hacker, for all their smart suits and ties, upper-crust accents and slavish adherence to the party line, were often just as bemused by events as the rest of us.

And who was responsible for that bemusement? Men like Sir Humphrey.

Sir Humphrey: "Bernard, what is the purpose of our defence policy?"

Bernard: "To defend Britain."

Sir Humphrey: "No, Bernard. It is to make people believe Britain is defended."

Bernard: "The Russians?"

Sir Humphrey: "Not the Russians, the British! The Russians know it's not."

The power of language becomes clear to us; not the Orwellian double-think with which an obfuscating politician will pretend to answer all our questions while not actually answering any whatsoever, but just little words that we all understand, and now we understand them a bit better. Like the way Sir Humphrey will congratulate the minister on a policy, by telling him that it's "courageous." Meaning "brave"; meaning "rather you than me"; meaning "shall I have somebody clean out your desk this afternoon? Or would you rather do it when you come in to say goodbye?"

Or there was the time Hacker, still new to the office, made a lighthearted quip, then apologized because it was so lazy.

Hacker: "I suppose they all say that, do they?"

Sir Humphrey: "Certainly not, Minister. Not quite all . . ."

Even terms of endearment become brutally barbed weaponry. The prime minister's own political advisor is the extraordinarily capable and deeply suspicious Dorothy Wainwright (Deborah Norton). It is only natural that Sir Humphrey, ever the old world charmer, should refer to her affectionately as "dear lady." It is only more natural that he should be well aware that such a phrase drives her to distraction every time he utters it.

Hacker is not, initially, alone in his battles with his smarmy advisor. In fact, he has an advisor of his own, the razor-sharp but unfortunately named Frank Weisel . . . unfortunate, because no matter how many times he explains that the name is correctly pronounced "Wise-ell," both Sir Humphrey and Bernard insist on calling him "Weasel." Which is, to be truthful, fairly accurate.

Weisel is not, however, around for long. Another feature of the early 1980s was the creation of what the (real-life) government termed quasi-autonomous non-governmental organizations, swiftly abbreviated to "quangos" and even more swiftly becoming derogatory shorthand for any example of government waste, piling further layers of useless bureaucracy onto an already creaking edifice of unnecessary paper-pushers. Friend Weisel is placed in charge of a new quango, set up to investigate the efficiency of . . . other quangos. That alone ranks among *Yes Minister*'s finest, driest, moments of wit.

Because it *was* a very dry show, assuming an awareness and intelligence on the part of its audience that the average eighties sitcom simply eschewed altogether, and then rewarding viewers with a humor that was rarely less than deft. No playing a situation for laughs; no absurd coincidences; no vicars walking up the path just as the lady of the house's knickers get snagged and torn off by the clothes horse. Just sharp scripting, wry badinage and sometimes daring observation. Daring, but not dangerous. Such as the occasion when Hacker, Bernard and Sir Humphrey are discussing the national press—and not disguising their targets by inventing new names for the papers.

Hacker: "Don't tell me about the press. I know exactly who reads the papers: the *Daily Mirror* is read by people who think they run the country; *The Guardian* is read by people who think they ought to run the country; *The Times* is read by people who actually do run the country; the *Daily Mail* is read by the wives of the people who run the country; the *Financial Times* is read by people who own the country; the [Communist] *Morning Star* is read by people who think the country ought

to be run by another country; and the *Daily Telegraph* is read by people who think it [already] is."

Sir Humphrey: "Prime Minister, what about the people who read *The Sun?*"

Bernard: "*Sun* readers don't care who runs the country, as long as she's got big tits."

The Sun, at that time (and for years before and after, too) was the home of the daily, topless, Page Three Girl, many of whom did indeed have big tits.

That was, however, a rare descent into ribaldry, and one that did not affect the show's standing even among the country's most ferocious television critics—Alf Garnett's old adversary Mary Whitehouse, for example. In January 1984, her National Viewers' and Listeners' Association, a watchdog body dedicated to rooting out smut and filth from British screens (and forerunners of the modern Mediawatch-UK) honored *Yes Minister* with an award for its adherence to decent family values. Even more remarkably at the ensuing awards ceremony, Paul Eddington and Nigel Hawthorne appeared in a short sketch that costarred and, according to some sources, was written by their other greatest fan, Margaret Thatcher.

Neither actor was, apparently, thrilled at the prospect of appearing onstage with the Iron Lady; neither rated the sketch, either. Nevertheless, Jonathan Lynn (who cowrote the series with Antony Jay) warmly thanked Mrs. Thatcher "for taking her rightful place in the field of situation comedy." The object of his gratitude, apparently, failed to even crack a smile.

The enduring popularity of *Yes Minister* is perhaps best signified both by its standings in the opinion polls and by the success of a 2013 revival on the UK satellite channel Gold. Starring David Haig as Jim Hacker and Henry Goodman as Sir Humphrey, both reviving parts they had played in a twenty-first-century stage production of the show, it lasted just one season. But, unusually for a TV remake, it was a good season.

A Proper B'Stard

Yes Prime Minister was still under way when a second politician burst onto the screen. But whereas the older show remained staunchly apolitical, at least so far as its affiliations were concerned, *The New Statesman* was wholly committed to one particular impression of the right wing of British politics. Why else would its hero have been named Alan Beresford B'Stard?

Devised by and starring Rik Mayall, written by Laurence Marks and Maurice Gran, and destined for a four-season life span, *The New Statesman* was everything that *Yes Prime Minister* was not. Crude, violent, obnoxious and utterly sociopathic, B'Stard was Member of Parliament for the constituency of Haltemprice—a fictional region that nevertheless shared its name with what had, until 1983, been a real constituency in Yorkshire (it was later restored to the political map, but only once *The New Statesman* had ended its run).

Still in his early thirties, B'Stard was openly based on the basest public perception of the classic eighties Thatcherite, motivated solely by greed and personal profit; callous, selfish and thoroughly dishonest. Rotten to the core. That many of his characteristics were based on, again, the basest public perception of various members of the ruling Conservative Party may or may not be an accurate addendum to that description, but the fact remains. If you had asked the average politically disaffected viewer to name a "typical" Conservative MP, B'Stard's name would not have been far from their lips.

Except B'Stard was actually worse than any of his real-life counterparts. Racist, sexist, homophobic, he not only hated the poor and loathed the foreign, he acknowledged the fact. (His real-life counterparts were at least vaguely circumspect in that department). Discussing Britain's membership of the European Union, and outlining his opposition to it, he was succinctness itself.

"Why should we, the country that produced Shakespeare, Christopher Wren, and those are just the people on our banknotes for Christ's sake, cower down to the countries that produced Hitler, Napoleon, the Mafia, and the . . . the Smurfs?"

So that's another difference between *Yes Minister* and *The New Statesman*, then. While Jim Hacker was motivated by his basic altruism, B'Stard acted only in the service of avarice and greed. And, while *Yes Minister* steadfastly avoided reference to any real-life political entities or characters whatsoever, *The New Statesman* gloried in them. Party leaders Margaret Thatcher and Labour's Neil Kinnock were both referenced, while Thatcher herself was depicted, too . . . brilliantly, by male impersonator Steve Nallon. Not even members of her cabinet, nor Kinnock's shadow cabinet, were safe.

B'Stard: "You're having an affair with him, aren't you?"

Sarah: "Of course I'm not, Alan. I mean he's fat and flabby, and, uh, he's got horrible greasy hair!"

B'Stard: "Didn't stop you with Nigel Lawson, did it?"

Accusations, however, that the show was somehow anti-Thatcher's government could easily be defused, however. No party was safe from the scathing humor of *The New Statesman*; all parties were painted in as shocking a light as was possible. Corruption, sleaze, spin, dirt, every negative term that has ever been flung at politics was daubed liberally across the entire landscape. Quite frankly, it was brilliant. But it was also faintly discomfiting.

What if this was what our politicians are really like?

Mayall, of course, was absolutely believable in the role; like so many of the great comics discussed in this book, from Tony Hancock to Rowan Atkinson (and beyond), he adopted a persona early in his career and spent the remainder of his life refining it.

True, it was not at all a likable one; like Atkinson's Blackadder, and Mayall's own role in *The Young Ones*, Alan B'Stard was the ultimate obnoxious antihero, rising to glory not through personal accomplishment, charm or demeanor, but because he was better at kicking other people out of his way. He even had his own Baldrick (or, perhaps, Percy) to help him do the dirtiest jobs, the vaguely aristocratic (and intensely stupid) Piers Fletcher-Dervish (Michael Troughton), a modern equivalent, if you will, of *Monty Python*'s Upper Class Twit of the Year.

To this already loathsome team can be added B'Stard's wife Sarah (Marsha Fitzalan), a bisexual nymphomaniac who is just as devious as her husband, and married him purely for his money. Whereas he married her because her father, Roland Gidleigh-Park (Charles Gray), is head of the local Conservative Party, and was responsible for B'Stard entering politics in the first place.

Yes Minister strove for realism; *The New Statesman* took the opposite tack altogether. Whereas the average politician could probably serve a lifetime with no more than one or two low-key scandals to rock their standing, B'Stard thrived on the things, and probably spent more time denying, defusing or otherwise dismissing the barrage of complaints about his behavior than he did serving the needs of the people who elected him. The fact that he triumphed against every aspect of adversity simply allowed us, the viewers, to hate him even more.

Nobody watching *The New Statesman* doubted that B'Stard was at least as dreadful as his media and political opponents painted him. What intrigued and amused were the lengths to which he would go to ensure that he was never brought to justice.

Some of the plots are, with the benefit of hindsight, shocking, or perhaps shockingly prescient. Midway through the 2010s, the British media became transfixed by police investigations into reports that a child abuse ring not only thrived in Westminster (the heart of British government) through the 1980s, but that Mrs. Thatcher was instrumental in suppressing any kind of investigation into it.

It was not exactly hot news—even at the time, rumor whisperingly insisted that there might be something rotten in the state apparatus; rumor that received its first public airing through the *New Statesman*. In the season-two episode "A Wapping Conspiracy," B'Stard is made the parliamentary patron of the newly formed Young Ladies' Recreational Association and is promptly photographed taking part in an orgy with several minors and a border collie.

As it happened, the photographs turn out to be fakes, and the story—which was published in *The Times* newspaper—a web of lies. B'Stard sues and wins a half-million-pound settlement (much to Sarah's delight, naturally), at which point the reporter who broke the story in the first place finally confesses that he and B'Stard invented the tale together, with the express intention of suing the paper. Which was probably true. But B'Stard is nothing if not an utter B'Stard. He denies the allegation, and announces he will now be suing the reporter for defamation of character.

On another occasion, in the 1990 special "Who Shot Alan B'Stard," he fakes his own shooting by a Basque mercenary, wholly to swing an upcoming vote on the restoration of capital punishment—which in turn will allow his father-in-law, the newly appointed Minister for Law and Order, to make a killing collecting kickbacks from the various contracts that will now need to be issued (someone has to build the gallows, make the rope, construct the trapdoors, etc.), while B'Stard himself will collect a million-pound payout from a bet he laid a few months earlier, when the odds on hanging being brought back were reckoned at 100-to-1.

So far, so good. But, tipped off by Sarah, talk show host Kerry Grout sets about unmasking the deception, setting off a chain of events that leads to Grout's own death (accidentally shot by the bumbling Piers) and B'Stard's arrest on a charge of murder.

He is found guilty and sentenced to hang, the first victim of the very same law that he schemed so hard to have passed. And before a live television audience (because, of course, who would not want to watch the death of such a B'Stard?), he is led to the gallows that one of his own companies had designed and built.

You Cannot Keep a Good B'Stard Down

A gallows that promptly collapses under its victim's weight. Faulty workmanship? Probably. In fact, definitely. Constructed by a subcontractor who was just as crooked as B'Stard himself, it was made of balsa wood, disguised to look like mahogany. But according to the law of the land, B'Stard's life was saved by an Act of God. He is freed, and receives a full pardon.

His political career does not recover, however, and *The New Statesman*'s third season saw B'Stard seemingly attempt to switch allegiance, to the left-wing Labour Party. Of course, it was all a ploy, designed to restore him to the ranks of his chosen party, but fate has not yet finished with him.

By the end of the season, he is again charged with murder, but this time in the Soviet Union, where he is working with a disaffected general to reawaken the Cold War. And there will be no last-minute reprieve, not even when Sarah arrives clutching a set of release papers. They are for Piers. B'Stard will be left to rot in the gulag, and when he tearfully asks his wife why she's done it, her answer comes straight out of his own lexicon: "Because I can."

That could have been the end of B'Stard. But it wasn't. One year later in television terms, but after three years in the icy hell of a Russian jail, B'Stard is released, to discover he is a forgotten man. More than that, he's a dead man. Politics have moved on without him—a new prime minister now runs the UK, John Major; a new MP now sits in Haltemprice; and Sarah has had him officially declared dead and gone off to live with a Danish nobleman, surrounded by all B'Stard's money.

He has no intention of remaining a corpse, however. Further plotting, fresh machinations, and soon Alan B'Stard MP is Alan B'Stard MEP—a member of the European Parliament for the German constituency of Obersaxony, and having all his foreign-language pornography rendered into English by the European Parliament's translation department. And it all ends with B'Stard returning home and engineering the greatest coup of his career, one that sees Britain and France on the brink of war, a coalition government ruling the country, the newly appointed prime minister in jail, and B'Stard declaring himself Lord Protector—a title unused in Britain since the days of the English Civil War, three centuries before, when the dictatorial Oliver Cromwell declared himself to be ruler of the land.

Wow.

The New Statesman finished its four-season run in December 1992, but Alan B'Stard was not yet finished with British politics. A 1994 special, while wrecking the show's continuity by completely ignoring the series finale, saw him back in t he Houses of Parliament, and back in the headlines again, and in 2006, the stage show "The Blair B'Stard Project" revealed that it was B'Stard, and not Tony Blair, who realigned the old socialist Labour party as the distinctly not-socialist New Labour party.

Ultimately, it would take Mayall's death, at the age of fity-six, on June 9, 2014, to finally ring the curtain down on one of the true legends of British political life. But one cannot escape the awful, sinking feeling that, though the man is gone, his spirit lives on. And the next time you switch on the television news and watch the latest slimeball politician wriggling his way out of a scandal that there's no way he didn't know was taking place, you will know that though the name may be different, at heart the man remains a B'Stard.

As Useless as a Marzipan Dildo

And so to Malcolm Tucker. And so to *The Thick of It*, a show not only conceived as a modern successor to *Yes Minister*, but inspired by the earlier program's success in the 2004 Best Sitcom poll.

That creator Armando Iannucci succeeded in both these aims was itself a remarkable triumph—rightly or wrongly, the viewing public has long regarded even the most amply proportioned revivals of favorite old television shows with considerably less enthusiasm than it treats, for example, reunions of favorite old bands, as though a bunch of warmed-up old jokes are somehow less funny than a bunch of warmed-up old musicians.

Where *The Thick of It* succeeded, however, was not only in the fact that the jokes were neither old nor warmed up. It was in illustrating just how politics, and the public perception of the people who control them, has changed. Or, as Tucker would put it when asked to refrain from using bad language by a decorous, old world civil servant, "I'm terribly sorry, you won't hear any more swearing from us, you massive gay shite. Fuck off."

No less than *That Was the Week That Was* realigning the hitherto deeply ingrained respect that people once had for their purported lords and masters; or *Yes Minister* lifting the lid off the machinations that lay behind them (but not, perhaps, *The New Statesman* revealing them all to be a bunch of crooks), *The Thick of It* focused on the one aspect of the modern game that most enraged and confounded people . . . the notion of "spin" (which

Peter Capaldi as the super-sweary Malcolm Tucker in *The Thick of It.*   *Photofest*

itself was unheard of before *Yes Minister* came along) . . . and then ran with it. Everything that followed simply illustrated the depths to which modern politics's respect for the electorate has sunk.

As with its predecessor, *The Thick of It* is set within a fictional but nevertheless believable government body, the Department of Social Affairs and Citizenship (DoSAC), a so-called super department that oversaw the operations of a number of other, smaller concerns.

The real-life government of the day had recently coined the term "joined-up politics," within which, to coin an old phrase, the left hand would finally have some awareness of what the right hand was doing. Of course it wouldn't work out like that, largely because so much effort and energy is put into thinking up such terms that nobody actually has the wherewithal to properly implement them. (Or, at least, we hope that's the reason. The notion that we are really being governed by sound bite and catchy phrase alone is too cynical to even entertain.)

Either way, Hugh Abbot (Chris Langham) is the minister charged with ensuring the smooth running of the department; Glen Cullen (James Smith) and Ollie Reeder (Chris Addison) are, respectively, senior and junior advisers; and media strategist Malcolm Tucker is the excoriating fireball of such relentless, abusive magnificence that the show actually hired a specialist swearing consultant, Ian Martin, to ensure that Tucker's outbursts were as inflammatory as they ought to be.

Appointed by the prime minister to ensure that the department adhered strictly to government policy, Tucker's role is therefore the absolute opposite to that of *Yes Minister*'s Sir Humphrey. But his effect on the daily routine of the department is just as telling.

For example, one of his charges is in trouble with the media, and it's Malcolm's job to shepherd her through the upcoming public apology.

> "Seeing as you're not used to this, I'll go through it for you, okay? What happens at a press conference is this. A bunch of press people are gonna appear, they've got things called cameras and microphones and mobile phones and hangovers and bad breath. Then you are gonna walk out and you're gonna read from what we call a 'prepared statement.'
>
> "In that, you will say 'I'm really fucking sorry for sounding like a hairy-arsed docker after twelve pints. I promise that I will never call an 8-year-old girl a cunt again. Can we now just draw a line over this, and fucking move on. Thank you.' Everybody goes home and then we wait and we see what happens. The best case is you get to keep your job, although you will forever be known as The Sweary Woman of Whitehall."

Another time, there are fears that a party member is about to break rank and reveal some information the government would prefer to keep to itself. So Malcolm has a quiet talk with him, in which he reveals, if so much as a word is breathed out of place, "I'll personally fucking eviscerate you, right? I mean, I don't have your education, I don't know what that means. But I'll start by ripping your cock off and I'll busk it from there. Okay?"

An MP's decision to send her children to private school, Tucker accuses, is the public equivalent of announcing that state schools are "knife-addled rape sheds"; when she uses her expense account to buy an extravagant office chair, he reminds her that the public would prefer MPs "lived in a fucking cave." And when she accidentally lets slip a piece of news to a journalist, he is not happy in the slightest.

"Fuck's sake! Jesus Christ! Well, now we've got another fuckin' adjective to add to fuckin' 'smug' and 'glum', haven't we? Fuckin' 'retarded'! Jesus Christ do you not think it would be germane to check who you're talking to?! It's a fuckin' newspaper office! It's not a fuckin' sanatorium for the fuckin' deaf, is it?! Are you so dense?! Am I gonna have to run around slapping badges on people with a big tick on some and a big cross on others, so you know when to shut your gob and when to open it?! Jesus Christ! Oh, but that'd probably confuse you as well, won't it?! That'd be too confusing, you'd see the cross and go 'oh, fuck, x marks the spot! I'd better tell this little person about the Prime Minister's fucking catastrophic erectile dysfunction!' Oh, but not to worry, not to worry. You've sent fuckin' Ollie [adviser Ollie Reeder] over there to deal with it. Fuckin' Ollie! He's a fuckin', he's a fuckin' knitted scarf, that twat! He's a fuckin' balaclava!"

Not that Tucker is the department's sole verbal vandal. Everybody has their moment in the vernacular sun. For instance, this commentary on youth offenders, delivered by MP Peter Mannion (Roger Allam): "I get people stopping me in the street and saying 'Are you still for locking up yobbos?' and I say 'Yeah, of course we are!' and then I think 'Are we?' because maybe I missed a memo. . . . Maybe I should understand yobbos, or not even call them yobbos. Call them young men with issues around stabbing."

Once again, there were no direct references to actual political parties, although sharp-eyed writing and a talent for mirroring current events left no room to doubt that the show was more or less set in the here and now—a notion that was confirmed in season four, in 2012, with the UK depicted as being led by a coalition government (as had been the case in the real world since 2010).

No matter. None of the parties are seen as being any better, in terms of health and efficiency, than any other, but all are instantly recognizable. There's one that is hideously riven by infighting and factions; another torn apart by its need to update its image and appeal to those voters who were not hidebound, gout-ridden old soldiers living out their less-than-golden years in southern English retirement homes; and a third an ineffective minority that tries to hold the middle ground between the pair and was thus effectively shifting its stance every couple of years, as it tried to keep up with the others' constantly contradictory positions on any issue that appeared to matter to the electorate (meaning, it was on the front page of one of the daily newspapers.)

There was the same revolving door of former public schoolboys passing quickly through government, en route to a big fat payday in the private sector; the same awarding of honors and knighthoods to the businessmen who made the biggest donations to party coffers; the same vainglorious orgy of snouts-to-the-trough of which each successive government accuses its predecessor.

All of that said, or implied, little of the action in the show relates to actual policies or governance. It is personal relations and, more importantly, clashes that dominate the agenda, and across twenty-one (untitled) episodes (four seasons) and three specials, we are privy not to the greatest affairs of state, but to the petty, self-aggrandizing and, most of all, downright nasty pressures by which government is run.

The urge to satisfy this lobbyist while pleasing that donor. The need to spin events one way for the media and another for the stock exchange. The ability to wear at least three different faces every day, because you never know who you will meet. And it was Malcolm Tucker's job to ensure that was done, by fair means and foul language.

Erring on the side of the latter, he usually succeeded.

Mocking the Media

Dropping Donkeys Absolutely Fabulously

According to the social hierarchy of pre-Revolutionary French politics, the First Estate was the clergy; the Second Estate was the nobility; and the Third Estate was the common folk. Us lot. Who eventually created, and took control of, the Fourth Estate, an independent press and media, through which we could comment and report on the other three.

It's a dream that took a long time to realize. For many years, even after the introduction of publishing and newspapers, the Fourth Estate remained in the hands of people who either operated within or were supportive of the first two (with politics eventually supplanting the nobility).

The popularity of privately produced chapbooks and pamphlets eroded the monopoly to an extent, but it would be the nineteenth and even the twentieth century before what would once have been called "seditious" literature was widely available to the public, and that only in the face of constant attempts to repress it. There's a reason, after all, why governments tend to prefer the status quo. Because they *are* the status quo.

Television and movies both followed in these general footsteps, adhering to the demands of various regulatory bodies, for to do otherwise would court swift and bitter sanction. Arguably, at least in the UK, it would be the early 1960s before the First and Second Estates finally acknowledged that the Third Estate was in its rights to at least smirk at, and—if this truly were a democracy—poke fun at them and question their actions. And that the Fourth Estate was their chosen platform.

The satire boom starts here.

And ended . . . somewhere. Arguably, the mainstream news-gathering element of the Fourth Estate is now deeper into the pockets and thrall of sundry establishment masters than at any time since World War II (when at least the powers that be had good reason to stop people from shooting their mouths off); while the entertainment industry lives in such constant fear of offending sundry superpowerful special interest groups that there are now almost as many banned words and sentiments as there are ones that can actually be spoken.

Wouldn't *that* be an excellent topic to parody?

Tomorrow's Litterbox Liner

Newsroom shows, whether print or media, have long been a staple of broadcasting, although the news that they gather, and the manner in which they do so, tends toward the sensationalized.

The excellent Canadian drama *E.N.G.* ran for five years from the end of the eighties, but was concerned more with the lives and loves of its characters than any commentary on news events themselves.

More recently, HBO's *The Newsroom* and the BBC's *The Hour* offered more pertinent commentaries on the behind-the-scenes battles that await any attempt to break a halfway sensitive news item, although *The Hour* was strictly historical (albeit set in an era, the late 1950s, that is certainly germane to the birth of TV satire), and *The Newsroom* feels very strictly balanced.

As, one would say, it ought to be. When a nation's electorate is split fifty-fifty (as so many countries' seem to be these days), why outrage half your potential audience by telling them that their political opinions are uninformed and moronic?

However, it is not only media tactics that can, and should, come under scrutiny. Ownership, bias, sponsorship, policy, all of these things impact on the art of news reportage; and they both merit inspection and can cause concern. Which was the primary target of one of the late 1980s' most enjoyable Britcoms, *Hot Metal*.

It was a period of considerable turmoil in the British press. News International, the company launched by press baron Rupert Murdoch, and publisher of the country's best-read paper, *The Sun* (home of the aforementioned big tits), was engaged in removing its titles from the traditional home of the British press on Fleet Street, to new premises on the freshly redeveloped Isle of Dogs, in east London. In real terms, it made no difference—who cares where a paper is published, so long as it *is* published? But symbolically it marked a major break with tradition—and the first, a growing band of Cassandras predicted, of many more to come.

Robert Maxwell, publisher of *The Sun*'s biggest rival, the *Daily Mirror*, was an avaricious robber baron engaged in buying up companies . . . any companies; newspapers, publishing houses, soccer teams . . . and running them into the ground, apparently for the fun of it (it would be a little longer before his death revealed the full extent of Maxwell's corruption and criminal tendencies—essentially he ate his employees' pension plans for breakfast).

Roland "Tiny" Rowlands, the poetically named owner of *The Observer*, was a businessman with no media experience, but he had been in the Hitler Youth, and was apparently good friends with Libyan President Gaddafi; and David Sullivan was widely condemned as a former pornographer, albeit one who launched the career of actress Mary Millington through his erotic magazines and movies, and probably did more to liberate his chosen subject from the gutter than any number of more "respectable" connoisseurs. He now owned the *Daily Sport*, and actually made a really good job of it, although his opponents would scarcely have agreed with that.

The point is not that all of these men (including Murdoch, despite him being the son of an Australian news magnate) were in some ways seen as the antithesis of the old-style newspaper man, with no feel or concern for the media's traditions. It was that they were not newspapermen to begin with. They were businessmen whose interests *included* newspapers, and who, in several cases, then used those papers to either promote their other interests or support the politicians who would follow their bidding.

Less a case of the tail wagging the dog, in other words, than of the tail eating the dog and then burying its bones with all the other skeletons in the cupboard: mobile phone records, bribes to law enforcement officers, media witch hunts, celebrity scandals, homosexual "outings," things like that.

This was the world that *Hot Metal* was concerned with, as a struggling (and fictional) daily newspaper, the *Daily Crucible*, is taken over by media hotdog Terence "Twiggy" Rathbone (Robert Hardy).

Hitherto renowned for its caution, steadfastness and journalistic integrity, the paper is now to be driven relentlessly downmarket. Its old-style editor, Harry Stringer (Geoffrey Palmer), is elevated to the powerless post of managing editor; in his stead come sensation specialist Russell Spam (also played by Hardy) and his gutter-press sidekick Greg Kettle (Richard Kane). Together, they will raise the *Daily Crucible* to depths previously unplumbed by man. The show documents the old school's battle for survival.

Sadly (because it really was funny), *Hot Metal* feels almost cripplingly dated today, and not only because *any* show whose historical background requires greater explanation than its plot is in trouble. It's just that we are so accustomed today to reading headline stories in which a reality TV star turns into a werewolf that it's hard to remember there was ever a time when that was *not* considered of front-page importance, and might even have been regarded as ever-so-slightly untrue.

So many of even our most respectable newspapers are more concerned with what they consider to be "entertainment" than anything like news, while so much of their content is now placed online that they are scarcely even newspapers any longer. *Hot Metal*, though it could never have known it, predicted that decline with chilling accuracy. Comical, but chilling.

Hold the Front Page

Where the newspapers fell, broadcasting tumbled.

It was the same story; local channels being devoured by media giants; businessmen tendering for up-for-sale franchises; the inexorable march of cable and satellite, themselves largely owned by the same voracious vampire squids that already owned the newspapers and had their hooks in the terrestrial channels, too. Serious news TV in the early 1990s already saw itself as an endangered species, and *Drop the Dead Donkey* was its last cry for help.

Again, Robert Maxwell and Rupert Murdoch were firmly positioned at the heart of the incoming terror—Murdoch was the founder, in 1990, of the satellite network BSkyB in the UK, and owner of 20th Century Fox and the old Metromedia in the US; Maxwell headed not only the ingloriously named Maxwell Cable TV and Maxwell Entertainment, but also 50 percent of MTV Europe, and sundry channels in Eastern Europe too.

Now, *Drop the Dead Donkey* arranged for us to meet a third media mogul, Roysten Merchant, a ruthless businessman who might have shared his initials with those two tycoons (it was no coincidence), but who had one thing that neither rival would ever get, a knighthood from the Queen (which also wasn't a coincidence).

He is also the new owner of GlobeLink News, a fictional television news company that, like the *Daily Crucible*, is about to see its hard-won reputation for honesty, impartiality and accuracy sacrificed to the trifold gods of sensationalism, profit and gossip.

The show's title says a lot. Although *Drop the Dead Donkey* is not, contrary to widespread opinion, a common phrase in the British news industry, still it is indicative of a certain kind of reportage.

Back in 1987, both *The Sun* and the *Daily Star* newspapers locked horns to see who could be first to rescue Blackie, a mistreated donkey that one of their readers (or reporters) had discovered in Spain. A British donkey, apparently.

A tremendous public furor was raised, a ruthless hue and cry, and ultimately the donkey was brought back home. As well it ought to have been.

But cute furry animals with big brown eyes have always sold newspapers, and many a cynic suggested that the only thing that could have sparked a bigger outrage (and thus sold even more papers) was if the donkey had been found dead. Sad but true.

(Sadder but truer: *The Sun* repeated the stunt in 2010, after discovering a donkey in Russia that had been sent parasailing by a marketing company, as an advertising gimmick. They brought that one home, too.)

Now imagine that, with this story already scheduled in an evening's news broadcast, an even bigger one broke on the horizon. One involving kittens, for example.

There could be just one solution, and the call would come down from the editor's desk. "Drop the dead donkey." And soon it *would* become a common phrase in the British news industry, because how did *The Sun* headline its 2010 animal rescue story in the first place? "Drop the Red Donkey."

Again, the focus (in the show, not the donkey saga) is on the struggle by the TV station's existing team to maintain the standards they were once so proud of. But it won't be easy. Led by editor George Dent (Jeff Rawle), GlobeLink's journalists find themselves forced to contend not with one Greg Kettle, but with three.

Gus Hedges (Robert Duncan) is Sir Royston's Chief Executive, and one of those smarmy little weasels who always appears to be telling folk precisely what they want to hear, but whose grasp of meaningless management-speak lays in sufficient get-out clauses that nothing is ever what it seems. Assuming you can even begin to decipher what he's saying in the first place.

The modern trend for business jargon was still in its relative infancy at the time, but already the show's writers had spotted its potential to become the Cockney Rhyming Slang of the information age, one meaningless term piled onto another for the sake of saying something very short and sweet in as complicated a manner as possible.

News anchor Sally Smedley (Victoria Wicks) was handpicked by Sir Roysten for her beauty, glamor and appeal to women's magazine picture editors, and that despite her appalling vapidity, absolute snobbery and the fact that most of her colleagues positively hate her.

And Damien Day (Stephen Tompkinson), already regarded as something of a black sheep in the GlobeLink family, on account of his ability to transform any disaster into a sideshow, is utterly adored by both Sir Roysten and Gus for his unerring ability to always find the most appealingly heartstring-tugging human angle in any story, no matter what that story might be.

Still, even they are appalled (and impressed) to learn that whenever Damien travels to an earthquake zone (for example), he always carries a child's teddy in his luggage. Just in case his report requires some additional pathos.

He has also been known to punch small children, so there's always a crying child in shot, and he once threw a hand grenade over a wall, to ensure a backdrop of suitable panic as he reported from a war zone.

At the time, a lot of viewers simply marveled at the wit of the writers who could create such a callous monster. Today, they are more likely to be astounded at how many real-life reporters appear to have learned from him.

Against these paragons of venal greed are ranged the champions of all a good news-gathering operation should stand for. Editor Dent is a sad and put-upon little man who is a martyr to his own hypochondria, and more or less about as effective as a cardboard raincoat; Alex Pates (Haydn Gwynne) is a cynical, determined professional who, as George's assistant editor, is usually the one to stand firm where he is nervously vacillating; Helen Cooper (Ingrid Lacey), who replaces Alex from the third season on, shares her commitment to real news gathering, and her impatience with George's insecurity; anchorman Henry Davenport (David Swift) learned his trade in the old days of gentleman newsreaders, and hates anything that reeks of modernity—Sir Royston included; deputy subeditor Dave Charnley (Neil Pearson) doesn't really land on either side, but is more likely to infuriate Gus than George (mainly because George has given up caring); and Joy Merryweather (Susannah Doyle) is the most efficient production assistant George has ever worked with, but is so grudgeful, resentful and downright surly that her very name feels like the most grotesque typo.

So five against three. It should be a walkover. But Sir Royston's supporters have Sir Royston's support, and so the studio is in a constant state of uproar as, say, one side battles to drop the dead donkey and replace it with a story that actually matters, and the other fights to keep it, because . . . well, because cute furry animals with big brown eyes boost ratings much more than another cut in interest rates.

As, it seems, did the show's premise. Deservedly popular across half a dozen seasons, *Drop the Dead Donkey* won kudos not only for its cynical portrayal of a real-life situation that was growing increasingly alarming, but also for its topicality.

Borrowing a trick from the satire shows of old (and from the manic puppets of *Spitting Image*), the show's scripts were generally completed just a week before broadcast, allowing the writers to insert references to any suitable current event. Some scenes would be inserted on the day of broadcast, while voice-over credits were taped at the very last minute, to allow the staff to discuss that same day's news.

Deliberately, the show ripped into the clichés that hallmark lazy news journalism. For almost twenty-five years, for example, it had been considered politic to refer to the then-ongoing sectarian warfare in Northern Ireland as "the troubles."

"What a bloody stupid phrase," snaps Henry. "What do they think two thousand people have died from? Stress?"

Even more entertaining was the show's response to the news that one of Sir Royston's real-life rival RMs, Robert Maxwell, had died, falling over the side of a yacht and drowning. Caution was suggested in the newsroom, because "we don't want to go overboard with the story."

Of course, it was not all about ideology. Interoffice relations were a major focus of the show, and the staff's private lives as well. We meet Alex's ex-husband, a slum landlord whose nose she happily breaks when he asks her to try and spike a story revealing the true extent of his corruption; and we cringe at the sight of George's daughter, who counters her father's weakness by running roughshod and riot over any sign of authority (and who seems to have a habit of burning down schools).

Dave will attempt to bed anything in a skirt, which includes most of his female coworkers; while Sally, who *does* resist his roguish demeanor, is not so impervious to the charms of what might euphemistically be termed "a bit of rough"—her favored lovers are dockers, navvies, lorry drivers, any man with a bit of brawn and a taste for posh totty. (Another euphemism—a well-brought-up young lady.)

Gus is lonely, sexless and terrified of going insane; Henry is an alcoholic, gambler and incorrigible womanizer; Helen is a single parent and a lesbian who lives in fear of her daughter discovering the latter; Damien is a thrill junkie; and so on. The lives and loves of the characters alone would have been the recipe for a gripping sitcom. The news angle simply adds further fat to the flames.

Despite the conflicts tearing it apart from within, GlobeLink survived five seasons intact, before the sixth concentrated on its closure, and the subsequent fates of its staff. Some will do well, some will do poorly, and

Damien will be proclaimed a god by a tribe he was filming in the Amazon, and who never allowed him to leave.

Observers of various real-life reporters will doubtless find several analogies for that.

A Crisp, Darling, a Crisp

The third great media expose of the early-mid 1990s was *Absolutely Fabulous*, the story of PR agent Edina "Eddie" Monsoon (Jennifer Saunders) and magazine editor Eurydice Colette Clytemnestra Dido Bathsheba Rabelais Patricia Cocteau "Patsy" Stone (Joanna Lumley) as they fight to remain relevant, cool and trendsetting in a world that has, frankly, grown younger than they.

As such, *Absolutely Fabulous* is less about the industry itself than it is about the ghastly spectacle of middle age creeping up on people who still believe they're in touch with upper echelons of the entertainment business, when all they really represent is the awful self-delusion that engulfs anyone who fails to accept there's a time when you just have to stop shopping for miniskirts, designer drugs and idiosyncratic sunglasses.

In their youth, these people took acid to make the world look weird. Now they take Prozac in the hope that they might look normal.

But five seasons, and several specials, of *Absolutely Fabulous* (loathsomely abbreviated to *AbFab*, probably by the same kind of people who once called *Coronation Street* "Corrie"), beginning in the UK in November 1992, established it among both the BBC and BBC America's top-rated comedies, and while its period ambience does often seem quaint today, still Saunders and Lumley represent one of television's most glorious double acts.

Neither woman is in great shape. Working to a mantra of "I want total sensory deprivation and back-up drugs," Eddie's taste for sex, pills and alcohol has long since left her more than mildly pickled, to a point of such helpless dissolution that her teenage daughter Saffron (Julia Sawalha) is forced to look after her, an onerous task that has transformed the girl into a bitter little beast (or a "little bitch troll from hell," as Patsy once put it) with very little patience left.

"Ooo, she's so cold, sweetie," Eddie says of the girl once. "I'll just bet she has her period in cubes."

Patsy, meanwhile retains (most of) her health, but persists in disporting herself in a manner that brings the phrase "rancid mutton dressed as newborn lamb" screaming into focus.

Absolutely Fabulous—Left to right: Jennifer Saunders, Julia Sawalha and Joanna Lumley.

Photofest

Not a typical vehicle for great comedy, then, and there are indeed moments when Eddie, in particular, can only merit groans of despair from any viewer who has come to care about her.

This is especially emphasized when one traces *Absolutely Fabulous* back to what was effectively the show's pilot, a short sketch during the third season of Saunders and Dawn French's *French & Saunders* show.

"Modern Mother and Daughter" features the same tragic relationship as Eddie and Saffron would suffer; indeed, the child (French) already bears that name, and has long since grown wearily accustomed to being the middle-aged mom of the house, while her parent, here named Adrianna (Saunders), is the flighty teenage fruitcake. (The character's eventual name, Edina Monsson, was derived from Saunders' husband, Adrian *Ed*mondson, and his nickname "Monsoon." The same combination also titled the Comic Strip movie *Eddie Monsoon: A Life?*, written by Edmondson in 1984.)

French would not appear in *Absolutely Fabulous* itself, beyond a single cameo appearance. Instead, Saunders turned to Lumley, a veteran British actress with credits and fame that dated back to the 1960s—not at all coincidentally the golden era that Eddie and Patsy spend their time rhapsodizing over.

Both Patsy and Eddie were considered raging beauties in their day and swiftly established themselves as successful career women too. Times, however, have changed, and if Eddie's self-destructive behavior is obvious to all, Patsy's is no less damaging, albeit less apparent.

By effectively keeping her friend in a state of permanent befuddlement (if not stupor), the commendably chain-smoking Patsy can continue to convince herself that they are still as young as she believes she feels, when every night was another party, every celebrity was a potential conquest and everything was absolutely fabulous.

It isn't, and that is largely what the show is about—codependency among the lead characters; desperate dependency between Eddie and Saffron (and, occasionally, her own mother, played by comedy veteran June Whitfield); and "depends if anything better comes along" between both women and a variety of potential opportunities.

Patsy: "I can get you a man."

Eddie: "Well, how?"

Patsy: "Pay."

Edina (Jennifer Saunders) and Patsy (Joanna Lumley) prepare for an absolutely fabulous night in the tiles.   *Photofest*

A vivid taste of the tone of the show can be gauged from this encounter, as Eddie tries to convince her daughter to move back home, after she heads off for college.

Saffie: "Mum, what is the problem? I have my life and you have yours. This is what you wanted."

Eddie: "I feel orphaned, you know."

Saffie: "What is the matter?"

Eddie: "Well, darling, you have just sort of abandoned me in this sort of wilderness of potential greatness and fabulousness, haven't you? All my walls have gone "flop," "flop" . . . I'm just like this kind of prisoner that's released . . . darling, that is walking out into the squinting sun. I mean, you've cast me adrift with no oars."

Saffie: "You have oars."

Eddie: "I haven't."

Saffie: "You have. You're just too lazy and fat to use them."

Of course, this tragic state of affairs only reinforces one of the traditional subtexts of a successful British sitcom—that the audience is at its happiest when it is encouraged to feel superior, morally, culturally or class-wise, to the characters on the screen. It isn't a hard and fast rule—more or less any comedy starring either Penelope Keith, Peter Bowles or Paul Eddington automatically has class woven into its very DNA.

But from *Hancock's Half Hour* to *Steptoe and Son*, from *Some Mothers Do 'Ave 'Em* to *Mr. Bean*, across the decks of *Red Dwarf* and into the bowels of *Blackadder*-ized history, the most popular characters tend to be the most wretched ones—by conventional standards, if not their own.

Absolutely Fabulous differed in that its nobodies had once been very much somebody. But if we really want to discuss lax moral values, a cavalier attitude toward promiscuity and, quite coincidentally, a return to the same golden age that Patsy and Eddie so desperately crave, then you should look no further than *Coupling*. The return, after too long, of the Great British Sex Comedy.

Everybody Behaving Badly

Friends with Benefits

A lot of people have lost faith in Steven Moffat. Once the golden boy of British television writing, his stewardship of the long-running, and awesomely popular, sci-fi series *Doctor Who* saw him transform it from a human drama dripping with wit, pathos and excitement, to a tangle of one-liners and failed, wannabe catchphrases, bellowed with increasing desperation by a stream of unfinished ciphers.

One hopes it's just a one-off. Because he once was very good.

In the UK, Moffat came to attention with the teen drama *Press Gang*; in the US, it was *Joking Apart*, a sitcom about his own messy divorce (!) that aired late night on mid-nineties PBS, and was initially prone to pass people by. And then came the episode when its hero was visited by a giant manifestation of his own penis. Giant as in about six feet tall.

Things like that do catch the eye.

The show is painful. Painfully funny, yes. But painfully painful as well. Mark (Robert Bathurst) and Becky (Fiona Gillies) have accepted that their relationship is over. But whereas Fiona, whose infidelity caused the breach in the first place, is effortlessly able to move on, Mark—a TV sitcom writer—is finding the transition harder.

He is also, unsurprisingly, bitter. On one occasion, Becky mentions that her new lover is a fan of Mark's latest television program. "Well, did he have to shag my wife?" Mark retorts. "Most people just write in!"

As with so much of Moffat's work, a great deal of the dialogue, Mark's parts in particular, is comprised of one-liners. On this occasion, however, it works; the character himself thinks in those terms, and Moffat later admitted that it was his own tendency to do that which helped bring about his own divorce.

Robert Bathurst mourns the loss of Fiona Gillies on the DVD of Steve Moffat's *Joking Apart*.

Becky, too, tires of it; she did not, after all, sign up to be Mark's "lawfully wedded straight man," and that is something else that Mark now finds he has to contend with. He has nobody to bounce his material off; no one to practice his jokes on. And his coping mechanism is as defective as his ability to have a normal conversation.

You want to sympathize with Mark, you really, really do. But sometimes, you want to punch him as well.

Two seasons of *Joking Apart*, aired some three years apart, did not grant the show the audience it deserved, at least in the UK. Moffat, however, worked on.

He wrote for Dawn French's *Murder Most Horrid*, and he marched toward the new century with *Chalk*—a late-nineties schoolroom comedy that tried a little too hard to be compared to *Fawlty Towers*, but was really just *Please Sir!* (John Alderton's late sixties schoolroom comedy) with added shouty bits.

But he bounced straight back with *Coupling*, commissioned by new wife, TV producer Sue Vertue, and from the outset it was obvious that this was no normal millennial laughfest.

The Girl with Two Breasts

If you've never watched *Coupling*, don't worry. Just imagine *Friends* with benefits. The very first joke in the very first episode is a pun about oral sex ("one swallow does not a girlfriend make"), and things go deliciously downhill from there.

Three seasons illustrated *Coupling* at its best—there was a fourth, but it is scarcely worth mentioning, the televisual equivalent of eating the last piece of cake on the plate, only to find it isn't actually a piece of cake. (Insert your own stomach-turning substitute here.)

According to Moffat, *Coupling* continued the autobiographical thread that bound *Joking Apart* together, but this time he focused on a happier sequence of events—his initial meetings with his wife-to-be, Vertue, and the manifold little quirks that manifest around the first months of any new relationship.

Including, one assumes, well-hung ex-boyfriends with a closet full of videos of every sexual encounter they have ever had; nymphomaniac ex-girl-friends who can't believe they are now an ex; faintly demented Welshmen whose entire existence is spent in the fruitless pursuit of some kind of meaningful (or -less, he's not fussy) sex; and a slightly older, slightly bitter, very neurotic best friend.

And such is everyday life in modern London.

The focus of the show, then, is the relationship between the malleably hapless Steve Taylor (Jack Davenport) and the borderline shrew Susan Walker (Sarah Alexander); and it is her coterie of friends around whom the action revolves—former lover Patrick Maitland (Ben Miles) and best friend Sally Harper (Kate Isitt), while she also works alongside Jeff Murdock (Richard Coyle), who happens to be Steve's best friend. Into this mix arrive Steve, who the others swiftly grow to like, and his ex-girlfriend, Jane Christie (Gina Bellman), who they grow to fear.

Have you ever had one of those friends who can sail unconcernedly . . . in fact, without even noticing . . . through some of life's most terrible traumas, but will probably wind up killing themselves over a slice of burned toast, or a bumpy bus ride?

That is Jane. Utterly self-obsessed, maniacally possessive, and so tragically desperate for male attention that she winds up scaring every man off, even her friends start referring to her as mad (albeit in the fourth season, so it probably doesn't count), while her job as a radio traffic reporter has driven the entire city to distraction.

Jane's the one who rides in the early morning helicopter, reporting on all the traffic problems, but who changes the street names because the real ones are dull.

In fact, a lot of things strike her as dull, and she changes them as well. Including, apparently, herself.

Jane: "I once went on holiday and pretended to be twins. It was amazing fun. I invented this mad, glamorous sister and went around really annoying everybody. And d'you know, I could get away with anything when I was my crazy twin Jane."

Sally: "But *you're* Jane."

Jane: "Kinda stuck. It's a long story."

There again, Jane is the only thing she's really interested in.

Jane: "I'm being stalked, actually, so I'm pretty secure in my attractiveness."

Susan: "You're being stalked?"

Jane: "Is that so hard to believe?"

Sally: "My god!"

Jane: "Every day on my way home from work, a man follows me. It's true."

Susan: "Well, have you been to the police?"

Jane: "They said I was being silly and paranoid. I heard them laughing after I left."

Sally: "That's terrible!"

Susan: "Well, have you confronted the man who follows you?"

Jane: "Well, there's no point, is there? It's never the same man twice. Sometimes they switch over when I'm halfway home. It's so well organized!"

Patrick is a lot like Jane, in that he is totally self-obsessed. But where she is possessive, he is cavalier; where she is scattered, he is calm. And where she is insecure, he is so maddeningly self-possessed that women not only throw themselves at him, but are grateful for even the briefest one-night-stand. The fact, as we are reminded on several occasions, that his nicknames include "donkey" and "tripod" probably doesn't hurt, of course, with even the determinedly left-wing Sally intrigued, despite her distaste for his right-wing politics.

He is a successful businessman, but he is also prone to saying the first thing that comes into his head, regardless of how appropriate, or even relevant, it might be. This, says Sally, is because there's not sufficient blood in his body to service both ends at once.

Sally: "What do you call [women] you go out with, but don't try to sleep with?"

Patrick: "Men."

Sally herself might be the most intriguing character in the show, simply because, though she appears to be the most balanced, she is also wholly defined by her neuroses—which are, in no particular order, growing old, growing ugly, getting wrinkles, going gray, and dying alone in a one-room apartment with cats that will eat her the moment she passes.

Obsessed with her own appearance, she shuns anything that reminds her of the fate awaiting her; attending a funeral, she is accosted by a truly ancient, wrinkled old lady, who informs Sally that once "I was as pretty as you." Poor paranoid Sally's moisturizer collection probably trebled in size overnight.

Patrick: "You can't prevent death with face cream."

Sally: "Yeah? That's what everyone thinks, but no one's ever used it in the quantities I do."

And then there's Jeff, the runt of the litter in so many ways, but the source of so much of *Coupling*'s humor. Steve is genuinely trying to make a go of things with Susan, but Jeff knows his weak spots and exploits them constantly, by embroiling his buddy in the kind of situations that are guaranteed to raise the needy girl's ire.

It is Jeff who discovers "the Giggle Loop," a process by which laughter, once unleashed, can never be halted until all are insensible. It is Jeff who warns Steve of Captain Subtext, the malevolent fiend who benighted Jeff's childhood with a little pair of scissors, and a needle and thread.

Jeff: "If I ever told any lies, he'd sneak into my room when I was asleep and perform surgical operations on me. Every morning I'd check and my penis would be a tiny bit smaller. Every time I told a lie he'd sneak in and remove another segment. That's how my mother would know if I'd been fibbing. 'Keep up with all your lying, Jeffrey, I've always wanted a daughter!' Aah, mothers, eh?"

And it is Jeff who even succeeds in cracking Patrick's perfect armor by introducing him to the melty man, a dark and sinister being who creeps up on the most sexually confident male lover, and turns steel to jello in a matter of seconds.

Jeff: "All of us, in our time, are visited by the melty man."

Patrick: "The what?"

Jeff: "Don't say his name, Patrick. Don't even *think* his name or he will rise from the shadow dimensions to do his evil work on your terrified pants."

Patrick: "Terrified pants?"

Steve: "There's nothing funny about the melty man, Patrick."

Patrick: "You know about the melty man, too?"

Steve: "We all know the melty man."

Patrick: "Who is he?"

Steve: "The archenemy of trouser confidence."

Jeff: "Professor Moriarty. In groin form."

Steve: "Darth Vader."

Jeff: "Without the helmet."

Even bottoms have a backstory in Jeff's so-singular universe.

"Arses are the human race's favorite thing. We like them on each other, we like them on magazine covers, we even like them on babies! When it itches, we like to scratch them; when it's cold, we like to warm them; and who among us, in a lonely moment, hasn't reached back for a discreet fondle? When God made the arse, he didn't say, 'Hey, it's just your basic hinge, let's knock off early.' He said, 'Behold ye angels, I have created the arse. Throughout the ages to come, men and women shall grab hold of these, and shout my name!'"

His theories about a shadowy underworld of unprovable theories and bizarre happenstances are rivaled only by his desperation to make an impression on women, even trying to convince one that he has lost a leg, in the hope of attracting her sympathy. And once he has started down this route, there is no stopping him.

Lie will pile upon lie, mangled explanation upon twisted observation; he is the sort of person who, having dug themselves into a hole, will then continue digging in the vain hope that they might break through to the other side eventually, and be able to make their escape.

He never does, but he lives in hope, and until that day arrives, he finds other means of gratification.

Jeff: "I love the word naked, it's brilliant isn't it, 'naked'. When I was a kid I used to write the word 'naked' on a bit of paper hundreds of times and rub my face in it."

or . . .

Jeff: "If you're gay, see . . . if you're gay, masturbation is practice. Y'know, you can have a good old practice on your own, and then later, when you're ready, when you've got the hang of it, you have a go on someone else's. It's a piece of piss . . . See, it's different . . . it's different when you're a straight bloke. When we finally get our hands on the gear, let me tell you, it's not a drill. Gays have their own practice kit, but you don't get any practice women. We're supposed to fly those babies the first time we get in 'em!"

All six, then, are seriously flawed characters, but flawed in a manner that makes them more human. Perhaps their quirks *are* exaggerated, by the simple process of placing them in a sitcom situation. But they remain recognizable all the same; as has been mentioned before, we all know people exactly like them; *Coupling* simply renders them in even greater relief.

Steve, for example, is well aware that Susan will not approve of the majority of his antics, and he is forever attempting to do the right thing; at the same time as continuing not to. This swiftly establishes the primary dynamic between Susan and himself. He is the evasive little weasel, always trying to get away with something (even if there is actually nothing to be getting away with); she is the disproportionately suspicious terrier who suspects his motives even when he's behaving. It's George and Mildred Roper all over again, only without Mildred's sexual frustrations and minus George's war stories. Or the budgerigar.

Susan: "Well, you know what it's like at the start, when they're all fiery-eyed, and eager, and they haven't seen you naked yet. And it's like he's smashing at your door with his mighty battering ram. And he's promising to ravish you forever. So you brace yourself for man overload, and throw open the doors, and what do you find standing there? An oversized toddler who wants his dinner. And before you can say, 'There's been a terrible mistake,' he's snoring on your sofa, the fridge is full of empty bottles and the whole place smells of feet."

You know when Susan is really annoyed, though. She says "apparently" a lot.

In among the exaggerations, however, there are some priceless moments of reality, most of which revolve around Steve and Susan.

The little tics that eventually sneak into every relationship, for example. Every time Steve moves in his seat or his sleep, she demands "where are you

Six friends, two (sometimes) couples, umpteen problems. The cast of *Coupling* (*back row left to right*) Gina Bellman as Jane Christie, Richard Coyle as Jeffrey "Jeff" Murdock, Kate Isitt as Sally Harper, Ben Miles as Patrick Maitland; (*center*) Jack Davenport as Steve Taylor; (*front*) Sarah Alexander as Susan Walker.   *Photofest*

going?" Every time she asks his opinion, he answers, "It's up to you." (A word of warning, however. Do not watch this episode, the season-two finale, with your significant other in the room. One of you will laugh too heartily, and it definitely won't be her.)

Even purchasing something as mundane as cushions can become both an expansive trial and a soul-destroying battleground, but there's probably no need to elaborate on that.

The success of *Coupling*, then, was not wholly down to its sexual humor. It pioneered, or at least popularized, some remarkably adventurous techniques.

Nonlinear narratives were a favorite device, as situations would be explored first from one person's perspective, then from another's. A scene in which Jeff, in his customary bumbling fashion, attempts to chat up an Israeli girl who speaks only Hebrew, without the benefit of either subtitles or an interpreter, is fabulous; so is the split screen that follows both Steve and Susan through their day in the aftermath of a temporary separation.

The show also mined a comedic genre that dated back to *The Likely Lads*, blossomed with *Man About the House* and had since reached its apogee with *Friends* and *Seinfeld*, exploring the dynamics between friends, not family.

That many of the situations had a sexual context may or may not be an accurate representation of the average "gang's" overriding concern; certainly there are other groups, just as eccentric as the *Coupling* crew, whose primary passions extend to fine wine or keep-fit, long-distance gardening or *Carry On* movies; and, within the confines of those obsessions, could likely sustain a similar sitcom. (Although one hopes that the majority of them won't.).

Coupling, however, made its bed, rumpled the sheets, put on some soft music and lowered the lights, and now it was inviting everyone to lie with it. Indeed, when NBC attempted to launch an American version of the show in 2003, some of the most vociferous complaints were that it was far more sexual than any homegrown sitcom would ever have ventured. It was an accusation that had frequently been leveled at other Britcoms in the past, but surely this one was different?

(Besides, how could anyone complain about sexually based humor in the land that gave us *Married with Children*—itself perhaps the least self-conscious tribute to the genre ever shot? Peggy Bundy hailed from Wanker County, for goodness sake. You could scarcely even *think* that word on British television.)

Everybody had loved *Coupling*, after all, when it was screened on BBC America. And those in the know saw a grand and grandiloquent circle being closed, one that looked back at life at 23 The Cuttings, and Tony Hancock's twisted vision of the stupidity of normalcy; that reflected on the week that was, and placed modern culture into the context it deserved; and which grasped the Anglo love of lowbrow sexual humor and transformed it into an artform.

It would be way too generous, and absurdly hyperbolic, to describe *Coupling* as the apogee of British situational comedy . . . Britcoms. Because it wasn't. But in so skillfully summarizing so much of all that we consider most precious, sacred and above all, funny about the past sixty years of its Britcomic predecessors, *Coupling* could be considered a crash course in all that makes the funny bone funny.

And maybe it opened the door for the next band of gate crashers come to rewrite the way we laugh at things. They're just around the corner, after all.

Epilogue

I s that it? We've reached the end of the book and there's barely been a mention of:

All Gas and Gaiters	*The League of Gentlemen*
Bread	*Little Britain*
Chance in a Million	*Men Behaving Badly*
The Dustbinmen	*Morecambe & Wise*
Father Dear Father	*The Office*
Hale & Pace	*Reeves & Mortimer*
Hark at Barker	*The Royle Family*
Keeping Up Appearances	*Two Pints of Lager . . .*

And several hundred more. *The High Life*, for example. An almost preternaturally youthful Alan Cumming as an almost supernaturally camp airline steward. *How could* we have overlooked that? Or *The I.T. Crowd*, or *Doctor in the House*, or . . . or . . . or . . .

Sorry. No room. And besides, by the time you've read this far, no doubt two or three more shows will have burst onto the screens, with their own multifarious reasons to watch. That's the beauty of television. There's always something new, always something better, and whether or not you personally agree with the selections included in this volume, well . . . maybe they don't agree with you.

Everyone wins.

It is often said, usually by desperate television executives looking to justify the new season's schedules, that the golden age of television is *now*.

This may or may not be true. With the best will, and the most analytical mind in the world, it is difficult to look at any year's programming from start to finish and agree that everything was startling and fresh. And that's as true of the 1960s as it is of the 2010s.

There may have been more shows under way that you now remember fondly, and which you pile up on the DVD player to watch in marathon sessions.

But there was also a lot of garbage on, too, because garbage is everything that you *don't* watch. And whatever your personal golden age might be . . . yes, there was still a lot of garbage around. Earlier in this book, discussing the alternatives to alternative comedy in the early 1980s, mention was made of *One Man and His Dog*, a weekly show about sheepdog trials.

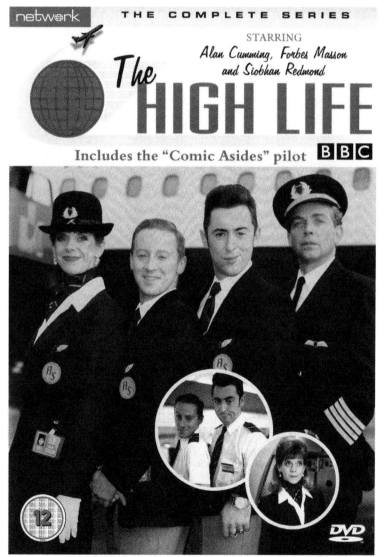

Siobhan Redmond, Forbes Masson, Alan Cumming and Patrick Rycart welcome you aboard this Air Scotia flight. But you probably won't want to stay.

Thirty-some years later, as I started writing this book, what was one of the flagship shows of Britain's independent television network? *Flockstars*—or, if we want to get forensic on its ass, *Celebrity One Man and His Dog.* A weekly show about Z-list nonentities attempting to compete in sheepdog trials.

To be lined up alongside shows featuring celebrity dancing, celebrity cooking, celebrity singing, celebrity hobbit-bashing and, perhaps if Jeff

Nina Baden-Semper, Rudolph Walker, Kate Williams and Jack Smethurst starred in the 1970s comedy *Love Thy Neighbour.* © *www.timeincukcontent.com*

from *Coupling* was involved in the decision-making process, celebrity mutual masturbation.

Yes, it's a golden age of something, all right, but in thirty or forty years' time, there will be an entire generation waxing tearfully rhapsodic about the best shows of their youth. None of which you've probably even glanced at, and maybe that's why there are so few shows included here from the past few years of television scheduling. Because it takes more than a few years for you to remember how much you used to like them.

Television was never intended to be analyzed, though; was never meant to be preserved. Probably wasn't even supposed to be remembered. It was ephemeral, fleeting, transitory, a way of filling the dead air that hung accusingly shroud-like in the sky, once man had invented the TV in the first place. Which, when you consider it, was a remarkable leap of faith. Can you even imagine inventing something that won't actually work until someone else has thought up something to do with it?

(Please note: That was a very simplistic and slightly facetious aside. Obviously the television program was invented first, else there'd have been nothing to test the television with.)

Nevertheless, no wonder those early executives wiped all the tapes. They were probably astonished to realize they had anything on them in the first place.

They did, though, and across the course of the past twenty-five chapters, we have attempted to look at a tiny fraction of a minority genre within a minuscule island's broadcast output, from half a century's worth of switching on the box. Some of it you'll agree with, some of it you won't, and some of it you'll cast aside because you'd much rather read about something else instead.

Which probably isn't in here.

No matter.

Change the channel, make some tea, go out for some cigarettes, go down to the pub. Then, when you get back, read a different chapter.

There's always something else on later, after all.

Appendix One
Episode Guide

Shows appear in the order they are discussed in the book, not in alphabetical order.

Hancock's Half Hour (radio)

* denotes episode missing from archive
Note: Shows are listed in the order that they appear in this book.

Season One

The First Night Party
The Diamond Ring*
The Idol
The Boxing Champion
The Hancock Festival*
The New Car
The Department Store Santa*
Christmas at Aldershot*
The Christmas Eve Party*
Cinderella Hancock
A Trip to France
The Monte Carlo Rally
A House on the Cliff
The Sheikh
The Marriage Bureau
The End of the Series

Season Two

A Holiday in France*
The Crown Jewels*
The Racecourse*
A Visit to Swansea*
The Holiday Camp

The Chef That Died of Shame
Prime Minister Hancock*
The Rail Strike
The Television Set
The Three Sons*
The Marrow Contest
The Matador*

Season Three

The Pet Dog
The Jewel Robbery
The Bequest
The New Neighbour*
The Winter Holiday*
The Blackboard Jungle
The Red Planet*
The Diet
A Visit to Russia*
The Trial of Father Christmas*
Cinderella Hancock* (rerecording)
The New Year Resolutions
Hancock's Hair
The Student Prince
The Breakfast Cereal*
How Hancock Won the War
The Newspaper*
The Greyhound Track
The Conjurer
The Test Match

Season Four

Back from Holiday
The Bolshoi Ballet
Sid James's Dad
The Income Tax Demand
The New Secretary
Michelangelo 'Ancock

Anna and the King of Siam
Cyrano De Hancock
The Stolen Petrol
The Expresso Bar
Hancock's Happy Christmas
The Diary
The 13th of the Series
Almost a Gentleman
The Old School Reunion
The Wild Man of the Woods
Agricultural 'Ancock
Hancock in the Police
The Emigrant
The Last of the McHancocks

Season Five

The New Radio Series
The Scandal Magazine
The Male Suffragettes
The Insurance Policy
The Publicity Photograph
The Unexploded Bomb
Hancock's School
Around the World in Eighty Days
The Americans Hit Town
The Election Candidate
Hancock's Car
The East Cheam Drama Festival
The Foreign Legion
Sunday Afternoon at Home
The Grappling Game
The Junkman
Hancock's War
The Prize Money
The Threatening Letters
The Sleepless Night
Bill and Father Christmas

Season Six

The Smugglers
The Childhood Sweetheart
The Last Bus Home
The Picnic
The Gourmet
The Elopement
Fred's Pie Stall
The Waxwork
Sid's Mystery Tours
The Fete
The Poetry Society
Hancock in Hospital
The Christmas Club
The Impersonator

Hancock's Half Hour (television)

* denotes episode missing from archive

Season One

The First TV Show*
The Artist*
The Dancer*
The Bequest*
The Radio Show*
The Chef That Died of Shame*

Season Two

The Alpine Holiday
Lady Chatterley's Revenge*
The Russian Prince*
The New Neighbour*
The Pianist*
The Auction*

Season Three

The Continental Holiday*
The Great Detective*
The Amusement Arcade*
A Holiday in Scotland*
Air Steward Hancock
The Regimental Reunion*
The Adopted Family*
The Elocution Teacher*
The Lawyer: The Crown v James S.
How to Win Money and Influence People
There's an Airfield at the Bottom of My Garden
Hancock's Forty-Three Minutes

Season Four

Ericson the Viking
Underpaid! or, Grandad's SOS*
The Set That Failed
The New Nose
The Flight of the Red Shadow*
The Horror Serial*
The Italian Maid*
Matrimony—Almost*
The Beauty Contest*
The Wrong Man*
The Oak Tree
The Knighthood
The Servants

Season Five

The Economy Drive
The Two Murderers
Lord Byron Lived Here
Twelve Angry Men
The Train Journey
The Cruise
The Big Night

The Tycoon
Spanish Interlude
Football Pools

Season Six

The Cold
The Missing Page
The Emigrant
The Reunion Party
Sid in Love
The Baby Sitters
The Ladies' Man
The Photographer
The East Cheam Centenary
The Poison Pen Letters

Season Seven (now titled *Hancock*)

The Bedsitter aka Hancock Alone
The Bowmans
The Radio Ham aka Mayday
The Lift aka Going Down
The Blood Donor
The Succession—Son and Heir

The Goons

* denotes episode missing from archive; some off-air recordings exist and
have been remastered for subsequent release

Season One*

Seventeen untitled episodes + Xmas Special: Cinderella

Season Two*

Seventeen untitled episodes (episodes one, three, only exist)

Season Three*

Fred of the Islands
The Egg of the Great Auk
I Was a Male Fan Dancer
The Saga of HMS Aldgate
The Expedition for Toothpaste
The Archers
Robin Hood
Where Does Santa Claus Go in the Summer?
The Navy, Army, and Air Force
The British Way of Life
A Survey of Britain
Flint of the Flying Squad
Seaside Resorts in Winter
The Tragedy of Oxley Tower
The Story of Civilisation
The Search for the Bearded Vulture
The Mystery of the Monkey's Paw
The Mystery of the Cow on the Hill
Where Do Socks Come From?
The Man Who Never Was
The Building of the Suez Canal
The De Goonlies
The Conquest of Space
The Ascent of Mount Everest
The Story of the Plymouth Hoe Armada
Special: Coronation edition

Season Four

The Dreaded Piano Clubber*
The Man Who Tried to Destroy London's Monuments*
The Ghastly Experiments of Dr. Hans Eidelburger*
The Building of Britain's First Atomic Cannon*
The Gibraltar Story*
Through the Sound Barrier in an Airing Cupboard*
The First Albert Memorial to the Moon*
The Missing Bureaucrat*
Operation Bagpipes*

The Flying Saucer Mystery*
The Spanish Armada*
The British Way*
The Giant Bombardon*
Ten Thousand Fathoms Down in a Wardrobe*
The Missing Prime Minister*
Dr. Jekyll and Mr. Crun*
The Mummified Priest*
The History of Communications*
The Kippered Herring Gang*
The Toothpaste Expedition*
The Case of the Vanishing Room*
The Great Ink Drought*
The Greatest Mountain in the World
The Collapse of the British Railway Sandwich System*
The Silent Bugler*
Western Story*
The Saga of the Internal Mountain*
The Invisible Acrobat*
The Great Bank of England Robbery*
The Siege of Fort Knight*
Special: Short insert in "Christmas Crackers"*
Special: Archie in Goonland*
Special: The Starlings*

Season Five

The Whistling Spy Enigma
The Lost Gold Mine of Charlotte
The Dreaded Batter-Pudding Hurler of Bexhill-on-Sea
The Phantom Head Shaver of Brighton
The Affair of the Lone Banana
The Canal
Lurgi Strikes Britain
The Mystery of the Marie Celeste Solved
The Last Tram from Clapham
The Booted Gorilla Found?
The Spanish Suitcase
Dishonoured, or The Fall of Neddie Seagoon

Forog
Ye Bandit of Sherwood Forest
Nineteen-Eighty-Five
The Case of the Missing Heir
China Story
Under Two Floorboards—A Story of the Legion
The Missing Scroll
Nineteen-Eighty-Five (remake)
The Sinking of Westminster Pier
The Fireball of Milton Street
The Six Ingots of Leadenhall Street
Yehti
The White Box of Great Bardfield
The End

Season Six

The Man Who Won the War
The Secret Escritoire
The Lost Emperor
Napoleon's Piano
The Case of the Missing CD Plates
Rommel's Treasure
Foiled by President Fred
Shangri-La Again
The International Christmas Pudding
The Pevensey Bay Disaster
The Sale of Manhattan
The Terrible Revenge of Fred Fu-Manchu
The Lost Year
The Greenslade Story
The Hastings Flyer—Robbed
The Mighty Wurlitzer
The Raid of the International Christmas Pudding
Tales of Montmartre
The Jet-Propelled Guided NAAFI
The House of Teeth
Tales of Old Dartmoor
The Choking Horror

The Great Tuscan Salami Scandal
The Treasure in the Lake
The Fear of Wages
Scradje
The Man Who Never Was (remake)
Special: The Missing Christmas Parcel—Post Early for Christmas
Special: The Goons Hit Wales
Special: China Story

Season Seven

The Nasty Affair at the Burami Oasis
Drums Along the Mersey
The Nadger Plague
The MacReekie Rising of '74
The Spectre of Tintagel
The Sleeping Prince
The Great Bank Robbery
Personal Narrative
The Mystery of the Fake Neddie Seagoons
What's My Line?
The Telephone
The Flea
Six Charlies in Search of an Author
Emperor of the Universe
Wings over Dagenham
The Rent Collectors
Shifting Sands
The Moon Show
The Mysterious Punch-up-the-Conker
Round the World in Eighty Days
Insurance, the White Man's Burden
The Africa Ship Canal
Ill Met by Goonlight
The Missing Boa Constrictor
The Histories of Pliny the Elder
Special: Robin Hood
Special: Operation Christmas Duff
Special: The Reason Why

Season Eight

Spon
The Junk Affair
The Burning Embassy
The Great Regents Park Swim
The Treasure in the Tower
The Space Age
The Red Fort
The Missing Battleship
The Policy
King Solomon's Mines
The Stolen Postman
The Great British Revolution
The Plasticine Man
African Incident
The Thing on the Mountain
The String Robberies
The Moriarty Murder Mystery
The Curse of Frankenstein
The White Neddie Trade
Ten Snowballs That Shook the World
The Man Who Never Was (remake)
World War One
The Spon Plague
Tiddleywinks
The Evils of Bushey Spon
The Great Statue Debate
Series "Vintage Goons"
The Mummified Priest
The Greatest Mountain in the World
The Missing Ten Downing Street
The Giant Bombardon
The Kippered Herring Gang (remake)
The Vanishing Room
The Ink Shortage
The Mustard and Cress Shortage
The Internal Mountain
The Silent Bugler
The Great Bank of England Robbery

The Dreaded Piano Clubber
The Siege of Fort Night
The Albert Memorial

Season Nine

The Sahara Desert Statue
I Was Monty's Treble
The £1,000,000 Penny
The Pam's Paper Insurance Policy
The Mountain Eaters
The Childe Harolde Rewarde
The Seagoon Memoirs
Queen Anne's Rain
The Battle of Spion Kop
Ned's Atomic Dustbin
Who Is Pink Oboe?
The Call of the West
Dishonoured—Again
The Scarlet Capsule
The Tay Bridge
The Gold Plate Robbery
The £50 Cure

Season Ten

The Christmas Carol
The Tale of Men's Shirts
The Chinese Legs
Robin's Post
The Silver Dubloons
The Last Smoking Seagoon

1972 Reunion Special

"The Last Goon Show of All"

On the Buses episode guide

Season One

The Early Shift
The New Conductor
Olive Takes a Trip
Bus Drivers' Stomach
The New Inspector
The Canteen
The Darts Match

Season Two

Family Flu
The Used Combination
Self Defence
Aunt Maud
Late Again
Bon Voyage

Season Three

First Aid
The Cistern
The Inspector's Niece
Brew It Yourself
Busmen's Perks
The Snake
Mum's Last Fling
Radio Control
Foggy Night
The New Uniforms
Going Steady
The Squeeze
On the Make

Season Four

Nowhere to Go
The Canteen Girl
Dangerous Driving
The Other Woman
Christmas Duty
The 'L' Bus
The Kids' Outing
The Anniversary
Cover Up
Safety First
The Lodger
The Injury
Not Tonight

Season Five

The Nursery
Stan's Room
The Best Man
The Inspector's Pets
The Epidemic
The Busmen's Ball
Canteen Trouble
The New Nurse
Lost Property
Stan's Uniform
The Strain
The New Telly
Vacancy for Inspector
A Thin Time
Boxing Day Social

Season Six

No Smoke Without Fire
Love Is What You Make It
Private Hire
Union Trouble

Bye Bye Blakey
The Prize

Season Seven

Olive's Divorce
The Perfect Clippie
The Ticket Machine
The Poster
The Football Match
On the Omnibuses
Goodbye Stan
Hot Water
The Visit
What the Stars Foretell
The Allowance
Friends in High Places
Gardening Time

Steptoe and Son episode guide

Season One

The Offer
The Bird
The Piano
The Economist
The Diploma
The Holiday

Season Two

Wallah, Wallah Catsmeat
The Bath
The Stepmother
Sixty-Five Today
A Musical Evening
Full House
Is That Your Horse Outside?

Season Three

Homes Fit for Heroes
The Wooden Overcoats
The Lead Man Cometh
Steptoe a la Cart
Sunday for Seven Days
The Bond That Binds Us
The Lodger

Season Four

And Afterwards at . . .
Crossed Swords
Those Magnificent Men and Their Heating Machines:
The Siege of Steptoe Street
A Box in Town
My Old Man's a Tory
Pilgrim's Progress

Season Five

*black and white only, color episodes missing
A Death in the Family*
A Winter's Tale*
Any Old Iron?*
Steptoe and Son—and Son!*
The Colour Problem*
T.B. or Not T.B.?*
Men of Property*

Season Six

*black and white only, color episodes missing
Robbery with Violence*
Come Dancing
Two's Company*
Tea for Two*
Without Prejudice*
Pot Black*

The Three Feathers*
Cuckoo in the Nest

Season Seven

Men of Letters
A Star Is Born
Oh, What a Beautiful Mourning
Live Now, P.A.Y.E. Later
Loathe Story
Divided We Stand
The Desperate Hours
The Party

Season Eight

Back in Fashion
And So to Bed
Porn Yesterday
The Seven Steptoerai
Upstairs, Downstairs, Upstairs, Downstairs
Seance in a Wet Rag and Bone Yard
A Perfect Christmas

Till Death Us Do Part episode guide

* denotes episode missing from archive

Season One

Till Death Us Do Part*
Arguments, Arguments . . .
Hair Raising!*
A House with Love in It
Intolerance*
Two Toilets? . . . That's Posh*
From Liverpool with Love*
Claustrophobia*

Season Two

Peace and Goodwill
Sex Before Marriage*
I Can Give Up Any Time I Like*
The Bulldog Breed*
Caviar on the Dole*
A Woman's Place Is in the Home*
A Wapping Mythology*
In Sickness and in Health . . .
State Visit
Alf's Dilemma
Till Closing Time Us Do Part

Season Three

The Phone
Blood Donor
Monopoly*
The Funeral*
Football*
The Puppy*
Aunt Maud

Special

Up the Polls

Season Four

To Garnet a Grandson
Pigeon Fancier
Holiday in Bournemouth
Dock Pilfering
Up the Hammers
Alf's Broken Leg
Christmas Special

Season Five

TV Licence
The Royal Wedding
Strikes and Blackouts
Party Night
Three Day Week
Gran's Watch
Paki-Paddy

Season Six

Outback Bound
Phone Call to Elsie
Marital Bliss
Wedgie Ben
The Letter
The Wake
Christmas Club Books

Season Seven

Moving In with Min
Min the Housekeeper
Drunk in Charge of a Bicycle
Window
A Hole in One
Unemployment

Monty Python's Flying Circus

Season One

Whither Canada?
Sex and Violence
How to Recognise Different Types of Trees from Quite a Long Way Away
Owl-Stretching Time
Man's Crisis of Identity in the Latter Half of the 20th Century
It's the Arts
You're No Fun Anymore

Full Frontal Nudity
The Ant, an Introduction
Untitled
The Royal Philharmonic Orchestra Goes to the Bathroom
The Naked Ant
Intermission

Season Two

Dinsdale!
The Spanish Inquisition
Deja Vu
The Buzz Aldrin Show
Live from the Grill-o-Mat
It's a Living
The Attila the Hun Show
Archaeology Today
How to Recognise Different Parts of the Body
Scott of the Antarctic
How Not to Be Seen
Spam
Royal Episode
Montreux Special

Season Three

Njorl's Saga
Mr. and Mrs. Brian Norris' Ford Popular
The Money Programme
Blood, Devastation, Death, War and Horror
The All-England Summarise Proust Competition
The War Against Pornography
Salad Days
The Cycling Tour
The Nude Man
E. Henry Thripshaw's Disease
Dennis Moore
A Book at Bedtime
The British Showbiz Awards

Season Four

The Golden Age of Ballooning
Michael Ellis
The Light Entertainment War
Hamlet
Mr. Neutron
Party Political Broadcast

Dad's Army episode guide

Season One

The Man and the Hour
Museum Piece
Command Decision
The Enemy Within the Gates
The Showing Up of Corporal Jones
Shooting Pains

Season Two

* denotes episode missing from archive
Operation Kilt
The Battle of Godfrey's Cottage
The Loneliness of the Long Distance Walker*
Sgt. Wilson's Little Secret
A Stripe for Frazer*
Under Fire*

Season Three

The Armoured Might of Lance Corporal Jones
Battle School
The Lion Has 'Phones
The Bullet Is Not for Firing
Something Nasty in the Vault
Room at the Bottom
Big Guns
The Day the Balloon Went Up

War Dance
Menace from the Deep
Branded
Man Hunt
No Spring for Frazer
Sons of the Sea

Season Four

The Big Parade
Don't Forget the Diver
Boots, Boots, Boots
Sgt.—Save My Boy!
Don't Fence Me In
Absent Friends
Put That Light Out!
Mum's Army
The Test
A. Wilson Manager?
Uninvited Guests
Fallen Idol
Battle of the Giants!

Season Five

Asleep in the Deep
Keep Young and Beautiful
A Soldier's Farewell
Getting the Bird
The Desperate Drive of Corporal Jones
If the Cap Fits . . .
The King Was in His Counting House
All Is Safely Gathered In
When Did You Last See Your Money?
Brain Versus Brawn
A Brush with the Law
Round and Round Went the Great Big Wheel
Time on My Hands

Season Six

The Deadly Attachment
My British Buddy
The Royal Train
We Know Our Onions
The Honourable Man
Things That Go Bump in the Night
The Recruit

Season Seven

Everybody's Trucking
A Man of Action
Gorilla Warfare
The Godiva Affair
The Captain's Car
Turkey Dinner

Season Eight

Ring Dem Bells
When You've Got to Go
Is There Honey Still for Tea?
Come In, Your Time Is Up
High Finance
The Face on the Poster
My Brother and I
The Love of Three Oranges

Season Nine

Wake-Up Walmington
The Making of Private Pike
Knights of Madness
The Miser's Hoard
Number Engaged
Never Too Old

It Ain't Half Hot, Mum

Season One

Meet the Gang
My Lovely Boy
The Mutiny of the Punka Wallahs
A Star Is Born
The Jungle Patrol
It's a Wise Child
The Road to Bannu
The Inspector Calls

Season Two

Showing the Flag
Down in the Jungle
The Natives Are Revolting
Cabaret Time
The Curse of the Sadhu
Forbidden Fruits
Has Anyone Seen My Cobra?
The Night of the Thugs

Season Three

The Supremo Show
Mind My Maharajah
Bang Goes the Maharajah
The Grand Illusion
Pale Hands I Love
Don't Take the Micky

Season Four

Monsoon Madness
Kidnapped in the Khyber
A Fate Worse Than Death
Ticket to Blighty
Lofty's Little Friend
Flight to Jawani

We Are Not Amused
Twenty-One Today

Season Five

Front Line Entertainers
Bridge Over the River Hipong
The Pay Off
Puddings from Heaven
The Superstar
The Eternal Quadrangle

Season Six

The Stars Look Down
The Big League
The Great Payroll Snatch
The Dhobi Wallahs
Lead Kindly Light
Holidays at Home
Caught Short

Season Seven

That's Entertainment?
The Guinea Pigs
Dog in the Manger
The Great Broadcast
Class of 1945
Star Commandos

Season Eight

Gloria's Finest Hour
Money Talks
Aquastars
The Last Warrior
Never the Twain Shall Meet
The Long Road Home
The Last Roll Call

The Goodies

Season One

Tower of London
Snooze
Give Police a Chance
Caught in the Act
The Greenies
Cecily
Radio Goodies

Season Two

* denotes episode missing from archive
Scotland
Commonwealth Games
Pollution
The Lost Tribe
The Music Lovers
Culture for the Masses
Kitten Kong*
Come Dancing
Farm Fresh Food
Women's Lib
Gender Education
Charity Bounce
The Baddies
Kitten Kong: Montreux Edition
A Collection of Goodies

Season Three

The New Office
Hunting Pink
Winter Olympics
That Old Black Magic
For Those in Peril on the Sea
Way Outward Bound
Superstar

Season Four

Camelot
Invasion of the Moon Creatures
Hospital for Hire
The Goodies and the Beanstalk
The Stone Age
Goodies in the Nick
The Race

Season Five

The Movies
Clown Virus
Chubbie Chumps
Wacky Wales
Frankenfido
Scatty Safari
Kung Fu Kapers
Lighthouse Keeping Loonies
Rome Antics
Fleet Street Goodies
South Africa
Bunfight at the OK Tea Rooms
The End
Goodies Rule OK?

Season Six

Lips, or Almighty Cod
Hype Pressure
Daylight Robbery on the Orient Express
Black and White Beauty
It Might as Well Be String
2001 and a Bit
The Goodies Almost Live

Season Seven

Alternative Roots
Dodonuts
Scoutrageous
Punky Business
Royal Command
Earthanasia

Season Eight

Goodies and Politics
Saturday Night Grease
A Kick in the Arts
U-Friend or UFO?
Animals
War Babies

Season Nine

Snow White
Robot
Football Crazy
Big Foot
Change of Life
Holiday
Animals are People Too

The Mighty Boosh

Season One

Killeroo
Mutants
Bollo
Tundra
Jungle
Charlie
Electro
Hitcher

Season Two

Call of the Yeti
The Priest and the Beast
Nanageddon
Fountain of Youth
The Legend of Old Gregg
The Nightmare of Milky Joe

Season Three

Eels
Journey to the Centre of the Punk
The (Power of the) Crimp
The Strange Tale of the Crack Fox
Party
The Chokes

I Didn't Know You Cared

Season One

Cause for Celebration
A Knitter in the Family
The Old Tin Trunk
After the Ball Was Over
Aye . . . Well . . . Mm . . .
Large or Small, Big or Tall
The Axe and Cleaver

Season Two

The Way My Wife Looks at Me
Chez Us
A Woman's Work
A Signal Disaster
You Should See Me Now
Good Wood, God!

Season Three

Men at Work
A Grave Decision
Party Games
A Bleak Day
Stout Deeds
Paradise Lost
The Last Tram

Season Four

The Love Match
Love Is a Many Splendoured Thing
A Tip Top Day
Don't Answer That
The Great Escape
What's in a Name
The Great Day

Last of the Summer Wine

Season One

Of Funerals and Fish
Short Back and Palais Glide
Inventor of the 40-Foot Ferret
Pate and Chips
Spring Fever
The New Mobile Trio
Hail Smiling Morn or Thereabouts

Season Two

Forked Lightning
Who's That Dancing with Nora Batty Then?
The Changing Face of Rural Blamire
Some Enchanted Evening

A Quiet Drink
Ballad for Wind Instruments and Canoe
Northern Flying Circus

Season Three

The Man from Oswestry
Mending Stuart's Leg
The Great Boarding House Bathroom Caper
Cheering Up Gordon
The Kink in Foggy's Niblick
Going to Gordon's Wedding
Isometrics and After

Season Four

Ferret Come Home
Getting on Sydney's Wire
Jubilee
Flower Power Cut
Who Made a Bit of a Splash in Wales Then?
Greenfingers
A Merry Heatwave
The Bandit from Stoke-on-Trent
Small Tune on a Penny Wassail

Season Five

Full Steam Behind
The Flag and Its Snags
The Flag and Further Snags
Deep in the Heart of Yorkshire
Earnshaw Strikes Back
Here We Go into the Wild Blue Yonder
Here We Go Again into the Wild Blue Yonder
And a Dewhurst up a Fir Tree
Whoops

Season Six

In the Service of Humanity
Car and Garter
The Odd Dog Men
A Bicycle Made for Three
One of the Last Few Places Unexplored by Man
Serenade for Tight Jeans and Metal Detector
From Wellies to Wetsuit
All Mod Conned

Season Seven

The Frozen Turkey Man
The White Man's Grave
The Waist Land
Cheering Up Ludovic
The Three Astaires
The Arts of Concealment
Getting Sam Home
The Loxley Lozenge

Season Eight

The Mysterious Feet of Nora Batty
Keeping Britain Tidy
Enter the Phantom
Catching Digby's Donkey
The Woollen Mills of Your Mind
Who's Looking After the Cafe Then?
Uncle of the Bride

Season Nine

Why Does Norman Clegg Buy Ladies' Elastic Stockings?
The Heavily Reinforced Bottom
Dried Dates and Codfanglers
The Really Masculine Purse
Who's Feeling Ejected Then?
The Ice-Cream Man Cometh

Set the People Free
Go with the Flow
Jaws
Edie and the Automobile
Wind Power
When You Take a Good Bite of Yorkshire, It Tastes Terrible
Merry Christmas, Father Christmas
Big Day at Dream Acres

Season Ten

The Experiment
The Treasure of the Deep
Dancing Feet
That Certain Smile
Downhill Racer
The Day of the Welsh Ferret
Crums

Season Eleven

Come Back, Jack Harry Teesdale
The Kiss and Mavis Poskitt
Oh Shut Up and Eat Your Choc Ice
Who's That Bloke with Nora Batty Then?
Happy Anniversary Gough and Jessie
Getting Barry Higher in the World
Three Men and a Mangle
What's Santa Brought for Nora Then?

Season Twelve

Return of the Warrior
Come In, Sunray Major
The Charity Balls
Walking Stiff Can Make You Famous
That's Not Captain Zero
Das Welly Boot
The Empire That Foggy Nearly Built

Roll On
The Last Surviving Maurice Chevalier Impression
A Landlady for Smiler
Barry's Christmas

Season Thirteen

Quick, Quick, Slow
Give Us a Lift
Was That Nora Batty Singing?
Cash Flow Problems
Passing the Earring
Pole Star
Situations Vacant

Season Fourteen

By the Magnificent Thighs of Ernie Burniston
Errol Flynn Used to Have a Pair Like That
The Phantom of the Graveyard
The Self-Propelled Salad Strainer
Ordeal by Trousers
Happy Birthday, Howard
Who's Got Rhythm?
Camera Shy
Wheelies
Stop That Castle

Season Fifteen

How to Clear Your Pipes
Where There's Smoke, There's Barbecue
The Black Widow
Have You Got a Light Mate?
Stop That Bath
Springing Smiler
Concerto for Solo Bicycle
There Are Gypsies at the Bottom of Our Garden
Aladdin Gets On Your Wick

Welcome to Earth
The Man Who Nearly Knew Pavarotti

Season Sixteen

The Glory Hole
Adopted by a Stray
The Defeat of the Stoneworm
Once in a Moonlit Junkyard
The Space Ace
The Most Powerful Eyeballs in West Yorkshire
The Dewhursts of Ogleby Hall
The Sweet Smell of Excess

Season Seventeen

Forever or Till Teatime
Bicycle Bonanza
The Glamour of the Uniform
The First Human Being to Ride a Hill
Captain Clutterbuck's Treasure
Desperate for a Duffield
The Suit That Turned Left
Beware of the Elbow
The Thing in Wesley's Shed
Brushes at Dawn
A Leg Up for Christmas
Extra! Extra!

Season Eighteen

The Love-Mobile
A Clean Sweep
The Mysterious C. W. Northrop
A Double for Howard
How to Create a Monster
Deviations with Davenport
According to the Prophet Bickerdyke
Next Kiss Please

Destiny and Six Bananas
A Sidecar Named Desire
There Goes the Groom

Season Nineteen

Beware the Oglethorpe
Tarzan of the Towpath
Truly and the Hole Truth
Oh Howard, We Should Get One of Those
The Suit That Attracts Blondes
The Only Diesel Saxophone in Captivity
Perfection—Thy Name Is Ridley
Nowhere Particular
From Audrey Nash to the Widow Dilhooley
Support Your Local Skydiver

Season Twenty

The Pony Set
How Errol Flynn Discovered the Secret Scar of Nora Batty
Who's Thrown Her Tom Cruise Photos Away?
What's Happened to Barry's Nose?
Optimism in the Housing Market
Will Barry Go Septic Despite Listening to Classical Music?
Beware the Vanilla Slice
Howard Throws a Wobbler
The Phantom Number Bus
Ironing Day
Last Post and Pigeon

Season Twenty-One

Lipstick and Other Problems
Under the Rug
Magic and the Morris Minor
Elegy for Fallen Wellies
Surprise at Throstlenest
Just a Small Funeral

From Here to Paternity
Some Vans Can Make You Deaf
Waggoner's Roll
I Didn't Know Barry Could Play

Season Twenty-Two

Getting Barry's Goat
The Art of the Shorts Story
The Missing Bus of Mrs. Avery
Hey! Big Vendor
Enter the Hawk
Gnome and Away
A Hair of the Blonde That Bit You
A White Sweater and a Solicitor's Letter
Why Is Barry at an Angle?
The Coming of the Beast
Potts in Pole Position

Season Twenty-Three

A Brief Excursion in the Fast Lane
The Mystical Squeak of Howard's Bicycle
Mervyn Would Be Proud
The Incredible Ordeal of Norman Clegg
Beware of the Hot Dog
In Search of Childlike Joy and the Farthest Reaches of the Lotus Position
A Chaise Longue Too Far
Exercising Father's Bicycle
Sadly, Madly, Bradley
It All Began with an Old Volvo Headlamp
A Musical Passing for a Miserable Muscroft

Season Twenty-Four

The Lair of the Cat Creature
Ancient Eastern Wisdom: An Introduction
A Pick-Up of the Later Ming Dynasty
The Secret Birthday of Norman Clegg

In Which Gavin Hinchcliffe Loses the Gulf Stream
The Miraculous Curing of Old Goff Helliwell
The Frenchies Are Coming
The Man Who Invented Yorkshire Funny Stuff
The Second Husband and the Showgirls
All of a Florrie
Thirty Years of Last of the Summer Wine
A Short Burst of Fred Astaire

Season Twenty-Five

Jurassic No Parking
The General's Greatest Battle
Spores
Happy Birthday Robin Hood
Who's That with Barry and Glenda? It's Not Barry and Glenda
An Apple a Day
Barry Becomes a Psychopathic Killer, but Only Part Time
Things to Do When Your Wife Runs Off with a Turkish Waiter
Beware of Laughing at Nora's Hats
Yours Truly—If You're Not Careful
Variations on a Theme of the Widow Winstanley

Season Twenty-Six

The Swan Man of Ilkley
Watching the Clock
Has Anyone Seen a Peruvian Wart?
Hermione the Short Course
Who's That Mouse in the Poetry Group?
Available for Weddings
The McDonaghs of Jamieson Street
The Afterthoughts of a Co-op Manager
Lot Number
Little Orphan Howard
Merry Entwistle and Jackson Day

Season Twenty-Seven

Follow That Bottle
How to Remove a Cousin
Has Anyone Seen Barry's Midlife Crisis?
The Genuine Outdoors Robin Hood Barbi
Barry in Danger of Reading and Aunt Jessie
Who's That Merry Man with Billy, Then?
Who's That Talking to Lenny?
Oh Look! Mitzi's Found Her Mummy
Plenty of Room in the Back
A Tale of Two Sweaters

Season Twenty-Eight

The Second Stag Night of Doggy Wilkinson
What Happened to the Horse?
Variations on a Theme of Road Rage
In Which Howard Got Double Booked
Will the Nearest Alien Please Come In
Elegy for Small Creature and Clandestine Trackbike
The Crowcroft Challenge
Must Be Good Dancer
Howard Remembers Where He Left His Bicycle
Sinclair and the Wormley Witches

Season Twenty-Nine

Enter the Finger
Will the Genuine Racer Please Stand Up?
A Short Introduction to Cooper's Rules
Is Jeremy Quite Safe?
All That Glitters Is Not Elvis
Eva's Back in Town
In Which Romance Isn't Dead—Just Incompetent
The Mischievous Tinkle in Howard's Eyes
Of Passion and Pizza
It's Never Ten Years
Get Out of That, Then
I Was a Hitman for Primrose Dairies

Season Thirty

Some Adventures of the Inventor of the Mother Stitch
The Mother of All Mistakes—Or Is It?
Will Howard Cross the Atlantic Single-Handed?
Who's That Looking Sideways at Nelly?
Nobody Messes with Tony the Throat
Will Stella Find True Love with Norris Fairburn?
Will Randolph Make a Good Impression?
In Which Romance Springs a Leak
Variations on a Theme of Father's Day
Goodnight Sweet Ferret

Season Thirty-One

Behind Every Bush There Is Not Necessarily a Howard
Happy Camping
The Rights of Man Except for Howard
Howard and the Great Outdoors
Look Whose Wheel's Come Off
How Not to Cry at Weddings

The Likely Lads episode guide

* denotes episode missing from archive

Season One

Entente Cordiale
Double Date
Older Women Are More Experienced
Other Side of the Fence
Chance of a Lifetime
The Suitor

Season Two

Baby It's Cold Outside*
A Star Is Born*
Talk of the Town*

Last of the Big Spenders
Far Away Places*
Where Have All the Flowers Gone?*

Season Three

Outward Bound*
Friends and Neighbours*
Rocker
Brief Encounter*
The Razor's Edge*
Anchors Aweigh*
Love and Marriage*
Goodbye to All That

Whatever Happened to the Likely Lads?

Season One

Strangers on a Train
Home Is the Hero
Cold Feet
Moving On
I'll Never Forget Whatshername
Birthday Boy
No Hiding Place
Guess Who's Coming to Dinner?
Storm in a Tea Chest
The Old Magic
Count Down
Boys Night In
End of an Era

Season Two

Absent Friends
Heart to Heart
The Ant and the Grasshopper
One for the Road
The Great Race

Some Day We'll Laugh About This
In Harm's Way
Affairs and Relations
The Expert
Between Ourselves
The Go-Between
Conduct Unbecoming
The Shape of Things to Come
Special: Christmas Edition

The Lovers episode guide

Season One

Sardine Sandwiches
The Date
Freckle Face
Brainwashing
A Pipe and a Moustache
The Truth Game December

Season Two

The Engagement
Breaking It Off
Birthday
Joint Bank Account
The Better Homes Exhibition
A Trial Marriage
The Best Laid Plans . . .

Man About the House

Season One

Three's a Crowd
And Mother Makes Four
Some Enchanted Evening
And Then There Were Two
It's Only Money

Match of the Day
No Children, No Dogs

Season Two

While the Cat's Away
Colour Me Yellow
In Praise of Older Men
Did You Ever Meet Rommel?
Two Foot Two, Eyes of Blue
Carry Me Back to Old Southampton

Season Three

Cuckoo in the Nest
Come into My Parlour
I Won't Dance, Don't Ask Me . . .
Of Mice and Women
Somebody Out There Likes Me
We Shall Not Be Moved
Three of a Kind

Season Four

Home & Away
One for the Road
All in the Game
Never Give Your Real Name
The Tender Trap
My Son, My Son

Season Five

The Last Picture Show
Right Said George
A Little Knowledge
Love and Let Love
How Does Your Garden Grow
Come Fly with Me

Season Six

The Party's Over
One More for the Pot
The Generation Game
The Sunshine Boys
Mum Always Liked You Best
Fire Down Below
Another Bride, Another Groom

Robin's Nest

Season One

Sleeping Partners
The Bistro Kids
A Little Competition
The Maternal Triangle
Piggy in the Middle
A Matter of Note
Oh Happy Day

Season Two

As Long as He Needs Me
The Seven Pound Fiddle
Ups & Downs
Three Times Table
Great Expectations
Love & Marriage

Season Three

You Need Hands
The Candidate
Just Desserts
Away from All What?
England Expects
Once Two Is Three
Dinner Date

Everything You Wish Yourself
Be It Ever So Humble
Day Trippers
The Long Distance Runner
At Harm's Length
The Happy Hen

Season Four

Should Auld Acquaintance
Person Friday Required
Lost Weekend
Too Many Waiters Spoil the Bistro
September Song
Sorry Partner
Albert's Ball

Season Five

Christmas at Robin's Nest
Pastures New
A Man of Property
If You Pass "Go," Collect £200
Never Look a Gift Horse . . .
Just an Old-Fashioned Girl
Great Expectations

Season Six

No Room at the Inn
Move Over Darling
The Homecoming
No Smoke Without Fire
When Irish Eyes Are Smiling
Anniversary Waltz
Wish You Weren't Here
The Headhunters of S.W.6

Are You Being Served?

Season One

Are You Being Served?
Dear Sexy Knickers
Our Figures Are Slipping
Camping In
His and Hers
Diamonds Are a Man's Best Friend

Season Two

The Clock
Cold Comfort
The Think Tank
Big Brother
Hoorah for the Holidays

Season Three

The Hand of Fate
Coffee Morning
Up Captain Peacock
Cold Store
Wedding Bells
German Week
Shoulder to Shoulder
New Look
Christmas Crackers

Season Four

No Sale
Top Hat and Tails
Forward Mr. Grainger
Fire Practice
Fifty Years On
Oh What a Tangled Web
The Father Christmas Affair

Season Five

Mrs. Slocombe Expects
A Change Is as Good as a Rest
Founder's Day
The Old Order Changes
Take-over
Goodbye Mr. Grainger
It Pays to Advertise

Season Six

By Appointment
The Club
"Do You Take This Man?"
Shedding the Load
A Bliss Girl
Happy Returns

Season Seven

The Junior
Strong Stuff, This Insurance
The Apartment
Mrs. Slocombe, Senior Person
The Hero
Anything You Can Do
The Agent
The Punch and Judy Affair

Season Eight

Is It Catching?
A Personal Problem
Front Page Story
Sit Out
Heir Apparent
Closed Circuit
The Erotic Dreams of Mrs. Slocombe
Roots?

Season Nine

The Sweet Smell of Success
Conduct Unbecoming
Memories Are Made of This
Calling All Customers
Monkey Business
Lost and Found

Season Ten

Goodbye Mrs. Slocombe
Grounds for Divorce
The Hold Up
Gambling Fever
The Night Club
Friends and Neighbours
The Pop Star

Open All Hours

Season One

Full of Mysterious Promise
A Mattress on Wheels
A Nice Cosy Little Disease
Beware of the Dog
Well Catered Funeral
Apples and Self Service

Season Two

Laundry Blues
The Reluctant Traveller
Fig Biscuits and Inspirational Toilet Rolls
The New Suit
Arkwright's Mobile Store
Shedding at the Wedding
St. Albert's Day

Season Three

An Errand Boy by the Ear
The Ginger Men
Duet for Solo Bicycle
How to Ignite Your Errand Boy
The Man from Down Under
The Cool Cocoa Tin Lid

Season Four

Soulmate Wanted
Horse-Trading
The Housekeeper Caper
The Errand Boy Executive
Happy Birthday Arkwright
The Mystical Boudoir of Nurse Gladys Emmanuel

Bless This House

Season One

The Generation Gap
Mum's the Word
Father's Day
Be It Ever So Humble
Another Fine Mess
For Whom the Bells Toll
A Woman's Place
The Day of Rest
Make Love . . . Not War!
Charity Begins at Home
If the Dog Collar Fits, Wear It
The Morning After the Night Before

Season Two

Two Heads Are Better Than One
Love Me, Love My Tree
Another Lost Weekend

Parents Should Be Seen and Not Heard
Strangers in the Night
Get Me to the Match on Time
Wives and Lovers
Never Again on Sunday
People in Glass Houses
A Rolls by Any Other Name
A Touch of the Unknown

Season Three

It Comes to Us All in the End
Tea for Two and Four for Tea
To Tell or Not to Tell
Blood Is Thicker Than Water
One Good Turn Deserves a Bother
The Loneliness of the Short Distance Walker
Watch the Birdie
Will the Real Sid Abbott Please Stand Up
Aitishoo! Aitishoo! We All Fall Down
Entente Not So Cordiale
I'm Not Jealous, I'll Kill Him
A Girl's Worst Friend Is Her Father

Season Four

Money Is the Root Of . . .
And They Will Come Home
Who's Minding the Baby?
A Beef in His Bonnet
The Bells Are Ringing
The First Years Are the Worst

Season Five

They Don't Write Songs Like That Anymore
The Gypsy's Warning
The Biggest Woodworm in the World
Home Tweet Home

You're Never Too Old to Be Young
The Policeman, the Paint and the Pirates
Happy Birthday Sid
Freedom Is
Mr. Chairman . . .
And Afterwards At . . .

Season Six

The Frozen Limit
Beautiful Dreamer
Fish with Everything
The Naked Paperhanger
Remember Me?
Something of Value
Men of Consequence
Skin Deep
Friends and Neighbours
Well, Well, Well
The Phantom Pools Winner
A Matter of Principle
Some Enchanted Evening

Some Mothers Do 'Ave 'Em

Season One

The Salesman's Job
Visiting the Brother-in-Law
Crossing the Road and Phoning the Doctor
Going on Holiday
The Hospital Visit
The Psychiatrist
The Labour Exchange

Season Two

Frank Goes Over the Edge
The R.A.F. Reunion
The P.R. Course

Frank and Marvin
Father's Clinic
The Baby Arrives
Jessica's First Christmas
Learning to Drive

Season Three

Moving House
Wendy House
Scottish Dancing
Men as Women
Motorbike
Australia House
Learning to Fly

My Family

Season One

Serpent's Tooth
Pain in the Class
Droit de Seigneur Ben
The Last Resort
Farewell to Alarms
Death Takes a Policy
Awkward Phase
Much Ado About Ben

Season Two

All Roads Lead to Ramon
The Unkindest Cut
Parisian Beauty
Trust Never Sleeps
Death and Ben Take a Holiday
Driving Miss Crazy
I Second That Emulsion
Age of Romance
Get Cartier

'Tis Pity She's a Whore
The Last Supper
Ben Wants to Be a Millionaire
Breakable

Season Three

Absent Vixen, Cheeky Monkey
Shrink Rap
Desperately Squeaking Susan
Of Mice and Ben
Imperfect Strangers
The Second Greatest Story Ever Told
Waiting to Inhale
Misery
Auto Erotica
A Handful of Dust
The Lost Weekend
Ghosts
One Flew out of the Cuckoo's Nest
Ding Dong Merrily . . .

Season Four

Fitting Punishment
They Shoot Harpers, Don't They?
The Great Escape
Return of the Prodigal Prat
Owed to Susan
Deliverance
Blind Justice
Friday the 31st
Sitting Targets
Loco Parentis
Canary Cage
May the Best Man Win
It's a Window-Filled Life
Sixty Feet Under

Season Five

Reloaded
The Mummy Returns
You Don't Know Jack
What's Up, Docklands?
Luck Be a Lady Tonight
First Past the Post
My Will Be Done
My Fair Charlady
The Mouthtrap
While You Weren't Sleeping
Dentist to the Stars
A Wife Less Ordinary
The Book of Love
Going Dental
Glad Tidings We Bring
Comic Relief Special

Season Six

. . . and I'll Cry If I Want To
Bliss for Idiots
The Spokes Person
Dentally Unstable
Living the Dream
An Embarrassment of Susans
And Other Animals
The Art of Being Susan

Season Seven

The Heart of Christmas
The Ego Has Landed
Four Affairs and a Funeral
Once More with Feeling
Dutch Art and Dutch Courage
Susan of Troy
One of the Boys
Abi Ever After

Breaking Up Ain't Hard to Do
Life Begins at Fifty
Ho Ho No

Season Eight

The Parent Trap
Let's Not Be Heisty
Cards on the Table
The Wax Job
Neighbour Wars
Can't Get No Satisfaction
The Abi Habit
Have a Unhappy Christmas

Season Nine

Bully for Ben
Bringing Up Janey
A Very Brief Encounter
The Psyche of Mikey
A Difficult Undertaking
Dog Dazed
It's Training Men
The Guru
Kenzo's Project
2039: A Christmas Oddity

Season Ten

Wheelie Ben
The Son'll Come Out
Desperately Stalking Susan
The Melbourne Identity
He's Just Not That Into Ben
Slammertime
Ben Behaving Badly
Janey's Choice
Mary Christmas

Season Eleven

Labour Pains
Accusin' Susan
Germs of Endearment
Harper V Harper
Relationship Happens
Facebooked
A Decent Proposal
Darts All, Folks
Susan for a Bruisin'
A Night Out

The Good Life

Season One

Plough Your Own Furrow
Say Little Hen . . .
The Weaker Sex?
Pig's Lib
The Thing in the Cellar
The Pagan Rite
Backs to the Wall

Season Two

Just My Bill
The Guru of Surbiton
Mr. Fix-It
The Day Peace Broke Out
Mutiny
Home Sweet Home
Going to Pot?

Season Three

The Early Birds
The Happy Event
A Tug of the Forelock

I Talk to the Trees
The Wind-Break War
Whose Fleas Are These?
The Last Posh Frock

Season Four

Away from It All
The Green Door
Our Speaker Today
The Weaver's Tale
Suit Yourself
Sweet and Sour Charity
Anniversary
Silly, but It's Fun . . . .
When I'm 65

The Fall and Rise of Reginald Perrin

Season One

Hippopotamus
Nightmare in the Park
The Sunday Extraordinary Business Meeting
The Bizarre Dinner Party
The Speech to the British Fruit Association
Trying a Frenchman, Welshman, Scotsman and an Italian
The Memorial Service

Season Two

Remarried and Back at Sunshine Desserts
Elizabeth's New Admirer
Jimmy's Offer
The Unusual Shop
Re-Involvement
The Four Untrustworthy Men
Extreme Solution

Season Three

The Great Project
Staff Training
The Trickle of Visitors
Communal Social Evenings
Timebomb
Losing Face
Closure

Fawlty Towers

Season One

A Touch of Class
The Builders
The Wedding Party
The Hotel Inspectors
Gourmet Night
The Germans

Season Two

Communication Problems
The Psychiatrist
Waldorf Salad
The Kipper and the Corpse
The Anniversary
Basil the Rat

Rutland Weekend Television

Season One

Rutland Weekend Gibberish
Rutland Weekend Kung-Fu
Rutland Weekend Warning System
Rutland Weekend Whistle Test
Rutland Weekend Rain in Hendon

Rutland Weekend Budget Cuts
Christmas with Rutland Weekend Television

Season Two

Rutland Weekend Rutles
Rutland Weekend Cop Show
Rutland Weekend Sequel
Rutland Weekend Sprimpo
Rutland Weekend Insurance
Rutland Weekend Is Innocent
Rutland Weekend Showtime!

Ripping Yarns

Season One

Tomkinson's Schooldays
The Testing of Eric Olthwaite
Escape from Stalag Luft B
Murder at Moorstones Manor
Across the Andes by Frog
The Curse of the Claw

Season Two

Whinfrey's Last Case
Golden Gordon
Roger of the Raj

The Comic Strip Presents ...

Season One

Five Go Mad in Dorset
War
The Beat Generation
Bad News Tour
Summer School

Season Two

Five Go Mad on Mescalin
Dirty Movie
Susie
A Fistful of Travellers' Cheques
Gino: Full Story and Pics
Eddie Monsoon—A Life?
Slags

Specials

The Bullshitters: Roll Out the Gunbarrel
Consuela, or The New Mrs. Saunders
Private Enterprise

Season Three

The Strike
More Bad News
Mr. Jolly Lives Next Door
The Yob
Didn't You Kill My Brother?
Funseekers

Season Four

South Atlantic Raiders
South Atlantic Raiders: Argie Bargie!
GLC: The Carnage Continues . . .
Oxford
Spaghetti Hoops
Les Dogs

Specials

Red Nose of Courage
The Crying Game
Wild Turkey

Season Five

Detectives on the Edge of a Nervous Breakdown
Space Virgins from Planet Sex
Queen of the Wild Frontier
Gregory: Diary of a Nutcase
Demonella
Jealousy

Specials

Four Men in a Car
Four Men in a Plane
. . . Sex Actually
The Hunt for Tony Blair
Five Go to Rehab

The Young Ones

Season One

Demolition
Oil
Boring
Bomb
Interesting
Flood

Season Two

Bambi
Cash
Nasty
Time
Sick
Summer Holiday

Blackadder

Season One

The Foretelling
Born to Be King
The Archbishop
The Queen of Spain's Beard
Witchsmeller Pursuivant
The Black Seal

Season Two (Black-Adder II)

Bells
Head
Potato
Money
Beer
Chains

Season Three (Black Adder the Third)

Dish and Dishonesty
Ink and Incapability
Nob and Nobility
Sense and Senility
Amy and Amiability
Duel and Duality

Season Four (Blackadder Goes Fourth)

Captain Cook
Corporal Punishment
Major Star
Private Plane
General Hospital
Goodbyeee

Special

Blackadder's Christmas Carol

Mr. Bean

Season One + Specials

Mr. Bean
The Return of Mr. Bean
The Curse of Mr. Bean
Mr. Bean Goes to Town
The Trouble with Mr. Bean
Mr. Bean Rides Again
Merry Christmas Mr. Bean
Mr. Bean in Room
Do-It-Yourself Mr. Bean
Mind the Baby, Mr. Bean
Back to School Mr. Bean
Tee Off, Mr. Bean
Goodnight, Mr. Bean
Hair by Mr. Bean of London

To the Manor Born

Season One

Grantleigh
All New Together
Going to Church
Nations of Heritage
The Summer Hunt Ball
The Grape Vine
A Touch of Class
Christmas Special: The First Noel

Season Two

The New Farm Manager
The Spare Room
Never Be Alone
Tramps and Poachers
The Honours List
Vive le Sport

Season Three

The New Scout Hut
Station Closing
Horses Vs. Cars
Birds Vs. Bees
Cosmetics
Connections in High Places
Back to the Manor

Only Fools and Horses

Season One

Big Brother
Go West Young Man
Cash and Curry
The Second Time Around
A Slow Bus to Chingford
The Russians Are Coming
Christmas Crackers

Season Two

The Long Legs of the Law
Ashes to Ashes
A Losing Streak
No Greater Love . . .
The Yellow Peril
It Never Rains . . .
A Touch of Glass

Christmas Trees
Diamonds Are for Heather

Season Three

Homesick
Healthy Competition
Friday the 14th
Yesterday Never Comes
May the Force Be with You
Wanted
Who's a Pretty Boy?
Thicker Than Water

Season Four

Happy Returns
Strained Relations
Hole in One
It's Only Rock and Roll
Sleeping Dogs Lie
Watching the Girls Go By
As One Door Closes
To Hull and Back

Season Five

From Prussia with Love
The Miracle of Peckham
The Longest Night
Tea for Three
Video Nasty
Who Wants to Be a Millionaire?
A Royal Flush

Specials

The Frog's Legacy
Dates

Season Six

Yuppy Love
Danger UXD
Chain Gang
The Unlucky Winner Is . . .
Sickness & Wealth
Little Problems

Specials

The Jolly Boys' Outing
Rodney Come Home

Season Seven

The Sky's the Limit
The Chance of a Lunchtime
Stage Fright
The Class of '62
He Ain't Heavy, He's My Uncle
Three Men, a Woman, and a Baby

Specials

Miami Twice: "The American Dream"
Miami Twice: "Oh to Be in England"
Mother Nature's Son
Fatal Extraction
Heroes and Villains
Modern Men
Time on Our Hands
If They Could See Us Now . . . !
Strangers on the Shore . . . !
Sleepless in Peckham . . . !

Father Ted

Season One

Good Luck, Father Ted
Entertaining Father Stone
The Passion of Saint Tibulus
Competition Time
And God Created Woman
Grant unto Him Eternal Rest

Season Two

Hell
Think Fast, Father Ted
Tentacles of Doom
Old Grey Whistle Theft
A Song for Europe
The Plague
Rock a Hula Ted
Cigarettes and Alcohol and Rollerblading
New Jack City
Flight into Terror
A Christmassy Ted

Season Three

Are You Right There Father Ted?
Chirpy Burpy Cheap Sheep
Speed
The Mainland
Escape from Victory
Kicking Bishop Brennan up the Arse
Night of the Nearly Dead
Going to America

Murder Most Horrid

Season One

The Case of the Missing
The Girl from Ipanema
He Died a Death
A Determined Woman
Murder at Tea Time
Mrs. Hat and Mrs. Red

Season Two

Overkill
Lady Luck
A Severe Case of Death
We All Hate Granny
Mangez Merveillac
Smashing Bird

Season Three

Girl Friday
A Life or Death Operation
Dying Live
The Body Politic
Confess
Dead on Time

Season Four

Frozen
Going Solo
Whoopi Stone
Confessions of a Murderer
Elvis, Jesus and Zack
Dinner at Tiffany's

The Vicar of Dibley

Season One

The Arrival
Songs of Praise
Community Spirit
The Window & the Weather
Election
Animals
The Easter Bunny
The Christmas Lunch Incident

Season Two

Ballykissdibley
Engagement
Dibley Live
Celebrity Vicar
Love and Marriage
Red Nose Day Special: Celebrity Party

Season Three

Autumn
Winter
Spring
Summer

Specials

Merry Christmas
Happy New Year
Antiques Roadshow
The Handsome Stranger
The Vicar in White

Red Dwarf

Season One

The End
Future Echoes
Balance of Power
Waiting for God
Confidence & Paranoia
Me^2

Season Two

Kryten
Better Than Life
Thanks for the Memory
Stasis Leak
Queeg
Parallel Universe

Season Three

Backwards
Marooned
Polymorph
Bodyswap
Timeslides
The Last Day

Season Four

Camille
D.N.A.
Justice
White Hole
Dimension Jump
Meltdown

Season Five

Holoship
The Inquisitor
Terrorform
Quarantine
Demons & Angels
Back to Reality

Season Six

Psirens
Legion
Gunmen of the Apocalypse
Emohawk: Polymorph II
Rimmerworld
Out of Time

Season Seven

Tikka to Ride
Stoke Me a Clipper
Ouroboros
Duct Soup
Blue
Beyond a Joke
Epideme
Nanarchy

Season Eight

Back in the Red: Part I
Back in the Red: Part II
Back in the Red: Part III
Cassandra
Krytie TV
Pete: Part I
Pete: Part II
Only the Good . . .

Season Nine

Back to Earth: Part I
Back to Earth: Part II
Back to Earth: Part III

Season Ten

Trojan
Fathers & Suns
Lemons
Entangled
Dear Dave
The Beginning

Yes Minister

Season One

Open Government
The Official Visit
The Economy Drive
Big Brother
The Writing on the Wall
The Right to Know
Jobs for the Boys

Season Two

The Compassionate Society
Doing the Honours
The Death List
The Greasy Pole
The Devil You Know
The Quality of Life
A Question of Loyalty

Season Three

Equal Opportunities
The Challenge
The Skeleton in the Cupboard
The Moral Dimension
The Bed of Nails
The Whisky Priest
The Middle-Class Rip-Off

Special

Party Games

Yes, Prime Minister

Season One

The Grand Design
The Ministerial Broadcast
The Smoke Screen
The Key
A Real Partnership
A Victory for Democracy
The Bishop's Gambit
One of Us

Season Two

Man Overboard
Official Secrets
A Diplomatic Incident
A Conflict of Interest
Power to the People
The Patron of the Arts
The National Education Service
The Tangled Web

Yes, Prime Minister (2013)

Season One

Crisis at the Summit
The Poisoned Chalice
Gentlemen's Agreement
A Diplomatic Dilemma
Scot Free
A Tsar Is Born

The New Statesman

Season One

Happiness Is a Warm Gun
Passport to Freedom
Sex Is Wrong
Waste Not Want Not
Friends of St. James
Three Line Whipping
Baa Baa Black Sheep

Special

Alan B'Stard Closes Down the BBC

Season Two

Fatal Extraction
Live from Westminster
A Wapping Conspiracy
The Haltemprice Bunker
California Here I Come
May the Best Man Win
Piers of the Realm

Special

Who Shot Alan B'Stard?

Season Three

Labour of Love
The Party's Over
Let Them Sniff Cake
Keeping Mum
Natural Selection
Profit of Boom

Season Four

Back from the Mort
H*A*S*H
Speaking in Tongues
Heil and Farewell
A Bigger Splash
The Irresistible Rise of Alan B'Stard

Special

A B'Stard Exposed

Hot Metal

Season One

The Tell-Tale Heart
The Modern Prometheus
Beyond the Infinite
Casting the Runes
The Slaughter of the Innocent
The Respectable Prostitute

Season Two

Religion of the People
The Joker to the Thief
The Hydra's Head
The Twilight Zone
Crown of Thorns

Unleash the Kraken
The Satellite Years

Drop the Dead Donkey

Season One

A New Dawn
Sally's Arrival
A Clash of Interests
A Blast from the Past
Old Father Time
Sex, Lies and Audiotape
The New Approach
The Root of All Evil
Death, Disaster 'n Damien
The Big Day

Season Two

The Gulf Report
The Trevorman Cometh
Henry & Dido
Baseball
Drunk Minister
Alex and the Interpreter
Hoax
Don't Mention the Arabs
Damien Down and Out
The Evangelist
George's Daughter
Dave's Day
Xmas Party

Season Three

In Place of Alex
Sally's Accountant
Henry's Lost Love

Helen'll Fix It
Sally's Libel
Lady Merchant
The New Newsreader
Joy
Paintball
George and His Daughter
Awards

Season Four

The Undiscovered Country
Quality Time
The Day of the Mum
Births and Deaths
Helen's Parents
Sally in TV Times
Crime Time
No More Mr. Nice Guy
Henry's Autobiography
The Strike
The Wedding
Damien and the Weather Girl

Season Five

Inside the Asylum
The Godless Society
The Bird of Doom
What Are Friends For?
The Path of True Love
George's Car
Charnley in Love
Henry's Diary
Dave and Diana
Luck
The Graveyard Shift
Sex 'n Death

Season Six

The Newsmakers
Beasts, Badgers and Bombshells
The Diaries
But Is It Art?
George Finds Love
A Bit of an Atmosphere
The Final Chapter

Absolutely Fabulous

Season One

Fashion
France
ISO Tank
Birthday
Magazine

Season Two

Hospital
Death
Morocco
New Best Friend
Poor
Birth

Season Three

Door Handle
Happy New Year
Sex
Jealous
Fear
The End

Specials

The Last Shout: Part I
The Last Shout: Part II

Season Four

Parallox
Fish Farm
Paris
Donkey
Small Opening
Menopause

Special

Gay

Season Five

Cleanin'
Book Clubbin'
Panickin'
Huntin', Shootin', Fishin'
Birthin'
Schmoozin'
Exploitin'
Cold Turkey
White Box

Specials

Identity
Job
Olympics

Coupling

Season One

Flushed
Size Matters
Sex, Death & Nudity
Inferno
The Girl with Two Breasts
The Cupboard of Patrick's Love

Season Two

The Man with Two Legs
My Dinner in Hell
Her Best Friend's Bottom
The Melty Man Cometh
Jane and the Truth Snake
Gotcha
Dressed
Naked
The End of the Line

Season Three

Split
Faithless
Unconditional Sex
Remember This
The Freckle, the Key and the Couple Who Weren't
The Girl with One Heart
Perhaps, Perhaps, Perhaps

Season Four

½ Minutes
Nightlines
Bed Time
Circus of the Epidurals
The Naked Living Room
½ Months

Appendix Two
Recommended Viewing

An A–Z of Additional Britcoms for Your Viewing Pleasure

1950s/60s

A Life of Bliss
The Bedsit Girl
Beggar My Neighbour
Citizen James
The Complete and Utter History of Britain
Dear Mother, Love Albert
Dick and the Duchess
Doctor in the House
The Dustbin Men
Father Dear Father
Fire Crackers
The Fossett Saga
George and the Dragon
Hugh and I
It's a Square World
The Marriage Lines
Me Mammy
Meet the Wife
Nearest and Dearest
Never Mind the Quality, Feel the Width
Not in Front of the Children
Our House
Our Man at St. Marks
The Rag Trade
Sykes
The Worker

1970s

Agony
Bless Me Father
Butterflies
Citizen Smith
The Cuckoo Waltz
The Fosters
Get Some In
Girls About Town
Happy Ever After
It's Awfully Bad for Your Eyes, Darling
Love Thy Neighbour
Mind Your Language
The Misfit
Moody and Pegg
My Wife Next Door

No, Honestly
Open All Hours
Porridge
Queenie's Castle
Rings on Their Fingers

Rising Damp
The Squirrels
Top Secret Life of Edgar Briggs
Two's Company

1980s

Birds of a Feather
Brass
Bread
Brush Strokes
Chance in a Million
Colin's Sandwich
Dear John
Desmonds
Don't Wake Up
Duty Free
Ever Decreasing Circles
A Fine Romance
The Front Line
Help

Just Good Friends
The Lady Is a Tramp
Making Out
Nanny
Never the Twain
No Problem
Nobody's Perfect
Singles
Solo
Sorry
Three Up Two Down
Tutti Frutti
The Two of Us
Whoops Apocalypse

1990s

2point4 Children
Bad Boys
Birds of a Feather
Bread
The Brittas Empire
Brush Strokes
Chef
Common as Muck
Dad
Don't Wait Up
Gimme Gimme Gimme
Grace and Favour
The High Life
If You See God, Tell Him

Keeping Mum
Keeping Up Appearances
Love Hurts
Maid Marian and Her Merry Men
May to December
Men Behaving Badly
Mrs. Merton and Malcolm
Nelson's Column
Next of Kin
Oh, Doctor Beeching
Once Upon a Time in the North
One Foot in the Grave
The Royle Family
Satellite City

Sex, Chips and Rock 'n' Roll
So Haunt Me

The Thin Blue Line
Waiting for God

2000s

After You've Gone
At Home with the Braithwaites
Black Books
Come Dine with Me
Early Doors
The Green Green Grass
Grownups
The Inbetweeners
League of Gentlemen
The Life of Riley
Miranda

Not Going Out
The Old Guys
Outnumbered
Partridge
The Smoking Room
Spaced
Time Gentlemen Please
Two Pints of Lager and a Packet of Crisps
The Worst Week of My Life

Appendix Three
From Sitcom to Silver Screen

An Index of British Movies Based on Original Sitcom Series

Are You Being Served? (1977)

I Only Arsked! (1958—based on *The Army Game*)

The Bad Education Movie (2015—based on *Bad Education*)

Bless This House (1972)

Guest House Paradiso (1999—based on *Bottom*)

Dad's Army (1971)

Dad's Army (2015)

Father, Dear Father (1973)

For the Love of Ada (1972)

George and Mildred (1980)

The Inbetweeners Movie (2011)

The Inbetweeners 2 (2014)

Inn for Trouble (1960—based on The Larkins)

The League of Gentlemen's Apocalypse (2005—based on *The League of Gentlemen*)

The Lovers! (1973)

Love Thy Neighbour (1973)

Man About the House (1974)

Bean (1997)

Mr. Bean's Holiday (2007)

Mrs. Brown's Boys D'Movie (2014)

Nearest and Dearest (1972)

Never Mind the Quality, Feel the Width (1973)

On the Buses (1971)

Mutiny on the Buses (1972—based on *On the Buses*)

Holiday on the Buses (1973—based on *On the Buses*)

Please Sir! (1971)

Porridge (1979)

Rising Damp (1980)

Stella Street (2004)

Steptoe and Son (1972)

Steptoe and Son Ride Again (1973)

That's Your Funeral (1972)

In the Loop (2009—based on *The Thick of It*)

Till Death Us Do Part (1968)

The Alf Garnett Saga (1972—based on Till Death Us Do Part)

Up Pompeii (1971)

Up the Chastity Belt (1971—based on *Up Pompeii*)

Up the Front (1972—based on *Up Pompeii*)

Bottoms Up (1960—based on *Whack-O!*)

The Likely Lads (1976—based on *Whatever Happened to the Likely Lads?*)

Whoops Apocalypse (1986)

Appendix Four
Further Listening

A Selection of Britcom-Related 45s and LPs from the Golden Age of Vinyl

Note: In the decades before VHS and DVD, when repeats of shows you might want to see again were as rare as fish lips (if much more succulent), the only way to reliably relive one's favorite TV comedy moments was via the gramophone—either with straightforward reproductions of classic shows and sketches or through other examples of our heroes' humor. The following documents the Best of Britcoms, as recounted at 33 and 45.

Singles

Rowan Atkinson
I Believe (The Reagan Song)/Cana (Polydor POSP 899, 1987)

*Bad News (**The Comic Strip Presents**)*
Bohemian Rhapsody/Life with Brian (EMI EM 24, 1987)
Cashing In on Christmas/Bad News (EMI EM 36,1987)

*The Bonzo Dog Doo-Dah Band (**Do Not Adjust Your Set**)*
My Brother Makes the Noises for the Talkies/I'm Gonna Bring a Watermelon
    to My Gal Tonight (Parlophone R 5430, 1966)
Alley Oop/Button Up Your Overcoat (Parlophone R 5499, 1966)
Equestrian Statue/The Intro and Outro (Liberty LBF 15040, 1967)
Mister Apollo/Ready Mades (Liberty LBF 15201, 1969)
I Want to Be with You/We Were Wrong (Liberty LBF 15273, 1969)
You Done My Brain In/Mr. Slater's Parrot (Liberty LBF 15314, 1970)

*Dora Bryan (**Absolutely Fabulous, Last of the Summer Wine**)*
All I Want for Christmas Is a Beatle/If I Were a Fairy (Fontana TF 427, 1964)

Peter Cook

The Ballad of Spotty Muldoon/Lovely Lady of the Roses (Decca F 12182, 1965)

Peter Cook and Dudley Moore

Excerpts from *Beyond the Fringe*: Sitting on the Bench/The End of the World (with others) (Parlophone R 4969, 1962)

Goodbye-Ee/Not Only but Also (Dudley Moore Trio) (Decca F 12158, 1965)

Isn't She a Sweetie?/Bo Dudley (Decca F 12380, 1966)

The L. S. Bumblebee/The Bee Side (Decca F 12551, 1967)

Bedazzled/Love Me (Decca F 12710, 1967)

*Harry H. Corbett (**Steptoe And Son**)*

Junk Shop/The Isle of Clerkenwell (Pye 7N 15468, 1962)

Like the Big Guys On/The Green Eye (Pye 7N 15552, 1963)

The Table and the Chair/Things We Never Had (Pye 7N 15584, 1963)

Flower Power Fred/(I'm) Saving All My Love (with Unidentified Flower Objects) (Decca F 12714, 1967)

*Dirk and Stig (**Rutland Weekend Television**)*

Gin Gan Goolie/Mr. Sheene (EMI EMI 2852, 1978)

Marty Feldman

Joyous Time of Year/The B Side (Decca F 12857, 1968)

Funny He Never Married/Travel Agency (Pye 7N 17643, 1968)

David Frost (& Others)

Zookeeper/Deck of Cards (Parlophone R 5441, 1966)

The Goodies

All Things Bright and Beautiful/Winter Sportsman (Decca F13449, 1973)

The In Betweenies/Father Christmas Do No Touch Me (Bradley BRAD 7421, 1974)

Funky Gibbon/Sick Man Blues (Bradley BRAD 7504, 1975)

Stuff That Gibbon/Goodies Theme (Decca F 13578, 1975)

Black Pudding Bertha/Panic (Bradley BRAD 7517, 1975)

Nappy Love I Wild Thing (Bradley BRAD 7524)

Make a Daft Noise for Christmas/ Last Chance Dance (Bradley BRAD 7533, 1975)

M.l.C.K.E.Y.M.O.U.S.E./Funky Farm (EMI 2784, 1978)

A Man's Best Friend Is His Duck/Taking My Oyster Walkies/Rastashanty (Columbia DB 9053, 1978)

The Goons

My September Love (with Eric Sykes)/You Gotta Go Oww! (Parlophone R 4251, 1956)

I'm Walking Backwards for Christmas/Bluebottle Blues (Decca F 10756, 1956)

Bloodnok's Rock 'n' Roll/The Ying Tong Song (Decca F 10780, 1956)

Eeh! Ah! Oh! Ooh!/I Love You (Decca F 10885, 1957)

A Russian Love Song/Whistle Your Cares Away (Decca F 10945, 1957)

Ying Tong Song/I'm Walking Backwards for Christmas (Decca F 13414, 1973)

Raspberry Song/Rhymes (Decca F 13769, 1978)

Tony Hancock

Wing Commander Hancock—Test Pilot/The Threatening Letters (with Kenneth Williams) (Pye 7N 15575, 1963)

*Frankie Howerd (**Up Pompeii**)*

The Last Word on the Election/(Version) (Decca F 12028, 1964)

Up Je T'Aime/All Through the Night (Pye 7N 45061, 1970)

Up Pompeii/Salute (Columbia DB 8757, 1971)

*Frankie Howerd (**Up Pompeii**) and Margaret Rutherford*

Nymphs and Shepherds/All's Going Well (Phillips PB 214, 1956)

*Sidney James (**Hancock's Half Hour, Bless This House**) and Liz Fraser*

The Ooter Song/Double Bunk (Decca F 11328, 1961)

*Michael Medwin (**The Army Game**)*

The Army Game Signature Tune/What Do We Do in the Army? (HMV POP 490, 1958)

Spike Milligan

Wish I Knew/Will I Find My Love Today? (Parlophone R 4406 ,1958)

I'm Walking Out with a Mountain/The Sewers of the Strand (Parlophone R 4839, 1960)

Postman's Knock/Wormwood Scrubs Tango (Parlophone R4891, 1962)

The Olympic Team/Epilogue (with John Bluthal) (Pye 7N 15720, 1964)

Purple Aeroplane/Nothing at All (Parlophone R 5513, 1966)

Tower Bridge/Silent Night (Parlophone R 5543, 1966)

The Q5 Piano Tune/Ning Nang Nong (Parlophone Ft 5571, 1969)

Girl on a Pony/Old Man's Protest Song (Warner Bros. K 16240, 1973)

On the Ning Nang Nong/The Silly Old Baboon (Polydor 2058 524, 1974)

Cheese/Shipmates (Starline PSR 367, promo only, 1974)

One Sunny Day/Woe Is Me (with Ed Welch, United Artists UA 36489, 1979)

Sticky/None Today Thank You (CBS STICKY 1, 1982)

Himazas I There Ain't No Morning (with Peter Cook, Paramount PARA 101, 1983)

Warren Mitchell (Till Death Us Do Part)

The Writing on the Wall/Her Heart's in the Right Place (CBS 2824, 1967)

Get Me to the Church On Time/A Hymn to Him (Decca MFLS 2, 1987)

Dudley Moore Trio

Strictly for the Birds (Solo)/Duddly Dell (Parlophone R 4772, 1961)

Monty Python's Flying Circus

Spam Song/The Concert (Charisma CB 192, 1972)

Eric the Half a Bee/Yangste Song (extended) (Charisma CB 200, 1972)

Teach Yourself Heath (Python Productions, flexidisc free with *Zig Zag* magazine, 1972)

Lumberjack Song/Spam Song (Charisma CB 268, 1974)

Monty Python's Tiny Black Round Thing (NME/Charisma SFL 1259, flexi-disc free with the *New Musical Express* magazine, 1974)

Brian Song (Sonia Jones)/Always Look on the Bright Side of Life (Warner Bros K 17495, 1979)

I Like Chinese/I Bet You They Won't Play This Song on the Radio/Finland (Charisma CB 374, 1980)

Galaxy Song/Every Sperm Is Sacred (CBS WA 3495, 1983)

Mr. Bean

(I Want to Be) Elected/(Version) (London LON 319, 1992)

Neil (The Young Ones)

Hole in My Shoe/Hurdy Gurdy Mushroom Man (WEA YZ 10, 1984)

Not the Nine O'Clock News

Oh Bosanquet/Gob on You (After the Break NB 5, 1979)

Ayatollah Song (BBC RESL 8, 1980)

I Like Trucking/Supa Dupa (BBC RESL 102, 1981)

Not the Presidential Press/Holiday Habits (BBC RESL 150, 1984)

Bill Oddie (The Goodies)

Nothing Better to Do/Traffic Island (Parlophone R5153, 1964)

The Knitting Song/Ain't Got Rhythm (Parlophone R5346, 1965)

I Can't Get Through/Because She Is My Love (Parlophone R5433, 1966)

Jimmy Young/Irish Get Out (Decca F 12903, 1969)

On Ilkla Moor Baht'at/Harry Krishna (Dandelion 4786, 1970)

Bill Oddie and the Superspike Squad Featuring John Cleese
Superspike parts one and two (Bradley BRAD 7606, 1976)

*The Rutles (**Rutland Weekend Television**)*
I Must Be in Love/Cheese and Onions/With a Girl Like You (Warner Bros
    K 17125, 1978)

Let's Be Natural/Piggy in the Middle (Warner Bros K 17180, 1978)

Shangri-La/Joe Public/Baby S'il Vous Plait/It's Looking Good (Virgin VUSA
    117, 1996)

*Mike Sarne and Wendy Richard (**Are You Being Served?**)*
Come Outside/Fountain of Love (Parlophone R 4902, 1962)

*Alexei Sayle (**The Young Ones**)*
Didn't You Kill My Brother/Dedicated (CBS A 6653, 1985)

'Ullo John, Gotta New Motor (version) (Springtime IS 162, 1984)

Peter Sellers
Dipso-Calypso/Never Never Land (HMV B10724, 1954)

Any Old Iron/Boiled Bananas and Carrots (Parlophone R 4337, 1957)

I'm So Ashamed/A Drop of the Hard Stuff (Parlophone R 4491, 1958)

Puttin' On the Smile/My Old Dutch (Parlophone R 4605, 1959)

A Hard Day's Night/Help! (Parlophone R 5393, 1965)

After the Fox/The Fox-Trot (Burt Bacharach) (U. Artists Up 1152, 1966)

They're Parking Camels Where the Taxis Used to Be/Night and Day (United
    Artists BP 335, 1980)

She Loves You/She Loves You (Parlophone R 6043, 1981)

Peter Sellers and Sophia Loren
Goodness Gracious Me (with Sophia Loren)/Grandpa's Grave (Parlophone
    R 4702, 1960)

Bangers and Mash (with Sophia Loren)/Zoo Be Zoo Be Zoo (Sophia Loren)
    (Parlophone R 4724, 1961)

*Mel Smith (**Not the Nine O'Clock News**)*
Mel Smith's Greatest Hits/Richard & Joey (with Roger Taylor) (Mercury
    MEL 1, 1981)

Kenneth Williams (aka Ramblin Syd Rumpo)
Green Grow My Nadgers Oh!/The Ballad of the Woggier's Moulie (Parlophone R 5638, 1967)

The Young Ones and Cliff Richard
Living Doll/(All the Little Flowers Are) Happy (WEA YZ 65, 1986)

EPs

Peter Cook and Dudley Moore
Pete and Dud By Appointment (Decca DFE 8644, 1965)
Peter Cook and Dudley Moore (Parlophone GEP 8940, 1965)

The Goons
The Goons (Decca DFE 6396, 1956)

Tony Hancock
Little Pieces of Hancock (Pye NEP 24146, 1961)
Little Pieces of Hancock No. 2 (Pye NEP 24161, 1962)
Hancock's Half Hour (Pye NEP 24170, 1962)
The Blood Donor (Pye NEP 24175, 1963)

Monty Python's Flying Circus
Python on Song (EP, double pack, Charisma MP 001, 1976)

Peter Sellers
Best of Sellers #1 (Parlophone GEP 8770, 1959)
Best of Sellers #2 (Parlophone GEP 8784, 1959)
Best of Sellers #3 (Parlophone GEP 8809, 1959)
Songs for Swingin' Sellers #1 (Parlophone SGE 2013, 1960)
Songs for Swingin' Sellers #2 (Parlophone SGE 2016, 1960)
Songs for Swingin' Sellers #3 (Ep, Parlophone GEP 8832
Songs for Swingin' Sellers #4 (Parlophone SGE 2020, 1961)
Fool Britannia (Ember Emb Ep 4530, 1964)

Peter Sellers and Sophia Loren
Peter and Sophia #1 (Parlophone SGE 2021, 1961)
Peter and Sophia #2 (Parlophone SGE 2022, 1961)
Peter and Sophia #3 (Parlophone SGE 2023, 1961)

Peter Sellers, Spike Milligan and Harry Secombe
How to Win an Election (Philips AL 3464, 1964)

Peter Sellers and Peter Ustinov
Two Peters (with Peter Ustinov, Parlophone GEP 8853, 1961)

LPs

Rowan Atkinson
Not Just a Pretty Face (Polydor POLD 5217, 1988)

Bad News
Bad News (EMI EMC 3535, 1987)
Bootleg (EMI EMC 3542, 1988)

*Michael Bentine (**The Goons**)*
It's a Square World (Parlophone PMC 1179, 1962)

Bonzo Dog Doo-Dah Band
Gorilla (Liberty LBL 83056, 1967)
The Doughnut in Granny's Greenhouse (Liberty LBL 83158, 1968)
Tadpoles (Liberty LBS 83257, 1969)
Keynsham (Liberty LBS 83290, 1969)
Let's Make Up and Be Friendly (UA UAS 29288, 1972)

The Comic Strip
The Comic Strip (Springtime HAHA 6001, 1981)

Peter Cook
Peter Cook Presents Misty Mr. Wisty (Decca LK 4722, 1965)
Here Comes the Judge — Live in Concert (Virgin VR 4, 1979)

Peter Cook and Dudley Moore
Not Only Peter Cook but also Dudley Moore (Decca LK 4703, 1965)
Once Moore with Cook (Decca LK 4785, 1966)
Bedazzled (Soundtrack) (Decca LK 4923, 1968)
Not Only but Also (Decca LK 5080, 1971)
The Clean Tapes (Cube HIFLY 26, 1971)
Not Only. . . but Also (Decca LK 5080, 1971)
The World of Pete and Dud (Decca PA 311, 1971)
Behind the Fridge (Warner Bros. K 40503, 1973)
Derek and Clive Live (Island LCT 9434, 1976)
Derek and Clive Come Again (Virgin V 2094, 1977)
Derek and Clive Ad Nauseam (Virgin V 2112, 1978)

*Harry H. Corbett and Wilfred Brambell (**Steptoe and Son**)*
Steptoe and Son (Pye NPL 18051, 1964)
Love and Harold Steptoe (Pye NPL 18135, 1965)
Gems from the Steptoe Scrap Heap (Pye NPL 18153, 1966)
Steptoe a la Carte (Golden Guinea GGL 0373, 1967)

Dad's Army
Dad's Army (BBC REH 183, 1974)
Original Cast Recording (WEA K56186, 1975)

Marty Feldman
Marty (Pye NPL 18258, 1968)
I Feel a Song Coming Off (Decca SKL 4983, 1969)

David Frost (with others)
The Frost Report on Britain (Parlophone PMC 7005, 1966)
The Frost Report on Everything (Pye NPL 18199, 1967)

The Goodies
The Goodies Sing Songs from the Goodies (Decca SKL 5175, 1973)
The World of the Goodies (Decca SPA 416, 1975)
The New Goodies LP (Bradley BRADL 1010, 1975)
Nothing to Do with Us (Island ILPS 9452, 1976)
The Goodies' Beastly Record (Columbia SCX 6596, 1978)

The Goons
Unchained Melodies (Decca LF 1332, 1964)
Best of the Goon Shows (Parlophone PMC 1108, 1959)
Best of the Goon Shows #2 (Parlophone PMC 1129, 1960)
Goon but Not Forgotten (Parlophone PMC 7037, 1967)
Goon Show Greats (Parlophone PMC 7179, 1968)
Goon Again (Parlophone PMC 7062, 1968)
First Men on the Goon (Parlophone PMC 7132, 1971)
The Last Goon Show of All (BBC Records REB 142S, 1972)
Michael Parkinson Meets the Goons (BBC Records REB 165M, 1973)

Tony Hancock
This Is Hancock (Pye NPL 18045, 1960)
Pieces of Hancock (Pye NPL 18054, 1960)
The Blood Donor and the Radio Ham (Pye NPL 18068, 1961)
Face to Face (Piccadilly FTF 38500, 1963)
It's Hancock (Decca LK 4740, 1965)

Frankie Howerd
At the Establishment (Decca LK 4556, 1963)

Spike Milligan
Milligan Preserved (Parlophone PMC 1146, 1961)
The Best of Milligan's Wake (Pye NPL 18104, 1964)
Muses with Milligan (Decca LK 470L, 1965)
The World of the Beachcomber (Pye NPL 18271, 1969)
Live at Cambridge University (with Jeremy Taylor) (2-LP, Spark SRLO
    3001,1974)
Sing Songs from Q8 (with Ed Welch) (United Artists UAG 30223, 1979)

Warren Mitchell (Till Death Us Do Part)
Songs of World War One (Allegro ALL 840, 1967)
Af Garnett's Music Hall (Allegro ALL 850, 1967)
The Thoughts of Chairman Alf (Warner Brothers K56427, 1977)

Monty Python's Flying Circus
Monty Python's Flying Circus (BBC REB 73M, 1970)
Another Monty Python Record (Charisma CAS 1049, 1971)
Monty Python's Previous Record (Charisma CAS 1063, 1972)
The Monty Python Matching Tie and Handkerchief (Charisma CAS 1080, 1973)
Monty Python Live at Drury Lane (Charisma CLASS 4, 1974, No. 19)
*The Album of the Soundtrack of the Trailer of the Film of Monty Python and the Holy
    Grail* (Charisma CAS 1103, 1975)
The Monty Python Instant Record Collection (Charisma CAS 1134, 1977)
Monty Python's Life of Brian (Warners K 56751, 1979)
Monty Python's Contractual Obligation Album (Charisma CAS 1152, 1980)

Dudley Moore
From Beyond the Fringe (Atlantic 2465 017, 1970)

Neil
Neil's Heavy Concept Album (WEA WX 12, 1984)

Not the Nine O'clock News
Not the Nine O'clock News (BBC REB 400, 1980)
Hedgehog Sandwich (BBC REB 421, 1981)
The Memory Kinda Lingers (BBC REF 453, 1982)

The Rutles
All You Need Is Cash (Warner Bros. K 56459, 1978)
Archaeology (Virgin VUSLP 119, 1996)

Peter Sellers
The Best of Sellers (Parlophone PMD 1069, 1958)
Songs for Swingin' Sellers (Parlophone PMC 1111, 1959)
Sellers' Market (United Artists UAG 30266, 1979)
The Voice Behind the Mask (Guild 62002, 1981)

Peter Sellers and Sophia Loren
Peter and Sophia (Parlophone PMC 1131, 1960)

Eric Sykes and Hattie Jacques
Eric, Hattie & Things (Decca LK 4507, 1953)

Till Death Us Do Part
Till Death Us Do Part (Pye NPL 18154, 1966)
Sex & Other Thoughts. Alf Garnet and Family (from the B.B.C. Series 'Till Death Us Do Part') (Pye 18192, 1967)
Till Death Us Do Part—The Original Soundtrack from the Film (Polydor 583 717, 1968)
Till Death Us Do Part (Marble Arch MAL 1112, 1969)

Kenneth Williams
On Pleasure Bent (Decca LK 4856, 1967)
The Best of Rambling Syd Rumpo (Star|ine SRS 5034, 1970)
The World of Kenneth Williams (Decca SPA 64, 1970)

Various Artists

Beyond the Fringe (Parlophone PMC 1145, 1961)
Bridge on the River Wye (Parlophone PMC 1190, 1963)
Peter Cook Presents the Establishment (Parlophone PMC 1198, 1963)
Private Eye's Blue Record (Transatlantic TRA 131, 1965)
A Poke in the Eye with a Sharp Stick (Transatlantic TRA 331, 1976)
The Secret Policeman's Ball (Island ILPS 9601, 1979)
Comic Relief Utterly Utterly Live (WEA WX 51, 1986)
Private Eye Presents Golden Satiricals (Springtime HAHA 6002, 1981)
The Secret Policeman's Other Ball (Springtime HAHA 6003, 1981)
The Secret Policeman's Third Ball (Virgin V 2459, 1987)

Bibliography

Adams, Guy. *Leonard Rossiter: Character Driven: The Untold Story of a Comic Genius.* Aurum Press, London, 2010.

Adams, John. *Yes, Prime Minister: The Ministerial Broadcast.* Cambridge University Press, Cambridge, 1993.

Berman, Garry. *The Best of the Britcoms from Fawlty Towers to Absolutely Fabulous.* Taylor Publishing, Dallas, 1999.

Bright, Morris. *Carry On Uncensored.* Boxtree, London, 1999.

Bright, Morris & Ross, Robert. *Last of the Summer Wine.* BBC Books, London, 2003.

Campey, George. *BBC Book of That Was the Week That Was.* BBC Books, London, 1963.

Carpenter, Humphrey. *A Great Silly Grin—How Peter Cook, Dudley Moore, Michael Frayn, Jonathan Miller, Alan Bennett, David Frost and the British "Invasion" Changed the Face of Comedy.* Da Capo Press, Cambridge, MA, 2000.

Charles, Craig. *The Log: A Dwarfer's Guide to Everything.* Penguin Books, London, 1997.

Clayton, David. *The Richard Beckinsale Story.* The History Press, London, 2008.

Cook, Lin (editor). *Something Like Fire—Peter Cook Remembered.* Methuen, London, 1996.

Corbett, Susannah. *Harry H. Corbett: The Front Legs of the Cow.* The History Press, London, 2012.

Corner, John (editor). *Popular Television in Britain: Studies in Cultural History.* British Film Institute Publishing, London, 1991.

Creeber, Glen (editor). *Fifty Key Television Programmes.* Edward Arnold, UK, 2004.

Curtis, Richard & Mayhew-Archer, Paul. *The Vicar of Dibley—The Complete Companion to Dibley.* Michael Joseph, London, 2000.

Davies, Russell (editor). *The Kenneth Williams Diaries.* Harper Collins, London, 1994.

Eastaugh, Kenneth. *The Carry-On Book.* David & Charles, North Pomfret, VT, 1978.

Elton, Ben & Mayall, Rik. *Bachelor Boys—The Young Ones Book.* Sphere, London, 1984.

Esmonde, John, Webber, Richard, & Larbey, Bob. *A Celebration of the Good Life.* Orion Books, London, 2000.

Fiddy, Dick. *Missing Believed Wiped: Searching for the Lost Treasures of British Television.* British Film Institute Publishing, London, 2001.

Foster, Andy & Furst, Steve. *Radio Comedy 1938–1968—A Guide to 30 Years of Wonderful Wireless.* Virgin Publishing, London, 1996.

Frost, David & Sherrin, Ned. *That Was the Week That Was.* WH Allen, London, 1963.

Galton, Ray, Simpson, Alan, & Ross, Robert. *Steptoe and Son.* BBC Books, London, 2002.

Games, Alexander (compiler). *The Essential Spike Milligan.* Fourth Estate, London, 2002.

Goodwin, Cliff. *Sid James: A Biography.* Virgin Books, London, 2011.

Hancock, Freddie & Nathan, David. *Hancock.* William Kimber & Company, London, 1969.

Hewison, Robert. *Footlights! A Hundred Years of Cambridge Comedy.* Methuen, London, 1983.

Joffe, Edward. *Hancock's Last Stand—The Series that Never Was.* The Book Guild, Lewes, UK, 1998.

Johnson, Kim "Howard." *Life Before (and After) Python: The Solo Flights of the Flying Circus.* St. Martin's Press, New York, 1993.

Laing, Stuart. *Representations of Working-Class Life 1957–1964.* Macmillan, UK, 1986.

Landy, Marcia. *Monty Python's Flying Circus: TV Milestones Series.* Wayne State University Press, Detroit, MI, 2005.

Lewis, Roger. *The Life and Death of Peter Sellers.* Applause Books, New York, 1997.

Lewisohn, Mark. *Radio Times TV Comedy Guide.* BBC Books, London, 1998.

Llewellyn, Robert. *The Man in the Rubber Mask: The Inside Smegging Story of Red Dwarf.* Unbound, London, 2013.

Lynn, Jonathan & Jay, Antony: *The Complete Yes Minister: The Diaries of a Cabinet Minister by the Right Hon. James Hacker MP.* Salem House, Topsfield, MA, 1987.

McCann, Graham. *Dad's Army: The Story of a Classic Television Show.* Fourth Estate, London, 2002.

McCann, Graham. *Do You Think That's Wise . . . ? The Life of John Le Mesurier.* Aurum Press, London, 2012.

MacQueen, Adam. *Private Eye the First 50 Years: An A–Z.* London: Private Eye Productions, 2011.

Miller, Jeffrey S. *Something Completely Different: British Television and American Culture.* University of Minnesota Press: Minneapolis, 2000.

Morgan, David. *Monty Python Speaks!* First Spike Printing, Avon Books, New York, 1999.

Nathan, David. *The Laughtermakers.* Peter Owen, London, 1971.

Nobbs, David. *The Reginald Perrin Omnibus.* Arrow Books, London, 1999.

Oddie, Bill: *One Flew into the Cuckoo's Nest—My Autobiography.* Hodder Paperbacks, London, 2009.

Paskin, Barbara. *Dudley Moore—The Melancholy Clown, an Authorized Biography.* New Millennium Press, Beverly Hills, CA, 2000.

Perry, George. *Life of Python.* Boston: Little Brown & Company, 1983.

Pertwee, Bill. *Dad's Army—The Making of a Television Legend.* Conway, London, 2009.

Rigelsford, Adrian. *Are You Being Served? The Inside Story of Britain's Funniest and Public Television's Favourite Comedy.* San Francisco: KQED Books, 1995.

Ross, Robert. *Monty Python Encyclopedia.* New York: Barnes & Noble Books, 2002.

Saunders, Jennifer. *Absolutely Fabulous: Continuity.* Headline, London, 2001.

Speight, Johnny. *Thoughts of Chairman Alf: Alf Garnett's Little Blue Book or Where England Went Wrong.* Harper Collins, London, 1973.

Speight, Johnny. *The Garnett Chronicles: The Life and Times of Alf Garnett Esq.* Robson Books, London, 1996.

Stevens, Christopher. *Ray Galton and Alan Simpson: The Masters of Sitcom: From Hancock to Steptoe.* Michael O'Mara, London, 2011.

Taylor, Rod. *The Guinness Book of Sitcoms: Over 1000 Situation Comedies on British TV and Radio in the Last 60 Years.* London: Guinness World Records, 1994.

Thompson, Harry. *Peter Cook: A Biography.* Hodder & Stoughton, London, 1997.

Thompson, John O. *Monty Python: Complete and Utter Theory of the Grotesque.* British Film Institute Publishing, London, 1982.

Vahimagi, Tise (compiler). *British Television: An Illustrated Guide.* British Film Institute/Oxford University Press, Oxford, UK, 1994

Webber, Richard. *Rising Damp—A Celebration.* Boxtree, London, 2001.

Webber, Richard. *Some Mothers Do 'Ave 'Em—The Authorized Handbook.* Boxtree, London, 2002.

Webber, Richard, Clement, Dick, & LaFrenais, Ian. *Whatever Happened to the Likely Lads?* Orion, London, 2000.

Wilmut, Roger. *From Fringe to Flying Circus: Celebrating a Unique Generation of Comedy 1960–1980.* Eyre Methuen, London, 1980.

Wilmut, Roger & Grafton, Jimmy. *The Goon Show Companion—A History and Goonography.* London: Robson Books, 1998.

Index

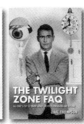

Nirvana FAQ
by John D. Luerssen
Backbeat Books
9781617134500......................$24.99

Pink Floyd FAQ
by Stuart Shea
Backbeat Books
9780879309503...................$19.99

Elvis Films FAQ
by Paul Simpson
Applause Books
9781557838582....................$24.99

Elvis Music FAQ
by Mike Eder
Backbeat Books
9781617130496.....................$24.99

Pearl Jam FAQ
by Bernard M. Corbett and Thomas Edward Harkins
Backbeat Books
9781617136122..........................$19.99

Prog Rock FAQ
by Will Romano
Backbeat Books
9781617135873......................$24.99

Pro Wrestling FAQ
by Brian Solomon
Backbeat Books
9781617135996......................$29.99

The Rocky Horror Picture Show FAQ
by Dave Thompson
Applause Books
9781495007477......................$19.99

Rush FAQ
by Max Mobley
Backbeat Books
9781617134517.......................$19.99

Saturday Night Live FAQ
by Stephen Tropiano
Applause Books
9781557839510......................$24.99

Seinfeld FAQ
by Nicholas Nigro
Applause Books
9781557838575....................$24.99

Sherlock Holmes FAQ
by Dave Thompson
Applause Books
9781480331495....................$24.99

The Smiths FAQ
by John D. Luerssen
Backbeat Books
9781480394490.................$24.99

Soccer FAQ
by Dave Thompson
Backbeat Books
9781617135989.....................$24.99

The Sound of Music FAQ
by Barry Monush
Applause Books
9781480360433...................$27.99

South Park FAQ
by Dave Thompson
Applause Books
9781480350649.................$24.99

Bruce Springsteen FAQ
by John D. Luerssen
Backbeat Books
9781617130939........................$22.99

Star Trek FAQ
(Unofficial and Unauthorized)
by Mark Clark
Applause Books
9781557837929......................$19.99

Star Trek FAQ 2.0
(Unofficial and Unauthorized)
by Mark Clark
Applause Books
9781557837936....................$22.99

Star Wars FAQ
by Mark Clark
Applause Books
978480360181......................$24.99

Quentin Tarantino FAQ
by Dale Sherman
Applause Books
9781480355880.................$24.99

Three Stooges FAQ
by David J. Hogan
Applause Books
9781557837882....................$22.99

TV Finales FAQ
by Stephen Tropiano and Holly Van Buren
Applause Books
9781480391444......................$19.99

The Twilight Zone FAQ
by Dave Thompson
Applause Books
9781480396180...................$19.99

Twin Peaks FAQ
by David Bushman and Arthur Smith
Applause Books
9781495015861......................$19.99

The Who FAQ
by Mike Segretto
Backbeat Books
9781480361034...................$24.99

The Wizard of Oz FAQ
by David J. Hogan
Applause Books
9781480350625...................$24.99

The X-Files FAQ
by John Kenneth Muir
Applause Books
9781480369740...................$24.99

Neil Young FAQ
by Glen Boyd
Backbeat Books
9781617130373........................$19.99

Frank Zappa FAQ
by John Corcelli
Backbeat Books
9781617136030........................$19.99

HAL•LEONARD®
PERFORMING ARTS
PUBLISHING GROUP

FAQ.halleonardbooks.com
0316

Prices, contents, and availability subject to change without notice.